POSITIVE ORGANIZING IN A GLOBAL SOCIETY

This book unites the latest research in diversity, inclusion, and positive organizational scholarship (POS) to investigate diversity and inclusion dynamics in social systems. Comprised of succinct chapters from thought leaders in the field, this book covers both micro- and macro-levels of analysis, covering topics such as authenticity, mentorship, intersectional identity work, positive deviance, resilience, resource cultivation and utilization, boundary spanning leadership, strengths-based development, positive workplace interventions to promote well-being, inclusive strategic planning, and the role of diversity in innovation.

Laura Morgan Roberts is Professor of Psychology, Culture, and Organization Studies at Antioch University, USA.

Lynn Perry Wooten is Associate Dean of Undergraduate Programs and Clinical Professor of Strategy, Management, and Organizations at the University of Michigan's Ross School of Business, USA.

Martin N. Davidson is Johnson and Higgins Professor of Business Administration at the Darden Graduate School of Business, University of Virginia, USA.

POSITIVE ORGANIZING IN A GLOBAL SOCIETY

Understanding and Engaging Differences for Capacity Building and Inclusion

Edited by Laura Morgan Roberts,
Lynn Perry Wooten, and
Martin N. Davidson

Routledge
Taylor & Francis Group

NEW YORK AND LONDON

First published 2016
by Routledge
711 Third Avenue, New York, NY 10017

and by Routledge
27 Church Road, Hove, East Sussex BN3 2FA

Routledge is an imprint of the Taylor & Francis Group, an informa business

© 2016 Taylor & Francis

The right of Laura Morgan Roberts, Lynn Perry Wooten, and Martin N. Davidson to be identified as the authors of the editorial material, and of the authors for their individual chapters, has been asserted in accordance with sections 77 and 78 of the Copyright, Designs and Patents Act 1988.

Library of Congress Cataloging-in-Publication Data
A catalog record for this book has been requested.

ISBN: 978-1-84872-575-1 (hbk)
ISBN: 978-1-84872-576-8 (pbk)
ISBN: 978-1-31579-464-8 (ebk)

Typeset in Bembo
by Apex CoVantage, LLC

Printed and bound in the United States of America by Publishers Graphics, LLC on sustainably sourced paper.

To our cherished marriage partners (Darryl, David, and Rachel) and our beloved children (Justin, Jada, Anaiah, and Isaiah), who strengthen us by revealing the beauty of differences and the power of inclusion, and our parents (Randall and Karen Morgan, Charles and Deloris Perry, and Arlanda and Jean Davidson), who were the first people to teach us about the positive power of diversity and to believe in our best selves.

CONTENTS

SECTION II
Authenticity

SECTION III
Resilience

ACKNOWLEDGMENTS

If you want to walk fast, walk alone, if you want to walk far, walk together!
—*African Proverb*

The writing of this book was truly an inclusive process, and we are grateful for everyone's contribution who walked on the bridge with us. First, we thank Kelle Parsons, who attended to so many of the details of the book's production from start to finish and cultivated all of the relationships that created this book. Kelle is an extraordinary and patient project manager who exemplified the practice of bringing her best self to this endeavor. We also thank Amy Lemley, who supported this project as the developmental editor of every chapter in the book. We believe Amy's magical touch as the developmental editor helped us to bridge the diversity of ideas written in this book. We thank Yen Azzaro who designed artwork for this project, and helped us to visualize the key concepts in this book in unconventional ways. We thank Anne Duffy, formerly of Psychology Press/Routledge at Taylor & Francis Group. Anne was our senior editor when we conceptualized and proposed this book. She was a guiding light and supporter of this book and of the published series of three edited books about Positive Organizational Scholarship and relationships, identities, and social change. We appreciate the support of the Ross School of Business at the University of Michigan for supporting Lynn Perry Wooten, and thank our colleagues at the Center for Positive Organizations for inspiring and energizing Positive Organizational Scholarship (POS). We thank the Darden Graduate School of Business at the University of Virginia for supporting Martin N. Davidson. We thank Antioch University's PhD Program in Leadership and Change for supporting Laura Morgan Roberts. We thank the participants in our 2010 Academy of Management professional development workshop on

Daring to Care about Diversity and POS, which planted the seeds for this collaborative book project. On a personal note, we thank our families for their inspiration, support, encouragement, and input during this project. Lastly, we express our sincere appreciation to the authors involved in this project who enthusiastically engaged new ideas, responded to feedback, and wrote stimulating chapters that are the core of this book. We are proud to have had the opportunity to work together as editors with a dynamic group of scholars and practitioners who are dedicated to positive organizing in our global society.

CONTRIBUTORS

Doyin Atewologun is a lecturer in leadership and learning at the School of Business & Management, Queen Mary University of London. Atewologun's research interests lie at the intersection of leadership development, identity work and diversity/inclusion. In addition to research and teaching, Atewologun works with organizations and individuals as consultant and coach to maximize the potential of diversity.

Myrtle Bell is professor of management at the University of Texas–Arlington. Bell's teaching and research focus on diversity, social issues, and human resources. Bell is past chair of the Gender and Diversity in Organizations division of the Academy of Management and author of *Diversity in Organizations* (2012).

Stacy Blake-Beard is a professor of management at the Simmons College School of Management where she teaches organizational behavior. Blake-Beard's research focuses on the challenges and opportunities offered by mentoring relationships, with a focus on how these relationships may be changing as a result of increasing workforce diversity. Blake-Beard is particularly interested in the issues women face as they develop mentoring relationships. Blake-Beard holds a B.S. in psychology from the University of Maryland at College Park and an M.A. and a Ph.D. in organizational psychology from the University of Michigan.

Lize A. E. Booysen is a full professor of leadership and organizational behavior in Antioch University's Leadership and Change Ph.D. Program. Booysen holds a doctorate in business leadership from the University of South Africa, and master's degrees in clinical psychology, research psychology, and criminology, all with distinction. Booysen is adjunct faculty and executive coach at the Center for

Creative Leadership, and senior research fellow at University of Johannesburg. Booysen participated in the GLOBE 65-nations cross culture leadership research project and is the past chair of the Business Leadership Member Interest Group of the International Leadership Association (ILA).

Hugo Canham teaches psychology at the University of the Witwatersrand in Johannesburg, South Africa. Canham's thesis explored employment equity and identity constructions in the banking sector in South Africa. Canham recently returned from a fellowship at Harvard University. Canham is an affiliated researcher to the Apartheid Archive Project. Canham is a psychologist and has worked in various capacities including heading transformation and equity initiatives at his university. Canham obtained an undergraduate degree from the University of Cape Town, an M.A. degree from the University of Natal, and his doctorate from the University of the Witwatersrand Graduate School of Business. Canham's research centers on methodological critiques of organizational inclusiveness.

Sandra Cha is an assistant professor of organizational behavior at Brandeis International Business School. Cha conducts research on leadership and identity, focusing on two aspects: leading through shared values (which are a core component of identity) and leading in the context of demographic diversity. Cha's research has appeared in publications including the *Journal of Applied Psychology*, *Leadership Quarterly*, and *Cultural Diversity and Ethnic Minority Psychology*. Cha has received multiple awards for her research, including the Accenture Award for a significant contribution to management and an approximately $100,000 grant from the Social Sciences and Humanities Research Council of Canada.

Arjun Chakravarti is assistant professor at the IIT Stuart School of Business in Chicago. Chakravarti's research interests focus on decision-making in managerial and consumer contexts. Specifically his work has addressed organizational learning and design issues related to information-sharing, relationship persistence, and productivity in small groups and across complex organizations. Chakravarti received his Ph.D. and MBA from the University of Chicago Booth School of Business.

Donna Chrobot-Mason is an associate professor at the University of Cincinnati and also serves as the director for the university's Center for Organizational Leadership. Chrobot-Mason is an organizational psychologist with expertise in leadership across differences and organizational initiatives designed to promote diversity and inclusion. Chrobot-Mason earned her Ph.D. in applied psychology from the University of Georgia. Chrobot-Mason coauthored the book *Boundary Spanning Leadership: Six Practices for Solving Problems, Driving Innovation, and Transforming Organizations* in 2011. Chrobot-Mason also serves as an adjunct scholar and leadership consultant with the Center for Creative Leadership.

Matthew L. Cole is assistant professor of management, chair of the Institutional Review Board, and chair of the Research Support Services Committee at Lawrence Technological University. Cole teaches biostatistics, business statistics, research design-quantitative methods, entrepreneurship, industrial/organizational psychology, and principles of management. Cole received his doctoral degree from Wayne State University (Detroit, MI) in Cognitive and Social Psychology across the Lifespan (CaSPaL). Cole's research interests, which focus on risk behaviors, the science of teams, positive organizational scholarship, OD, appreciative inquiry, and research methodology, have led to the publication of 20 peer-reviewed articles. Cole has facilitated national and international workshops, seminars, and strategic planning sessions on SOAR and Appreciative Inquiry with Jacqueline Stavros.

Stephanie J. Creary is an assistant professor of strategic management at the Cornell University School of Hotel Administration. Creary's research advances a resource-based perspective on identity to examine how identities at multiple levels of analysis influence generativity, workplace relationships, and strategic change. Creary received a PhD in management with a concentration in organizational studies from the Boston College Carroll School of Management. Creary also holds a B.S. in communication disorders (cum laude) and an M.S. in speech-language pathology from the Boston University College of Health and Rehabilitation Sciences: Sargent College; an MBA with high honors from the Simmons School of Management; and an M.S. in management with a concentration in organization studies from the Boston College Carroll School of Management.

Martin N. Davidson is Johnson and Higgins Professor of Business Administration at the University of Virginia's Darden Graduate School of Business. Davidson's research, teaching, and consulting helps leaders use diversity strategically to generate superior business performance in global organizations. Davidson's book, *The End of Diversity as We Know It: Why Diversity Efforts Fail and How Leveraging Difference Can Succeed*, introduces a research-driven paradigm for leaders in search of more innovative outcomes from the diversity (and diversity initiatives) in their organizations. Davidson's research also appears in *Harvard Business Review, Administrative Science Quarterly*, and *International Journal of Conflict Management* among other journals and books. Davidson teaches leadership in Darden's Executive Education and MBA programs, and consults with a host of corporations, government agencies, and NGOs in the Americas, Europe, and Asia. Davidson earned his A.B. from Harvard University and his Ph.D. from Stanford University. Davidson blogs and can be reached at www.leveragingdifference.com.

Jeff DeGraff is a professor at the University of Michigan, author, speaker and advisor to hundreds of the top organizations in the world, including General Electric, Bayer, Procter & Gamble, Prudential, and Coca-Cola. DeGraff operates the Innovatrium Institute for Innovation in Ann Arbor, Michigan, where innovation practices are tested and assessed, and he has created many of the most widely used innovation methodologies, practices, and processes used by top shelf companies and not-for-profits. DeGraff writes a syndicated column and hosts a public radio program on leading innovation. DeGraff is known as the "Dean of Innovation" because of his influence on the field. To learn more about DeGraff and his work on innovation, please visit www.jeffdegraff.com. Connect with him on Twitter @JeffDeGraff.

Stewart I. Donaldson is professor of psychology and community and global health, dean of the School of Social Science, Policy & Evaluation (SSSPE) and the School of Community & Global Health (SCGH), and director of the Claremont Evaluation Center (CEC) at Claremont Graduate University. Donaldson is on the Board of the International Positive Psychology Association (IPPA), director and cofounder of the Western Positive Psychology Association (WPPA), and was Congress Chair of IPPA's Third World Congress on Positive Psychology in Los Angeles, June 2013. Donaldson's recent publications in positive psychology include *Happiness, Excellence, and Optimal Human Functioning Revisited* (2014, *Journal of Positive Psychology* with Maren Dollwet & Meghana Rao); *Taming the Waves and Wild Horses of Positive Organizational Psychology* (2013, *Advances in Positive Organizational Psychology* with Maren Dollwet); *Applied Positive Psychology: Improving Everyday Life, Health, Schools, Work, and Society* (2011, Routledge, with Mihaly Csikszentmihalyi & Jeanne Nakamura); and *Positive Organizational Psychology, Behavior, and Scholarship: A Review of the Emerging Literature and Evidence Base* (2010, *Journal of Positive Psychology* with Ia Ko).

Bernardo M. Ferdman, Ph.D., is passionate about helping to create an inclusive world where more of us can be fully ourselves. Ferdman is distinguished professor of Organizational Psychology at the California School of Professional Psychology of Alliant International University in San Diego, and a leadership and organization development consultant and executive coach with three decades of experience working on diversity and inclusion. Ferdman edited *Diversity at Work: The Practice of Inclusion* (2014, Jossey-Bass) and is a fellow of the Society for Industrial and Organizational Psychology and the American Psychological Association, past chair of the Academy of Management's Diversity and Inclusion Theme Committee and of AOM's Gender and Diversity in Organizations Division, and a member of the Diversity Collegium. Ferdman consults, writes, speaks, teaches, and conducts research on inclusion and diversity, multicultural leadership, Latinos and Latinas in the workplace, and bringing one's whole self to work.

Lamont A. Flowers is the distinguished professor of educational leadership and the executive director of the Charles H. Houston Center for the Study of the Black Experience in Education in the Eugene T. Moore School of Education at Clemson University.

Lawrence O. Flowers is the department chair of biology and associate professor of biology at Livingstone College.

Tiffany A. Flowers is an assistant professor of education at Georgia Perimeter College.

Katherine Giscombe, Ph.D., works with Catalyst's knowledge base to engage with and provide member organizations with impactful experience, including consulting services to create business-driven diversity and inclusion initiatives. Giscombe directed Catalyst's groundbreaking study, Women of Color in Corporate Management: Opportunities and Barriers, and several subsequent in-depth research projects on diverse women. Drawing from this extensive background, Giscombe raises awareness of, and generates solutions to, the subtle obstacles that still must be overcome for women of color, and other marginalized groups, to succeed in the workplace.

Robby Griswold serves as Zingerman's Community Partnerships Coordinator and its Diversity and Inclusion Committee Chair. In the former, Griswold leverages his organization's philanthropic activities for the benefit of the greater nonprofit community in southeast Michigan, and as a community engagement opportunity for its 700 staff members. As chair of the Diversity and Inclusion Committee, Griswold leads a cross-level and cross-unit team of passionate organizational developers that handles an ambitious roster of activities with a reach that touches HR practice, cultural awareness and competence, systems for inclusive internal communication, and dialogue skills. Professional membership groups and community agencies seek out Griswold for his skills in facilitation, youth development and leadership, and diversity and inclusion program design and implementation. Griswold is a proud alumnus of the University of Michigan.

Jessica Halem is an MBA student at Simmons College School of Management. Previous to graduate school, Halem spent 20 years in social change work ranging from international women's issues to LGBT health to urban planning to comedy. Halem is the program manager for the LGBT Office at Harvard Medical School. Halem holds a B.A. in liberal arts from Sarah Lawrence College.

Demetria Henderson is a doctoral student in the department of management at the University of Texas–Arlington. Henderson's current research interests include diversity, positive organizational behavior, and career advancement. Prior to beginning her doctoral work, Henderson worked as a SAS programmer, utilizing her background in statistics. Henderson holds a B.S. in mathematics from Louisiana State University and an M.S. in organization development from the McColl School of Business at Queens University of Charlotte.

Patricia Faison Hewlin is an assistant professor at McGill University. Hewlin conducts research on how organization members and leaders engage in authentic expression, as well as factors that impede authenticity in every day work interactions. Hewlin's research has centered on employee silence, and the degree to which members suppress personal values and pretend to embrace those of the organization, a behavior she has termed as "creating facades of conformity." Hewlin's research interests also span to gaining insight on leadership dynamics and how members cope with perceived organizational value breaches in megachurches and other values-driven organizations.

Aurora Kamimura is a Ph.D. student in the Center for Higher and Postsecondary Education at the University of Michigan. Kamimura's research agenda examines organizational resilience of postsecondary institutions, and the impact of diverse learning environments. Kamimura has experience in statewide postsecondary access initiatives, multicultural affairs, and most recently served as an associate dean of student services. Kamimura earned her B.A. in social sciences from the University of California, Irvine, and her Ed.M. in administration, planning, and social policy from Harvard University.

Ellen Ernst Kossek (Ph.D., Yale) is Basil S. Turner Professor of Management at Purdue University's Krannert School of Management and research director of the Susan Bulkeley Butler Center for Leadership Excellence, which advances women's leadership. Kossek was elected a resident of the Work Family Researchers Network, fellow in APA & SIOP, to Academy of Management's Board of Governors, and chair of the Gender and Diversity Division. Kossek is a founding member of the Work Family Health Network, which seeks to change the structure of work to improve work-family relationships. Kossek's research has won awards for advancing gender, work-life and diversity, most recently the 2014 Families and Work Institute's Work Life Legacy award.

Vineetha Krothapalli is an academic associate at the Indian School of Business in Hyderabad, India, where she works on subjects related to organizational behavior and strategy. Prior to joining the Indian School of Business, Krothapalli was assistant manager, human resources at Oracle Financial Services Software Ltd, Bangalore, India, where she took care of the business HR functions at the organization. Krothapalli holds a B.E. (bachelor of engineering) in electronics and communications from the University of Madras, and MBA in human resources and marketing from the Bangalore University. Krothapalli is interested in research focusing on organizational culture, workforce diversity, and mentoring, and is working on these topics.

Michelle Kweder is a lecturer at Simmons College where she teaches classes about leadership and the city of Boston. A critical management scholar, Kweder's current research focuses on a critique of mainstream business curricula, intersectional critical discourse analysis, and leadership as seen through late night comedy. Kweder is particularly interested in moving from critique to emancipatory practice. She holds a BA in English and Women's Studies from Hamilton College, a MBA from Simmons College, School of Management, and a PhD in business administration, organizations and social change from the University of Massachusetts—Boston.

Amy Lemley is project manager at Lift Consulting, where she administers the Reflected Best Self Exercise survey as prework for executive education programs. As a freelance developmental editor, Lemley works with authors of both academic and trade books from the proposal through the draft and copyediting stages. Lemley is coauthor of eight nonfiction books, including *Work Makes Me Nervous: Overcome Anxiety and Build the Confidence to Succeed* (Wiley, 2010). Lemley was formerly a senior editor and multimedia content specialist at the University of Virginia Darden Graduate School of Business Administration.

Emily LeRoux-Rutledge is completing a Ph.D. in social psychology at the London School of Economics. LeRoux-Rutledge studies the impact of media on women's lives in developing countries. LeRoux-Rutledge's doctoral research looks at the ways in which narratives about women in the South Sudanese media resonate with South Sudanese women's own life narratives. LeRoux-Rutledge is also an international development consultant specializing in research, monitoring and evaluation for nongovernmental organizations with a media, information and communication focus. LeRoux-Rutledge has conducted research in more than 20 countries across Africa, Asia and Eastern Europe.

Tanya Menon is associate professor at Fisher College of Business, Ohio State University. Menon's research focuses on how people make social judgments in organizations, including how they experience envy, conflict, coalitions, and diversity. Menon is particularly interested in the implications of these processes for organizational learning and the cultural and network processes that affect such judgments. Menon's work has appeared in *Harvard Business Review*, *Organization Science*, *Journal of Personality & Social Psychology*, *Personality and Social Psychology Review*, *Management Science*, and *Organizational Behavior & Human Decision Processes*, among others.

James L. Moore III is an associate provost in the Office of Diversity and Inclusion, where he also serves as the director of the Todd Anthony Bell National Resource Center on the African American Male at Ohio State University. Additionally, Moore is a distinguished professor of urban education in the College of Education and Human Ecology.

Chris Mueller leads the Social and Public Innovation practice at the Innovatrium, which helps large complex organizations reinvent themselves amidst rapidly changing market conditions through developing teams of self-authorizing and resourceful leaders. Mueller's clients include school districts, cities, communities, foundations and nationally recognized art institutions.

Audrey Murrell, Ph.D., is the associate dean of the College of Business Administration at the University of Pittsburgh. Murrell conducts research on mentoring, careers in organizations, workplace/supplier diversity and social issues in management. This work has been published widely in management and psychology journals and within several books such as *Mentoring Dilemmas: Developmental Relationships Within Multicultural Organizations* (with Crosby and Ely); *Intelligent Mentoring: How IBM Creates Value Through People, Knowledge and Relationships* (with Forte-Trummel and Bing); and the forthcoming book entitled *Mentoring in Medical and Health Care Professions* (with South-Paul).

Tina Opie, Ph.D., began her path toward the study of valuing individual difference at the Darden School of Business, earning her MBA in Management in 1999. Opie received her Ph.D. in management from the Stern School of Business in 2010, where her emphasis of study was organizational behavior. Currently, Opie is an assistant professor in the management division at Babson College, teaching organizational behavior courses to MBA and undergraduate students. Opie's research focuses primarily on how organizations can create workplaces that successfully leverage individual difference and convey respect for individual contributions. Opie also created a research website, www.hairasidentity.com, whose mission is to promote and initiate discussion between men and women from diverse backgrounds around the relationships between hair and self-esteem and perceptions about professionalism.

Kelle Parsons is a research assistant at the University of Michigan Ross School of Business. Parsons completed her master of arts in higher education and master of public policy at the University of Michigan, and also holds a B.A. in organizational studies from the University of Michigan. Parsons has focused on higher education, organization development, organizational change, and public policy.

Julie R. Posselt is assistant professor of higher education in the Center for the Study of Higher and Postsecondary Education at the University of Michigan. Posselt's scholarship uses organizational and sociological theory to understand institutionalized inequalities in higher education and efforts to interrupt these historic tendencies and encourage diversity. Posselt has recently published in the *American Educational Research Journal*, *Chronicle of Higher Education*, and *American Journal of Education*, among others. Posselt also has a book forthcoming with Harvard University Press based on an ethnographic comparative case study of faculty gatekeeping in graduate admissions.

Lakshmi Ramarajan is an assistant professor in the Organizational Behavior Unit at Harvard Business School. Ramarajan's research examines how people can work fruitfully across social divides, with a particular emphasis on multiple identities and group differences in organizations. Ramarajan investigates work identities alongside other identities that are important to people, such as gender, ethnicity, community and family, and the impact of multiple identities on employee engagement, career success and satisfaction, quality of interpersonal and intergroup relations, and work performance. Ramarajan's research has been published in the *Academy of Management Review*, the *Academy of Management Annals*, and in edited volumes on Positive Organizational Scholarship. Ramarajan earned her B.A. (honors) in international relations from Wellesley College, her M.Sc. in international relations from the London School of Economics and Political Science, and her Ph.D. in management from the Wharton School of Business.

Meghana A. Rao is a researcher and consultant specializing in optimal human and institutional functioning. Rao serves as the president of the Work and Organizations Division of the International Positive Psychology Association (IPPA) and the associate director and cofounder of the Western Positive Psychology Association (WPPA). As research associate at the Claremont Evaluation Center (CEC), Rao leads research on positive work relationships, social flow, strengths-driven evaluation, cross-cultural issues in positive psychology, and positive psychology of gender. Rao has a master's degree in organizational development, an MBA in human resource management, and is pursuing a doctoral degree in positive organizational psychology at Claremont Graduate University.

Laura Morgan Roberts is an author, professor, researcher, leadership development coach, and organizational consultant. Roberts is the professor of psychology, culture and organization studies in Antioch University's Graduate School of Leadership and Change. Roberts is also a core faculty affiliate of the Center for Positive Organizations at the University of Michigan (Ann Arbor) and the Center for Gender in Organizations at Simmons School of Management (Boston). Roberts's research centers on authenticity, identity, diversity, strengths, and value creation. Roberts coedited *Exploring Positive Identities and Organizations* (with Jane Dutton) and has published several articles and case studies related to diversity and positive organizational scholarship. Roberts earned her M.A. and Ph.D. (organizational psychology) from the University of Michigan and B.A. (psychology, highest distinction) from the University of Virginia.

Vicki J. Rosenberg, president, Vicki Rosenberg & Associates, provides organizational development services to foundations, institutions of higher education, government and nonprofits with an emphasis on strategic planning and capacity building and a specialty in leveraging the competitive advantage of differences. Prior to launching her firm, Rosenberg served as vice president and COO of the Council of Michigan Foundations (CMF) for which she designed and led its *Transforming Michigan Philanthropy Through Diversity & Inclusion initiative* and as a senior program officer for the Getty Education Center, a program of the J. Paul

Getty Trust. Rosenberg has served on numerous state and national boards and task forces and is the author or lead editor of several articles and publications, many on diversity and inclusion. Rosenberg holds an MBA from the University of California, Los Angeles, and a B.A. from the University of Minnesota. Rosenberg lives in Saugatuck, Michigan, with her husband, sculptor Eddie Parach.

Sheldene Simola is an associate professor of business administration at Trent University, Ontario, Canada. Simola completed her MBA at the Laurier School of Business and Economics and her Ph.D. at Queen's University. Simola teaches individual ethical decision-making in business and organizations and ethics of corporate governance. Simola's research has focused primarily on relational and care ethics in business, social sustainability in organizations, moral courage, corporate crisis prevention and management, and teaching and learning in business education.

Jacqueline M. Stavros is professor of management and director of the DBA Program at Lawrence Technological University. Stavros teaches strategy, organization development and change, leading change, research design, qualitative research methods, and business sustainability. Stavros received her doctoral degree from Case Western Reserve University's Weatherhead School of Management in Cleveland. Stavros's research interests include positive organizational scholarship, organization development and change, Appreciative Inquiry, sustainability, and strategy. Stavros has written four books, 26 journal articles, and eight book chapters from her research agenda. Stavros has traveled to over a dozen countries as an invited speaker, consultant, and conference presenter on Appreciative Inquiry and SOAR.

Ilene C. Wasserman, Ph.D. has over 30 years of experience as a consultant to organizations and as an executive coach working with leaders and teams to enhance communication and collaboration by leveraging multiple dimensions of domestic and global diversity. Wasserman uses a whole system narrative approach based on the principles that we transform organizational cultures through engaging the whole system. In addition to leading a consulting group, Wasserman is well published and teaches graduate courses.

Skot Welch is the principal/founder of Global Bridgebuilders (GBB), a firm focusing on cultural transformation and inclusion that leads to innovation. Global Bridgebuilders is an international team providing services to enterprises across the globe. GBB bases its work in the core belief that inclusion is a business discipline and that it should be leveraged across all that the enterprise does. To gain this leverage, the firm applies a continuous improvement model, anchored in metrics.

Natasha N. Wilder conducts applied research on positive organizational cultures, cross-cultural competency, and diversity. As consultant based in San Francisco,

California, Wilder relishes working with organizations to support the engagement and well-being of their employees. Wilder is pursuing her Ph.D. in positive organizational psychology at Claremont Graduate University.

Heather Wishik, J.D., president, Heather Wishik Consulting, LLC, has been a global organization development, leadership development and diversity and inclusion consultant, coach and scholar since 1993, except for three and a half years when she served as the assistant vice president and director of global diversity and inclusion for the TJX Companies, Inc. Since 2001 Wishik has been a Batten Research Fellow at the Darden Graduate School of Business, University of Virginia, where she collaborates with faculty on global leadership research, and leveraging difference, diversity and inclusion theory and practice. Wishik holds an honours degree in industrial and organizational psychology and a certificate in group process facilitation from the University of South Africa, a J.D. from the University of San Diego School of Law, a B.A. from Goddard College, and group relations consultation training from the Tavistock Institute. With Martin Davidson, Wishik coauthored three chapters of the book *The End of Diversity as We Know It: Why Managing Diversity Efforts Fail and How Leveraging Difference Can Succeed* (Davidson, Berrett-Koehler, 2011).

Lynn Perry Wooten is a clinical professor of strategy, management and organizations and the associate dean of undergraduate programs at the University of Michigan's Stephen M. Ross School of Business. Wooten's current research bridges theory and practice and focuses on positive organizing routines, diversity management practices, and crisis leadership. Wooten's research has been published in journals such as Academy of Management Journal, American Behavioral Scientist, Decision Sciences Journal of Innovative Education, Human Resource Management, and Organizational Dynamics. Wooten has coauthored a book on crisis leadership, Leading Under Pressure: From Surviving to Thriving Before, During, and After a Crisis. Through her applied research projects, Wooten has worked with many organizations including the Council of Michigan Foundations, the Executive Leadership Institute, Google, General Motors, Trinity Health, and Whirlpool. Wooten earned a bachelor of science in accounting from North Carolina A&T State University, an MBA from the Fuqua School of Business at Duke University, and a Ph.D. from the University of Michigan.

Jeffrey Yip is an assistant professor at Claremont Graduate University and a visiting researcher with the Center for Creative Leadership. Yip's research seeks to advance a relational understanding of leader effectiveness and development. In particular, Yip focuses on the role of boundary spanning and developmental relationships. A Fulbright scholar, Yip has a Ph.D. in organizational behavior from Boston University and a master's in human development and psychology from Harvard University.

Alan James Yu is a Ph.D. student in leadership studies at the University of San Diego and a visiting researcher with the Center for Creative Leadership. As an educational specialist in creativity and adult learning, Yu is particularly interested in leadership education practices that employ the use of the creative arts. With the support of the Bali Institute for Global Renewal, Yu plans to pursue a dissertation study on the development of moral imagination through engagement in Balinese arts in leadership education programs in Bali, Indonesia. Prior to his doctoral studies, Yu worked as a professional graphic designer and creative consultant for various companies in Seattle.

INTRODUCTION

Martin N. Davidson, Lynn Perry Wooten,
Laura Morgan Roberts, and Kelle Parsons

> If we are to achieve a richer culture, rich in contrasting values, we must recognize the whole gamut of human potentialities, and so weave a less arbitrary social fabric, one in which each diverse human gift will find a fitting place.
>
> —*Margaret Mead*

Few would eschew being a part of a team, organization, or community that fostered high levels of productivity, creativity and innovation, and belongingness.

But when it comes to manifesting such a possibility, the devil is in the details. A variety of best practices has been discovered that leads to positive and generative pathways, filled with the energy and excitement that characterizes truly diverse and inclusive workplaces and communities. But rarely do you get there without travails. The experience of Richard Orange, a gifted teacher and management consultant on diversity and inclusion illustrates this journey. He worked with companies on overcoming racial discrimination and led training and workshops on the topic. The issues were sobering and interactions frequently elicited frustration, anger, sadness, and despair. Even though the sessions were consistently rated as valuable learning experiences, he came to believe that sending people out of the workshops emotionally and spiritually drained was wrong. Moreover, participants were often unable to convert their learning experience into sustainable change in their organizations. Orange decided he could not continue teaching the same way. He worked with his consulting colleagues to reenvision the training and together, they transformed the experience of the people with whom they worked by providing positive and generative reflections on diversity. They exposed participants to culturally diverse spiritual traditions that often served to buoy those who were most discouraged. In essence, Orange and his colleagues expanded the available responses to the issues of Diversity and Inclusion (D&I) by providing a positive lens through which participants could engage with what they learned about culturally diverse practices for strengthening individuals and organizations.[1]

In a similar vein, we collected the chapters in this volume to provide an expanded set of options for how scholars and practitioners can develop knowledge and practice about D&I. We had three large objectives in mind as we developed the volume. First, we wanted to provide D&I scholarship with a new lens through which inquiry could be framed: the lens of Positive Organizational Scholarship (POS). D&I scholarship provides substantial insights into how identity and behavioral differences affect organizing and the management of these differences.[2] Aspects of D&I scholarship explore these issues by studying discrimination, marginalization, exclusion, and injustices, which are profoundly painful and debilitating facets of organizing. Other streams of research focus on how people, groups, and organizations benefit from D&I practices, but there is still somewhat of an emphasis on reducing problems such as prejudices and oppression through fostering a positive vision, organizational learning, and actions for replacing undesired behaviors, policies, and systems.[3] Thus, we believe this inquiry has historically ignored how organizations and their members develop positive organizing practices for diversity and inclusion. As a result of this insight, we advocate that Diversity and Inclusion inquiry take on the set of generative assumptions in which POS is grounded:

> [the commitment to] revealing and nurturing the highest level of human potential, and [striving] to answer questions like: What makes employees feel like they're thriving? How can I bring my organization through

difficult times stronger than before? What creates the positive energy a team needs to be successful?[4]

In other words, POS is motivated by discovering life-giving dynamics, optimal functioning, and enhanced capabilities in organizational life. POS helps scholars and practitioners to identify individual and collective strengths that lead to positive outcomes, processes, and attributes of organizations and their members. Given the scope and aims of POS, it is our hope that the chapters in this book shine light on innovative ways of enhancing Diversity & Inclusion scholarship with the POS perspective.[5]

Our second objective is reciprocal: providing POS scholars a different way of envisioning positive organizing. As scholars, we are committed to understanding how differences could be understood and leveraged in positive and generative ways. The POS intellectual community is an ideal environment in which to share this research. It is vibrant and full of brilliant and accomplished scholars, both established and up and coming. It is filled with people with whom we have deep and powerful connections as colleagues, advisors, and mentors. We (Davidson, Wooten, and Roberts) have contributed to exciting collaborative efforts that have charted new terrain in POS research for positive relationships,[6] positive identities,[7] positive social change and organizations,[8] the *Handbook of POS*,[9] and positive leadership.[10] Each of these endeavors has stimulated our growing interest in building bridges between D&I and POS. Even so, this is our first foray into developing an ethos of insight and inquiry into difference to advance POS scholarship and practice as they relate to diversity and inclusion. As we have participated actively in POS research projects, teaching, coaching, and conferences, we have often raised questions of diversity and inclusion with our colleagues. Raising such questions about positive organizing and capacity building around Diversity and Inclusion has been like coming to a feast in which every imaginable dish is arrayed on the table. It is now our collective task to provide the plates and utensils with which to dine.

Hence, currently, Diversity and Inclusion research and Positive Organizational Scholarship represent two separate fields of scholarship, despite the fact that both examine capacity building among individuals, groups, and organizations. While a few recent articles and book chapters[11] (Creary, Caza, & Roberts, in press; Davidson & James, 2007; Dutton, Roberts, & Bednar, 2010; Ely, Meyerson, & Davidson, 2006; Myers & Wooten, 2009; Ramarajan & Thomas, 2011) have begun to build these bridges, a host of possibilities remains for deeper, more integrated investigations of diversity and inclusive practices as they relate to strengths and extraordinary outcomes.

This book advances scholarship in both domains by articulating the mechanisms and boundary conditions of capacity building and inclusion that frame inquiry into positive organizing in our global society. We believe that research and the practice of positive organizing will benefit profoundly by integrating diverse and often marginalized perspectives. These chapters point to a distinctive set of enablers to support this integration, captured in the six sections of the book: Multiple Identities and Resources, Authenticity, Resilience, Relating across Differences, Inclusive and Equitable Systems, and Innovative Thinking. We hope to inspire POS scholars to see their inquiry through the richness of Diversity and Inclusion lenses.

Finally, we crafted this book because we believed that making a difference in the world means that what we produce must be accessible to diverse audiences. We wanted the book to appeal to scholars—that is clear from our first two objectives. But we also wanted the book to provide value to practitioners who care about diversity, inclusion, and generative ways of leading and living. We wanted the volume to serve as a bridge between these two frequently segregated communities. To support this objective, we invited our contributors to submit concise chapters, rather than extended chapters. The contributors are scholar-practitioners who investigate, teach, and apply POS principles for understanding D&I dynamics in social systems. Their chapters feature 21st-century challenges for individuals, groups, and organizations that seek to promote Diversity and Inclusion, and they illuminate how appreciative, strength-based analyses and interventions can facilitate deeper understanding and critical change. Taken together, the chapters identify action steps for generating research, teaching, and practice-based pathways for promoting diversity and inclusion in contemporary organizations.

The Origins of This Book

This book project began nearly five years ago, with a convening of scholars at the Academy of Management meetings in August 2010 in Montreal, Canada. We (the editors) designed an innovative professional development workshop (PDW) that brought together micro- and macro-level diversity, inclusion, and POS researchers to address barriers and opportunities for building conceptual and empirical bridges between these fields. Many scholars shared our enthusiasm for "Daring to Care about Diversity Management Research by Bridging It with Positive Organizational Scholarship," the title of the PDW. Through the workshop, we began to create a community of exchange that would seed future collaborations across theoretical, ideological, and demographic differences. We invited several exciting, innovative, and well-regarded diversity and POS scholars to participate in this exchange as thought leaders[12] who facilitated discussions among our standing-room-only group of conference attendees. Through rich dialogue and exchange, we began to uncover potential connections between these fields, while also reflecting upon core assumptions that may challenge scholars who seek to bridge diversity, inclusion, and POS. At this PDW, we anchored in our discussion around an Emergent Learning Map. The Emergent Learning Map™ technique was designed to empower groups with a framework to address complex challenges by pooling know-how in peer learning events and transforming their collective ideas into practice. This technique involved the PDW participants dialoguing about what it would entail for us to bridge diversity management and inclusion research with POS research, based upon past experiences and envisioning actions for the future. Based on the discussion, we concluded our PDW session by identifying opportunities to share our collective learning. This edited book was at the top of the list: an opportunity to create a forum for exploring a wide range of topics that would stretch the field's current understanding of diversity, inclusion, and positive organizing.

Building the Bridge

Each of the chapters in this book represents a building block to bridge the disciplinary divide between Diversity and Inclusion and POS research. The chapters are written to engage scholar-practitioners who have a desire to investigate, teach, and apply principles of POS to D&I dynamics in social systems. These chapters speak to the 21st-century opportunities and challenges for individuals, groups, and organizations that seek to promote diversity and inclusion, and through their voices the chapters illuminate how appreciative, strength-based analyses and interventions can facilitate deeper understanding, resourcefulness, positive actions, and critical change.

To build this bridge, it was important to us that the chapters in this book include a diversity of voices. These voices challenge us to understand and engage differences for capacity building by exploring topics such as the intersection of gender, race, sexual orientation, family status, age, and nationality with organizational life. Moreover, the chapters bring a POS view of Diversity and Inclusion to life through an emic perspective by providing a discourse from a native's point of view.[13] The authors speak in first person, and in their chapters describe behaviors as seen from the perspectives of cultural insiders and interpret constructs based upon self-understanding, self-awareness, and personal experiences. As a result, the chapters present a holistic view of the topics in this book through the conceptualization of constructs, the sharing of empirical research, reflections of practices as scholars and consultants, provocative editorial commentaries, and interpretive descriptions of phenomena. Furthermore, the chapters were penned to direct the reader's attention to both the research framing of each topic and a phenomenon with practical implications.

Journeying on the Bridge with Us

As an editorial team, we had the task of organizing these chapters into themes that would guide the reader's journey. We first began with a "traditional" structure of three categories for organizing the chapters: (1) micro—the experiences of individuals in organizations; (2) meso—multiple levels of individual or group processes in organizations; and (3) macro—the behavior of entire organizations and interactions between organizations and their environments. After multiple meetings of the editorial team, however, we realized that this compilation of chapters not only represented the diversity of levels we traditionally observe when studying organizational behavior, but also could be organized into six themes: (1) Multiple Identities and Resources; (2) Authenticity; (3) Resilience; (4) Relating across Differences; (5) Inclusive and Equitable Systems; and (6) Innovation.

The first theme of chapters presented in this book is Multiple Identities and Resources. This theme explores how individuals bring multiple identities to an organization, and why this is an opportunity to engage differences. In addition, chapters in this section examine how diverse identities result in the enactment of an individual's strengths and resourcefulness. Also, the chapters in this section lead us to consider how cultural identity is not only an asset at the individual level, but also can be resource that contributes to organizational effectiveness.

This section begins with a chapter written by Wilder, Rao, and Donaldson that bridges POS and D&I work by discussing how the two bodies of research have connected in the past through exploring strengths-based approaches for the assets of diverse workers. When reading their chapter, we are prompted to reflect upon the role of workplace culture for creating an inclusive environment to engage differences and support the thriving of individuals across diverse affiliations and identities.

In the next chapter, Creary builds on the existing literature by depicting global diversity management in multinational organizations as an opportunity to apply POS principles. Using case studies as examples, she posits that "social identity resourcing" is a phenomenon whereby identity group–based differences are valued and considered as a factor for positive deviance. This chapter invites us to contemplate a social identity–based mechanism for both individual and collective flourishing in global organizations.

Continuing the conversation, Roberts and Cha focus specifically on the ways in which racial minorities mobilize racial, ethnic, and cultural identities as resources for personal and organizational effectiveness. They propose a typology of the non-dominant cultural capital that serves as a source of strength for minorities in the workplace. This typology brings to our attention how symbolic capital, social capital, psychological capital, and human/intellectual capital empower racial minorities to make significant contributions to their organizations while navigating racism.

Ramarajan and LeRoux-Rutledge explore the ideas of multiple identities and resourcing through the cases of three African entrepreneurs. Their integration of diversity research from a POS perspective contrasts the tensions between structural barriers to entrepreneurship in a developing economy and the identity of a marginalized social group as a resource. Through these case studies we witness the ways discrimination and identities can become resources that contribute to resilience, relationships, and novel perspectives that catalyze entrepreneurial success.

Pushing the conversation deeper, Atewologun describes her research on instances when professionals became temporarily acutely aware of one or more of their "nonwork" identities (ethnic, gender, or other identity), and how these experiences led to increased self-awareness, insight, and learning. This concept of a constellation of identities that become temporarily activated expands our understanding of multiple identities and the ways these identities can serve as resources in the workplace. Also, this chapter brings to our attention that we should adopt an integrated rather than strands-based approach to diversity and inclusion that acknowledges identity intersections and complexities.

The second theme of chapters examines Authenticity, the ability of individuals to be genuine, self-aware, and comfortable revealing their true selves. In this section, Hewlin's chapter begins the dialogue on authenticity by sparking a conversation on authentic engagement in environments where individuals bring divergent sets of values into the workplace. In this chapter, she contends that authenticity is an individual endeavor guided by one's values and the capability to incorporate these values into the work–life experience. Opie also discusses the importance of authenticity, with a particular focus on the costs and missed opportunities of inauthenticity among marginalized groups. She uses a specific case study of hairstyle to engage a POS lens and explore the ways that encouraging authenticity benefits individuals and organizations.

Branching the dialogue on authenticity, Ferdman discusses the relationship between inclusion efforts within organizations and feelings of comfort of individuals. He argues that inclusive work environments foster more comfort among previously marginalized identity groups, and they also involve a more equitable distribution of discomfort; Ferdman contends that those in previously privileged groups may share in some of the discomfort involved in making space for different identities.

Finally, Roberts, Wooten, Davidson, and Lemley examine how diverse cultures influence how effectively individuals can access and use sincere expressions of praise, appreciation, or gratitude—what they conceptualize as authentic affirmations. Authentic affirmations take into account the broad range of cultural consciousness while emphasizing relationships, self-awareness, and meaning-making as aspects of strength-based development. Based upon their experiences with using the Reflected Best Self Exercise™ in culturally diverse contexts, the authors propose mindful, culturally inclusive approaches toward strength-based leadership development and talent management.

For the third theme, Resilience, the authors initiate a conversation on how diverse individuals achieve desirable outcomes amidst adversity and their capacity to adapt, bounce back, and flourish when confronting challenging situations. Opening our conversation on resilience, Giscombe explores the interpretations of failure that lead to building resilience, particularly the enabling and inhibiting factors faced by members of marginalized group identities. Her chapter probes us to think about how organizational members burdened with stigmatized identities not only cope with, but also succeed in exclusionary environments. Henderson and Bell build on that idea by exploring the ways that racial socialization—the skills and knowledge to overcome discrimination—contributes to a quality of resilience through positive thought processes and behaviors in workplaces. Menon and Chakravarti continue the conversation by presenting the concept of *social resilience*, referring to individuals' willingness to persist despite uncomfortable social interactions, particularly interracial interactions. Taking lessons from a randomized control trial of college roommates, they discuss the organizational factors that facilitate social resilience in the workplace.

The fourth chapter theme shifts the conversation to Relating across Differences. The chapters in this section reinforce that great opportunities are given to us when relationships are inclusive and constructively value differences. Chrobot-Mason, Yip, and Yu's chapter begins this section by introducing the concept of a boundary spanning mindset, which is important, they argue, in solving "wicked problems" and improving intergroup interactions. Drawing on interviews with organizational leaders, they unpack the boundary spanning mindset concept and offer strategies for developing that mindset for leaders. In a similar vein, Blake-Beard, Murrell, Krothapalli, Halem, and Kweder push our understanding of mentoring relationships beyond the traditional understanding of similarity-based relationships. Using the concept of high quality connections (HQCs), they focus on building an understanding of the value of mentoring across diversity to individuals and organizations. Extending the conversation, Simola examines the ways individuals develop high-quality relationships, particularly across differences. She describes the role of "care ethics" in facilitating the development of high-quality relationships, particularly through the approach of life story–telling, which facilitates openness, authenticity, and understanding.

Contextualizing relational processes in health care organizations, Wasserman begins a conversation about the ways that discursive processes—the patterns people make as they communicate—foster authenticity and collaboration across differences. She identifies the skills that help individuals relate and engage across differences as well as the ways the conversational spaces can be designed to facilitate relationship building. Wishik draws upon her consulting experiences and discusses the ways that the new context of communications—where anyone can comment in the "digital river"—requires transcending from managing diversity to leveraging differences. To accomplish this, Wishik proposes "constructivist listening" as a practice that incorporates reflection and learning before the expression of opinion, and as a result enhances the quality of relationships. Turning the conversation to the global context, Booysen examines the sub-Saharan African concept of *Ubuntu*, which is generally considered a concept referring to interconnectedness, inclusion, and relational practice. She also considers its potential to lead to discrimination due to its emphasis on extended family, paternalism, and authority, and identifies ways to ensure the practice of *Ubuntu* is inclusive and positive.

The fifth theme of chapters, Inclusive and Equitable Systems, advances our thinking by conceptualizing how positive organizing can be integrated with diversity management to permeate the behaviors of organizations, communities of practices, and sectors. For instance, Wooten, Parsons, Griswold, and Welch examine key practices based on Positive Organizational Scholarship concepts that produce collective resourcefulness and generative dynamics for managing D&I. Using the case of a local business exemplifying positive deviance, they discuss the generative mechanisms of POS and the ways organizations can apply related practices to leverage D&I to create value for organizational stakeholders. Next, Canham uses a case study of a major South African bank to investigate the dynamics associated with the philosophical shift of diversity as something that has been externally imposed to an opportunity to foster individual and organizational thriving. Using the voices of case participants, we learn from Canham's experience the value of facilitating individuals' empowerment (a sense of self-determination, meaning, and impact) to promote positive deviance.

Focusing on the higher education sector, Flowers, Moore, Flowers, and Flowers outline three ways colleges and universities can promote inclusion among faculty, including assessing organizational culture, enabling underrepresented faculty members to serve in leadership positions, developing comprehensive plans to engage and support underrepresented faculty, and employing human-centered approaches to use underrepresented faculty to promote institutional and personal success. Rosenberg continues the conversation by focusing on a case involving the philanthropic sector. She explains the implementation of a peer-learning curriculum based on an Appreciative Inquiry model, which intended to promote intercultural competency. She describes the positive results of the program and focuses on the importance of a positive framing of diversity and inclusion on facilitating buy-in and commitment to such a program.

Stepping back to a cross-sector lens, Kossek starts a conversation about the importance of positive workplace strategies designed to support diversity in work-life inclusion. Kossek argues that effective organizations are even more so when they use organizational strategies that facilitate social support to allow individuals to synthesize personal identities with work demands.

The authors in the sixth and final theme of this book, Innovative Thinking, invite us to think about how fostering innovation through diversity yields positive outcomes. DeGraff and Mueller start a conversation about the ways that different perspectives, cultures, and strengths produce the requisite conflict that fosters innovative thinking. Using the Competing Values Framework, they outline how organizations foster constructive conflict to promote innovative thinking. Complementing the DeGraff and Mueller chapter, Kamimura and Posselt propose a conceptual framework to model the ways that identity diversity lead to innovation and knowledge creation in academic research teams, focusing specifically on the cognitive diversity and the specific communication processes by which diverse identities interactively influence knowledge creation in academic research teams. Sharing a research-based tool, Stavros and Cole describe how the Strengths, Opportunities, Aspirations, and Results (SOAR) tool can foster an inclusive approach to strategic thinking, planning, and leading. They summarize their empirical study using the SOAR profile in diverse team environments, showing that it promotes a focus on strengths and whole-system solutions that positively affect team performance. The closing chapter in this section, written by Davidson, offers a novel viewpoint on innovating. This chapter discusses bringing a marginalized group—so-called weird people—into the mainstream by leveraging their weirdness to co-create more effective teams and organizations.

As you read this book, please consider this introduction an invitation to join us on the bridge. We believe each of these chapters represent a brick for building the bridge that can fuse diversity and inclusion with Positive Organizational Scholarship. As a collection, they provide an assortment of paths by which to join us on this journey. There is a path for those who seek to identify new directions for classic research on Diversity and Inclusion and related theories. Likewise, there is a path for scholars who are currently investigating POS-related topics or employing appreciative methods, and who seek to examine Diversity and Inclusion dynamics in greater depth. Alternatively, you may want to venture on the path for educators who seek to bring into their classrooms the contemporary themes of diversity, inclusion, and organizational studies (for example, examining current issues through a POS lens). Or you may decide to take a different path, reading the chapters from a practitioner standpoint and using the knowledge in your consulting or coaching practice to increase clients' facility for generating learning and results from engaging Diversity and Inclusion. This bridge is built upon vivid portrayals of what is possible and practical ways to engage Diversity and Inclusion that are truly generative. No matter what path you take on the bridge, we hope that your journey through these chapters sparks interest in individuals, groups, and organizations that model Diversity and Inclusion at their best.

Notes

1. Personal communication between one of the editors and the late Richard Orange.
2. Roberson, Q. (2006). Disentangling the meanings of diversity and inclusion in organizations. *Group & Organization Management, 31*(2), 212–236.
3. Ferdman, B. M., & Deane, B. R. (2014). *Diversity at work: The practice of inclusion.* San Francisco, CA: Jossey-Bass.
4. Drawn from Introduction to Positive Organizational Scholarship at http://positiveorgs.bus.umich.edu/an-introduction/
5. Cameron, K., & Spreitzer, G. (2011). What is positive about positive organizational scholarship? In K. Cameron & G. Spreitzer (Eds.), *The handbook of Positive Organizational Scholarship.* New York: Oxford University Press.
6. Dutton, J., & Ragins, B. R. (2007). *Exploring positive relationships at work: Building a theoretical and research foundation.* Hillsdale, NJ: Lawrence Erlbaum Associates.
7. Roberts, L., & Dutton, J. (2009). *Exploring positive identities and organizations: Building a theoretical and research foundation.* New York: Psychology Press.
8. Golden-Biddle, K., & Dutton, J. (2012). *Using a positive lens to explore social change and organizations: Building a theoretical and research foundation.* New York: Psychology Press.
9. Cameron, K., & Spreitzer, G. (2011). *The Oxford handbook of positive organizational scholarship.* New York: Oxford University Press.
10. Dutton, J., & Spreitzer, G. (2014). *How to be a positive leader: Small actions, big impact.* San Francisco, CA: Berrett-Koehler.

11. Creary, S., Caza, B., & Roberts, L. (in press). Out of the box? How managing a sub-ordinates multiple identities affects the quality of a manager-subordinate relationship. *Academy of Management Review.*

    Davidson, M. N., & James, E. H. (2007). The engines of positive relationships across difference: Conflict and learning. In J. Dutton & B. R. Ragins (Eds.), *Exploring positive relationships at work: Building a theoretical and research foundation* (pp. 137–158). Hillsdale, NJ: Lawrence Erlbaum Associates.

    Dutton, J. E., Roberts, L. M., & Bednar, J. (2010). Pathways for positive identity con-struction at work: Four types of positive identity and the building of social resources. *Academy of Management Review, 35,* 265–293.

    Ely, R., Meyerson, D., & Davidson, M. N. (2006). Rethinking political correctness. *Harvard Business Review, 84*(9), 79–87.

    Ramarajan, L. & Thomas, D. A. (2011). A positive approach to studying diversity in organizations. In K. S. Cameron & G. M. Spreitzer (Eds.), *The Oxford handbook of posi-tive organizational scholarship* (pp. 552–565). New York: Oxford University Press.

12. Modupe Akinola, Sandra Cha, Gwendolyn Combs, Stephanie Creary, Erika James, Katherine Klein, Ellen Kossek, David Kravitz, Denise Lewin Loyd, Debra Meyerson, Valerie Myers, and Ryan Quinn.

13. Morris, M. W., Leung, K., Ames, D., & Lickel, B. (1999). Views from inside and out-side: Integrating emic and etic insights about culture and justice. *Academy of Manage-ment Review, 24,* 781–796.

SECTION I

Multiple Identities and Resources

Section Introduction

Amy Lemley, Laura Morgan Roberts,
Lynn Perry Wooten, and Martin N. Davidson

In 2014, women's fashion and lifestyle magazine *Marie Claire* announced the addition of Janet Mock to its contributing editor roster. The author of *Redefining Realness: My Path to Womanhood, Identity, Love & So Much More* is many things: Author. Speaker. Advocate. African American. Transgender woman. It was in the pages of

Marie Claire that Mock had come out as transgender three years earlier, revealing a secret that few people knew, even close colleagues at People.com, where Mock was a staff editor. In commenting about her new role at *Marie Claire*, Mock said she refused to be identified by a single distinction. She would not "just be thrown into a corner as the trans correspondent," she told the Poynter Institute. "I'll also give my perspective on beauty, pop culture, and politics" (Klinger, 2014). She acknowledges that no one identity characterizes her—or anyone. "Representation is so reductive and so basic," she told a crowd at the University of Delaware, adding, with a hint of humor, "Like, don't be basic!" (Jusczak, 2014). Although she is seen largely as a transgender advocate, she has said she wrote her memoir *Redefining Realness* for all women and girls, and many of her observations reach across all boundaries. "Self-definition and self-determination are about the many varied decisions that we make to compose and journey toward ourselves," she writes, "about the audacity and strength to proclaim, create, and evolve into who we know ourselves to be. It's okay if your personal definition is in a constant state of flux as you navigate the world" (Mock, 2014).

Race. Gender. Sexual orientation or identity. Country of origin. Socioeconomic background. Age. Consciously or unconsciously, organizations often marginalize according to characteristics such as these. Some organizations do acknowledge difference. Few embrace it as an asset. Looking to positive psychology for ways to engage differences rather than ignore them is the focus of this section's first chapter, "Positive Psychology's Contributions and Prospects for Engaging Differences at Work." In it, Wilder, Rao, and Donaldson provide an overview of related research in the two fields of study this book seeks to unite: Positive Organizational Scholarship (POS) and Diversity and Inclusion. Discovering there is little to go on as far as combined research is concerned, the authors offer vignettes and recommendations that set the stage for an engaging, surprising, hopeful, and challenging group of chapters exploring how positive psychology could—and has—engaged differences at work.

The second chapter, "Resourcefulness in Action: The Case of Global Diversity Management," considers how organizations can engage global diversity successfully. When an organization's spheres of activity span countries or continents or necessitate a multinational workforce, it may seem best to avoid a culture clash by ignoring or downplaying cultural differences. But Creary explains how, through social identity resourcing, there is an opportunity to leverage these potentially significant differences to create new resources rather than merely "handle" or "cope" with them. (Indeed, that is a recurrent theme in this book as authors integrate diversity, inclusion, and POS.)

Most of the time, the dominant culture is seen to have the most value. A Positive Organizational Scholarship lens invites an inquiry into how nondominant cultural capital creates value for the entire enterprise, as in "Sources of Strength: Mobilizing Minority Racial, Ethnic, and Cultural Identities as Resources." Among other things, minorities have had to develop valuable skills in confronting marginalization and stereotyping—leadership skills including self-reliance, creativity, diligence, perseverance, biculturalism, attunement to others' perceptions, and relationships with constituencies. Roberts and Cha argue that these skills can be leveraged for the individuals and for the organizations they are part of, allowing both to thrive.

Continuing with the exploration of turning a negative into a positive, "How Identities and Discrimination Catalyze Global Entrepreneurship" presents three vignettes about multiple identities as resources. In each, an entrepreneur's distinct experiences and characteristics, including cultural background, directly influenced the choices he or she made to boldly step forward. Ramarajan and LeRoux-Rutledge's chapter illuminates how multiple identities foster business development and innovation.

Building on the discussion of embracing and capitalizing on minority identities, the last chapter in this section explores what it means to have multiple, intersecting identities—some stereotyped, some lauded, some perhaps unknown in an individual's professional realm. In "Intersectional Identity Salience and Positive Identity Construction," Atewologun suggests that the key to fully expressing these identities with less fear of stereotyping or marginalization may lie in self-insight, social resources, and organizational culture, and a positive organizational framework may position both the individual and the group to benefit.

This collection of chapters bridges diversity, inclusion, and POS to explore the myriad ways that embracing multiple identities can generate valued resources and build individual and organizational capacity for our global society.

References

Jusczak, M. (2014, November 10). Not your "diverse learning experience": Trans author Janet Mock talks privilege, representation. *Review*. http://udreview.com/2014/11/10/not-your-diverse-learning-experience-trans-author-janet-mock-talks-privilege-representation/

Klinger, L. (2014, July 22). Janet Mock won't "be thrown into a corner as the trans correspondent" at Marie Claire. *Poynter Institute*. http://www.poynter.org/news/mediawire/259806/janet-mock-wont-be-thrown-into-a-corner-as-the-trans-correspondent-at-marie-claire/

Mock, J. (2014). *Redefining realness: My path to womanhood, identity, love so much more*. New York: Atria Books.

1

POSITIVE PSYCHOLOGY'S CONTRIBUTIONS AND PROSPECTS FOR ENGAGING DIFFERENCES AT WORK

Natasha N. Wilder, Meghana A. Rao, and Stewart I. Donaldson

Kyle[1] is a transgender man in his mid-30s who works at a boutique financial firm in San Francisco. Although he has not come out as transgender (or trans*) to his coworkers (who assume he is a cisgender[2] male), he finds himself uniquely positioned to bridge differences among employees and connect with them across gendered divides. Many of his cisgender female coworkers find him to be more sympathetic to their concerns than other men in the office. Similarly, cisgender male coworkers include him in conversations they would not typically engage in with female colleagues. In these instances, Kyle sometimes acts as a de facto translator, providing a subtle counterpoint perspective that his colleagues value. Kyle acknowledges that his socialization as a woman (prior to identifying as transgender) and his transition to living and being recognized as a man have helped him adapt his interaction style to match traditionally feminine and masculine modalities. He is especially attuned to gendered ways of employing tone, gestures, and language to connect with others, which facilitates access to spaces and relationships that might not otherwise be so readily available to him if he were cisgender.

Kyle's story illustrates how a gender minority experience can be an organizational asset. In this case, Kyle's transgender identity contributes to overall improved workplace communication. This framing of minority gender identity lies in contrast to how common discourse and psychological research often address gender diversity, typically following a problem orientation or deficit approach (e.g., Budge, Adelson, & Howard, 2013). For instance, prevailing consideration of trans* experiences highlights adverse health conditions (e.g., Clements-Nolle et al., 2001), social stigma, and precarious career opportunities (e.g., Badgett et al., 2007), all of which are outcomes that position trans* identity as a challenge that requires a solution. Similarly, the consideration of broader diversity topics such as gender or race often identifies attendant inequities (e.g., lower pay for women than men in the workplace), exemplifying a deficit approach. This approach is a well-worn path in social science research and has garnered valuable findings to improve the lives of many. But the field of positive psychology forges alternate routes toward social justice and workplace inclusion (see Donaldson, Csikszentmihalyi, & Nakamura, 2011).

Whereas Positive Organizational Scholarship primarily examines how organizational structures and practices can engender strength, generativity, and thriving for an organization as a whole, positive psychology also marshals inquiry into individual strengths, behaviors, psychological mechanisms, and conditions that foster thriving in the workplace (Donaldson & Dollwet, 2013; Donaldson & Ko, 2010). As the field of positive psychology enters its second decade, it is an apt time for us to take stock of its treatment of diversity in organizations. The basis for this chapter is our review of positive psychology research published in peer-reviewed journals between 1998 and 2013 (Donaldson, Dollwet, & Rao, 2014). From a total of 1,336 articles, we identified 10 that specifically addressed diversity topics. In the following sections, we use these articles to structure a brief discussion of positive psychological framing of gender, race, socioeconomic status, sexual orientation, and age in organizational literature, as well as implications for inclusive organizational practices.

Gender

Positive psychology holds promise for illuminating the organizational assets of women and noncisgender individuals. For instance, in the case of women in male-dominated industries, strengths-based coaching is one technique for stimulating positive work outcomes (Elston & Boniwell, 2011). This type of development encourages women to capitalize on their strengths, and also has the potential to broaden conversations about what constitutes an asset in the workplace. In this way, a strategy like strengths-based coaching could facilitate the exploration of behaviors that are often considered "feminine" and counterproductive (e.g., expressing emotions during meetings or utilizing collaborative decision-making processes that require a longer timeline), and stimulate a reexamination of the value of these behaviors in a work setting. A POS lens on gender in the workplace could illuminate additional benefits of gender-inclusive policies and practices.

Race and Ethnicity

Findings from the review of diversity research in positive psychology (Donaldson & Rao, in press) indicate that there is a relative absence of a focus on race and ethnicity. This mirrors a broader need for understanding and mobilizing factors that support the thriving of racial and ethnic minorities in organizations. Generating positive psychological knowledge about race in organizations necessitates methodological choices that take race into account, such as asking employees to self-identify their races in company surveys and understanding how this characteristic relates to other variables of interest (e.g., feeling comfortable speaking up in meetings). To build a knowledge base and apply it in organizations requires us, as scholars and practitioners, to inquire into whether our underlying assumptions take into account both (1) historical and existing structural inequities and (2) potential unique assets of racial and ethnic minorities. For example, research on Latinos who immigrate to the United States to work in construction jobs highlighted innovative strategies for upward career mobility in the absence of formal credentials, education, or English language skills (Hagan, Lowe, & Quingla, 2011). Building our understanding about race and work will allow us to coalesce a richer and more nuanced picture of diversity factors in the workplace, reducing our reliance on simplified narratives that are often rooted in stereotypes.

Socioeconomic Status

Socioeconomic status (SES) is closely tied to access to vocational opportunities, creating a salient need for positive work-identity formation in the working poor. Low-SES workers are more likely to hold jobs that carry social or moral stigma, known as "dirty work" (see Ashforth & Kreiner, 1999). A practice of employing moral imagination (i.e., situating a decision within its context, envisioning a positive future, developing awareness of one's own feelings, and empathically taking the perspective of others) can help "dirty workers" feel positively toward their work (Roca, 2010). Similarly, blue collar workers establish positive work identities by focusing on the universal dignity of all jobs, positive social exchanges, or the quality of their performance (Lucas, 2011). Research suggests that temporary workers (who often have low SES) place higher meaning than permanent workers on well-being at work (Mininni et al., 2010).

Sexual Orientation

The relative paucity of positive organizational psychological research addressing sexual orientation reflects a broader tendency toward organizations' refraining from collecting sexual orientation data from employees. Historically, companies have shied away from asking employees about their sexual orientation to mitigate the risk of equal opportunity employment issues or because they could not identify a reason for tracking this workforce demographic. Bolstering the case for positive organizational impact, a Williams Institute review uncovered that workplace climates and policies supportive of the LGBTQ (for lesbian, gay, bisexual, transgender, and queer [or sometimes "questioning"]) led to employee openness about identifying as LGBTQ, resulting in less discrimination, improved health outcomes for employees, and higher job satisfaction and organizational commitment (Badgett et al., 2013). Further, a provocative new study posits that sexual minority status may sometimes buffer against racial prejudice in a work setting. In the study, black men being perceived as gay appeared to mitigate negative stereotypes that white people hold of black men (e.g., as threatening), leading to significantly higher salary recommendations for gay black males than for straight black males (Pedulla, 2014). These findings support the idea that LGBTQ individuals may experience greater acceptance of a range of behaviors than those traditionally pre-scribed to their cisgender and straight coworkers. With employees' self-identifiers such as gender, age, and race to offer context, employers can leverage employees' contributions for the good of the organization while also enhancing their level of engagement. More research is needed to understand assets of LGBTQ employees and identify the conditions that foster positive workplace climates for all sexual minorities.

Age

Understanding and harnessing the contributions of workers of all ages requires a change in organizational narratives about the ideal worker when recruiting, hiring, and developing employees. In all workers, engagement is a key to retention and also to productivity. Schullery (2013) reviewed studies of workplace engagement in the United States across generations and noted that Baby Boomers reported the highest work engagement, and Millennials among the lowest. She suggests that Baby Boomers are often at the peak of their careers, while Millennials find themselves in entry-level positions that fail to meet their expectations of provid-ing challenging and meaningful tasks. Millennials seek to learn, be challenged, and understand the value of their contributions; when provided guidance and support, they are able to deliver exceptionally high performance (Tulgan, 2009). Like-wise, older workers possess higher *positive psychological* capital, intellectual capital, emotional intelligence, and social capital than younger workers, stemming from the development of self-awareness over a lifetime (Peterson & Spiker, 2005). This research implies a need for organizations to shift their focus from managing disen-gaged workers of particular generations to crafting jobs that are meaningful along generational preferences. A positive approach to engaging employees across ages would involve identifying the unique strengths of each generation, in addition to assessing an individual's characteristics, and cultivating a work culture in which all can thrive.

Conclusion

Historical legacies and current structures that privilege some groups over oth-ers can make it easier for organizations and academics to identify the assets of dominant groups (e.g., white cisgender, heterosexual males in the Silicon Valley information technology industry). To combat this effect and centralize minority experience as an essential organizational perspective, it is critical that positive orga-nizational research inquires into the assets of marginalized groups. As Kyle's story illustrates, and the rest of this chapter elucidates, minority experiences can translate into unique employee assets that benefit organizations. In Kyle's case, being a transgender man affords him communication tools that facilitate connecting across gendered divides at work. Similarly, strategies such as strengths-based coaching for gender minorities (e.g., women or nonbinary people in male-dominated industries) can help these employees to recognize and capitalize on their distinctive resources in the workplace. From an organizational perspective, broadening the understanding of the "ideal" worker may require looking beyond a specific age range, gender, race, or sexual orientation. The development of promising employees may require educating managers about unconscious bias that likely stimulates the aforementioned findings on promotions of black and white, gay and straight males (Pedulla, 2014). Accumulating knowledge about the conditions that support the thriving of individuals of diverse affiliations and identities can have a positive impact on employees and organizations alike. Those of us who come from an academic perspective can support original research in these areas and encourage cross-pollination from other disciplines that focus on diverse groups such as gender, LGBTQ, and race studies.

For organizational leaders, creating a work culture that is inclusive of diverse employees goes beyond acknowledging difference—especially as a singular focus on disenfranchisement or disadvantages of certain groups—to include cultivating assets and enriching the experiences of all employees. This ongoing process requires shifting the discourse (Rao, 2014) and assessing the entire employee experience, from recruiting to development/retention efforts, with attention to both a diversity lens and a positive psychology/Positive Organizational Scholarship objective. The process of empowering members who are different from the rest of the group requires leaders to build an inclusive organizational culture.

For Practitioners: Questions to Stimulate a Work Culture of Inclusion

- Where and how do you recruit potential employees? Do your recruiting practices make an effort to reach underrepresented groups in your company/industry? What does a picture of the "ideal employee" look like in your company? Is this archetype indicative of how you recruit, select, promote, and otherwise develop employees?
- How does your organization indicate who belongs or is a good "cultural fit"? Language, images on your website, metaphors used by senior leaders, and many other cultural artifacts and practices send messages to employees about belonging. For example, the absence of a gender-neutral bathroom (i.e., one with neither a sign featuring a pants-wearing or dress-wearing figure to specify who can enter), could

(*continued*)

feel alienating for an employee who is trans* (that is, who does not identify as male or female).

- If your company offers social events, do these systematically exclude some organizational members? For example, events occurring in the evenings may privilege employees who do not have to commute and may exclude those who leave promptly after work to attend to their families.
- Who participates in decision-making and meetings? How can you elicit the perspectives of members who are typically not included?
- When conducting surveys of employee opinions, what demographic data do you collect? Why do you choose to measure those specific characteristics? Do your questionnaires ask about biological sex (male, female, intersex, etc.) or gender (man, woman, trans, etc.); are there options on questionnaires that are inclusive to those outside of the sex binary? Are race and ethnicity options inclusive of multiple and mixed identities?
- Does your organization explicitly state a commitment to inclusivity? Are there practices and policies that support this commitment? How do employees perceive any existing practices or policies?
- Have you explored programs such as mentoring, employee resource groups, coaching, or other similar strengths-based approaches to develop underrepresented groups and individuals?

Notes

1. The name has been changed to protect identity.
2. Trans* is an inclusive term used to encapsulate identities such as transgender, transsexual, and outside the gender binary of man and woman. Cisgender is used to describe an identity in which an individual's self-perception of his or her gender (e.g., man or woman) matches the sex he or she was assigned at birth (i.e., male or female).

References

Ashforth, B. E., & Kreiner, G. E. (1999). "How can you do it?": Dirty work and the challenge of constructing a positive identity. *Academy of Management Review, 24*(3), 413–434.

Badgett, M.V.L., Durso, L. E., Kastanis, A., & Mallory, C. (2013). *The business impact of LGBT-supportive workplace policies* (pp. 1–37). Los Angeles: Williams Institute, University of California–Los Angeles.

Badgett, M.V.L., Lau, H., Sears, B., & Ho, D. (2007). Bias in the workplace: Consistent evidence of sexual orientation and gender identity discrimination. http://www.law.ucla.edu/williamsinstitute

Budge, S. L., Adelson, J. L., & Howard, K. S. (2013). Anxiety and depression in transgender individuals: The roles of transition status, loss, social support, and coping. *Journal of Consulting and Clinical Psychology, 81*(3), 545–557.

Clements-Nolle, K., Marx, R., Guzman, R., & Katz, M. (2001). HIV prevalence, risk behaviors, health care use, and mental health status of transgender persons: Implications for public health intervention. *American Journal of Public Health, 91*(6), 915–921.

Donaldson, S. I. (2011). Determining what works, if anything, in positive psychology. In S. I. Donaldson, M. Csikszentmihalyi, & J. Nakamura (Eds.), *Applied positive psychology: Improving everyday life, health, schools, work, and society* (pp. 3–11). London: Routledge.

Donaldson, S. I., & Dollwet, M. (2013). Taming the waves and horses of positive organizational psychology. *Advances in Positive Organizational Psychology, 1*, 1–22.

Donaldson, S. I., Dollwet, M., & Rao, M. A. (2014). Happiness, excellence, and optimal functioning revisited: Examining the peer-reviewed literature linked to positive psychology. *Journal of Positive Psychology, 9*(6), 1–11.

Donaldson, S. I., & Ko, I. (2010). Positive organizational psychology, behavior, and scholarship: A review of the emerging literature and evidence base. *Journal of Positive Psychology, 5*(3), 177–191.

Donaldson, S. I., & Rao, M. A. (in press). *Theory-driven positive psychology: A culturally responsive scientific approach.* New York: Routledge.

Elston, F., & Boniwell, I. (2011). A grounded theory study of the value derived by women in financial services through a coaching intervention to help them identify their strengths and practice using them in the workplace. *International Coaching Psychology Review, 6*(1), 16–32.

Hagan, J., Lowe, N., & Quingla, C. (2011). Skills on the move: Rethinking the relationship between human capital and immigrant economic mobility. *Work and occupations, 38*(2), 149–178.

Lucas, K. (2011). Blue-collar discourses of workplace dignity: Using outgroup comparisons to construct positive identities. *Management Communication Quarterly, 25*(2), 353–374. doi:10.1177/0893318910386445

Mininni, G., Manuti, A., Scardigno, R., & Rubino, R. (2010). Subjective wellbeing between organizational bonds and cultural contaminations. *World Futures: The Journal of General Evolution, 66*(6), 387–397.

Pedulla, D. S. (2014). The positive consequences of negative stereotypes: Race, sexual orientation, and the job application process. *Social Psychology Quarterly, 77*(1), 75–94. doi:10.1177/0190272513506229

Peterson, S. J., & Spiker, B. K. (2005). Establishing the positive contributory value of older workers: A positive psychology perspective. *Organizational Dynamics, 34*(2), 153–167.

Rao, M. A. (2014). Cultivating openness to change in multicultural organizations: Assessing the value of appreciative discourse. *Organization Development Journal, 32*(3), 75–88.

Roca, E. (2010). The exercise of moral imagination in stigmatized work groups. *Journal of Business Ethics, 96*(1), 135–147. doi:10.1007/s10551-010-0454-9

Schullery, N. M. (2013). Workplace engagement and generational differences in values. *Business Communication Quarterly, 76*(2), 252–265.

Tulgan, B. (2009). *Not everyone gets a trophy: How to manage generation Y.* San Francisco, CA: Jossey-Bass.

2

RESOURCEFULNESS IN ACTION

The Case for Global Diversity Management

Stephanie J. Creary

> Your vision has to be a vision that resonates around the globe. If it doesn't resonate around the globe, people can feel like they can opt out of the vision because it really doesn't apply to them. . . . [In addition,] any diversity strategy not aligned with the core messaging, core deliverables of the company is doomed to failure.
> —*A diversity leader (DL002), interviewed by the author*

Without a doubt, organizational diversity initiatives can and do fail (Davidson, 2011; Jacobsen, 2014; Visconti, 2011). But, as this diversity leader suggests, and a growing body of research on global diversity management echoes, a relatable vision and strategy can prevent such failure (Mor Barak, 2014; Nishii & Ozbilgin, 2007; Sippola & Smale, 2007). Yet developing and mobilizing a vision and strategy for diversity management can be difficult for diversity leaders given that these actions require them to adopt a business perspective (Creary, 2008; Lahiri, 2008; Mitchell & Creary, 2009). Notably, scholars have argued that a business perspective on diversity management may be too reductive; further, it could mask a moral imperative to address issues of inclusion and exclusion along sociodemographic lines in organizations (Ramarajan & Thomas, 2010; Wrench, 2005). Regarding race in particular, Wrench (2005) stated, "The problem is that fighting racism and discrimination will now only be seen as important if there is a recognizable business reason for it." As a result, diversity leaders who have been interested historically in addressing issues of inequality in their organizations may find it difficult to embrace a business-oriented strategic partner role (Lahiri, 2008; Mitchell & Creary, 2009).

In this chapter, I use the case of global diversity management in 14 large multinational organizations (12 American, one European, one Asian) to illustrate how diversity leaders took a positive approach to global diversity management in spite of the tension they were experiencing in their roles. In doing so, I also offer a Positive Organizational Scholarship (POS) perspective on global diversity management in which I examine a phenomenon whereby identity group-based differences are seen as valuable and focus on an established condition of positive deviance (e.g., Ramarajan & Thomas, 2010). Specifically, I propose "social identity resourcing" as a generative mechanism whereby individuals' social identities are engaged as organizational assets to create new resources. "Social identities" refers to one or more social categories or memberships (e.g., race, ethnicity) represented in an individual's self-concept in which he or she shares some degree of emotional involvement with other in-group members and that describe and prescribe how one should think, feel, and behave as a group member (Tajfel & Turner, 1979). "Resourcing," refers to the creation in practice of assets such that they enable actors to enact schemas or knowledge structures (Feldman, 2004; Sonenshein, 2014)—making the most of what is available. Thus, I use "social identity resourcing" to describe the practice through which diversity leaders engage organizational members' social identities as assets for creating a vision and strategy for global diversity management.

In taking a POS approach to global diversity management, this chapter departs from past research on global diversity management that draws comparisons between a global approach and a multidomestic (i.e., country-level) approach to diversity management (e.g., Nishii & Ozbilgin, 2007; Sippola & Smale, 2007) or discusses a conceptual framework for managing global diversity (Mor Barak, 2014). Instead, it invites diversity and POS scholars, practitioners, and educators to consider a social identity-based mechanism that promotes both individual and collective flourishing in global organizations.

Rethinking Diversity Management: The Development of Global Diversity Initiatives

Prior to 2008, the diversity practices within each of the organizations I studied concentrated largely on increasing the representation of individuals from historically underrepresented groups in frontline and leadership positions in different markets around the world, or "developing diverse talent." In some organizations, this practice was motivated largely by a legal push for equal opportunity and social justice. In others, it reflected the organization's desire to draw on the insights individuals have attained through their membership in different social groups to understand and gain entrée into diverse markets around the world (for a larger discussion of similar dynamics, please refer to Ely & Thomas, 2001; Thomas & Ely, 1996). While the current practice was met with skepticism, particularly from majority group members, it was recognized widely, especially within North American and European markets, as the going approach.

Between 2008 and 2009, all the organizations I studied began increasing efforts to globalize their operations, starting with the development of an overarching strategy that could be viewed as relevant not just within individual markets, but in different markets around the world. As a consequence, they needed to reconsider existing diversity practices so they could support the execution of such a strategy. Yet commitment to a more global approach to diversity management was not widespread. For example, one diversity leader compared the challenges in her company to elections for public office:

> You've got a base, and you've got to figure out how you keep your base and then extrapolate to the new potential voters or constituents. The base of diversity truly has been a U.S. thing. So how do you keep that base engaged, happy, feeling like they're important and people care about them while you drive a global strategy?
>
> *(DL002)*

Encountering perspectives such as this motivated the diversity leaders in my sample to take actions that would enable a wider group of stakeholders (supporters and nonsupporters) to become more engaged in global diversity management. Hence, they began reconceptualizing their existing approaches to diversity management.

Social Identity Resourcing

The diversity leaders I studied engaged in social identity resourcing to create a vision and strategy for diversity management that was more global in orientation—which required engaging organizational members' social identities as assets. Social identity resourcing took two forms: harnessing and integrating. *Harnessing* refers to practices that provided organizational members from different social groups with opportunities to share their perspectives on how global diversity management should be approached. For each organization, this meant creating venues in which organizational members of all sociodemographic backgrounds would be invited to contribute to the development of the vision and strategy. In U.S.-based companies, harnessing involved the creation of task forces comprising senior leaders from different demographic groups (e.g., women, African Americans, people with disabilities, people of various generations, etc.) to talk about global diversity. One diversity leader described her organization's approach to global diversity management:

> We have ten global teams that are truly global, made up of senior leaders from all of our business units and a representation of our geographies in both developed and developing markets. We're asking them, "How do we accelerate leadership and create a more globally inclusive environment?" And for our businesses that are focused externally, "How do we positively influence the buying decision of customers?" And "Are there key external stakeholders that we need to be collaborating with, in your constituency?"
>
> *(DL010)*

While the American approach to global diversity management continued to prioritize talent development, it was broadened to include the notion that the company should be, in the words of this diversity leader (DL010), "a place where people around the globe, no matter who they are, where they come from . . . have a genuine opportunity to come to this company to contribute and be successful."

In contrast, I found that the diversity leaders in the European and Asian companies were concentrating on convincing their executive teams that they were not, in the words of one leader, "trying to push the American agenda." Hence, their harnessing practices centered much more on developing "cross-culturally competent" leaders. For example, a diversity leader in the Asian company revealed that her organization decided to develop an "agenda on culture" since the number one diversity challenge in her organization was to help Eastern and Western employees work together more effectively across difference.

Where harnessing emphasizes soliciting perspectives from members of different social groups on global diversity management, *integrating* reflects the actual use of these perspectives to mobilize a vision and strategy for global diversity management. Diversity leaders in many U.S.-based organizations discussed using employee affinity groups (i.e., a women's, African American, LGBTQ, or intergenerational network, etc.) as tools for integration. One diversity leader explained:

> Our network groups are still focused on employee development. [Yet,] to some extent, they support marketplace research or ideas or they support research the company is doing. Like the LGBT network has been helpful in looking at potential partnerships for [the company] or potential market opportunities and the women's networks have looked at some opportunities as well.
>
> *(DL008)*

Finally social identity resourcing had the consequence of altering the sense of ownership for diversity management in each of the companies. Whereas diversity management under the previous approach was considered wholly owned by the diversity leader, the new approach to global diversity management fostered a shared sense of ownership between senior leadership and diversity leaders. For example, the American diversity leader in the Asian company worked with her organization's chairman and senior leadership team to promote cross-cultural competence in their organizations. She shared an example of their progress:

> Our chairman spent three hours with the new hires talking with them about the history of the company, his vision, and he talked about culture. He talked about being a global company, the importance of teamwork across culture, value and diversity.
>
> *(DL013)*

As a result of experiencing that shared sense of ownership, many diversity leaders reported that they found it easier to embrace their strategic partner role. One diversity leader commented:

> I really see my role as enabling the organization to [manage diversity] at the business unit level, and that's about as far as I can go. My executive champion meets monthly for half a day with the CEO and all of his peers, and [diversity management] is an agenda item, and I'm not at that meeting. . . . So he behaves in a way that [suggests that diversity] is really important. And he's causing others to behave in that way as well.
>
> *(DL005)*

Social Identity Resourcing: Future Inquiries

In this chapter, I advance a POS perspective of global diversity management by identifying social identity resourcing as a mechanism that addresses issues of inclusion and exclusion in organizations while also maintaining a business perspective of diversity management (cf. Ramarajan & Thomas, 2010). Given its dual focus, social identity resourcing is an important mechanism for engaging differences for capacity building and inclusion in global organizations. Specifically, the *harnessing* form recognizes that giving organizational members from different sociodemographic backgrounds the opportunity to contribute to the development of a vision and strategy for global diversity management is critical to the organization's overall success. The *integrating* form goes one step further to suggest that actually engaging these organizational members in implementation initiatives helps create a shared responsibility for diversity management and one that extends beyond the diversity leader's purview.

In creating this framework for social identity resourcing, I depart from past research on global diversity management, which focuses on revealing the differences between a global and a multidomestic (i.e., country-level) approach to diversity management (e.g., Nishii & Ozbilgin, 2007; Sippola & Smale, 2007) or highlights a conceptual framework for managing global diversity (Mor Barak, 2014). Instead, this chapter draws on both diversity management research (Ely & Thomas, 2001; Ramarajan & Thomas, 2011; Thomas & Ely, 1996) and a POS perspective (Feldman, 2004; Fredrickson & Dutton, 2008; Sonenshein, 2014) to reveal a social identity–based mechanism that promotes individual and collective flourishing in global organizations. Future research and practice on diversity and inclusion and POS should continue this line of inquiry by revealing (1) other mechanisms through which individuals' social identities, particularly those that have been stigmatized or marginalized historically, can contribute to individual and collective flourishing and (2) how engaging leaders at different levels of the organization can enable this work.

For Practitioners: Tips for Addressing Inclusion/Exclusion as Well as Advancing a Business Perspective

- Share the responsibility for global diversity management. The diversity leader should work with the CEO and other key leaders to devise a plan for engaging other organizational leaders as diversity allies.
- Invite organizational members from different sociodemographic backgrounds to share their perspectives on how global diversity management should be approached in the organization. Engage them as partners in implementation initiatives.
- Customize your effort by engaging members of existing employee affinity groups (e.g., women's, Latino, and African American networks) to conduct market research. To promote learning, consider inviting them to conduct research with a constituency of which they are not members.

References

Creary, S. J. (2008). *Leadership, governance, and accountability: A pathway to a diverse and inclusive organization.* New York: Conference Board.

Davidson, M. (2011, October 29). Why diversity efforts fail and how to make them succeed. *Washington Post.* http://www.washingtonpost.com/business/why-diversity-efforts-fail-and-how-to-make-them-succeed/2011/10/24/gIQAJeuLTM_story.html

Ely, R. J. & Thomas, D. A. (2001). Cultural diversity at work: The effects of diversity perspectives on work group processes and outcomes. *Administrative Science Quarterly, 46*(2), 229–273.

Feldman, M. S. (2004). Resources in emerging structures and processes of change. *Organization Science, 15*(3), 295–309.

Fredrickson, B. & Dutton, J. (2008). Unpacking positive organizing: Organizations as sites of individual and group flourishing. *Journal of Positive Psychology, 3*(1), 1–3.

Jacobsen, M. (2014, July 3). Google finally discloses its diversity record, and it's not good. *PBS.* http://www.pbs.org/newshour/updates/google-discloses-workforce-diversity-data-good/

Lahiri, I. (2008). *Creating a competency model for diversity and inclusion practitioners.* New York: Conference Board.

Mitchell, C. & Creary, S. J. (2009). *Diversity and inclusion: Global challenges and opportunities.* New York: Conference Board.

Mor Barak, M. E. (2014). *Managing diversity: Toward a globally inclusive workplace* (3rd ed.). Thousand Oaks, CA: Sage.

Nishii, L. H. & Ozbilgin, M. F. (2007). Global diversity management: Towards a conceptual framework. *International Journal of Human Resource Management, 18*(11), 1883–1894.

Ramarajan, L. & Thomas, D. A. (2011). A positive approach to studying diversity in organizations. In K. S. Cameron & G. Spreitzer (Eds.), *The Oxford handbook of positive organizational scholarship* (pp. 552–565). New York: Oxford University Press.

Sippola, A. & Smale, A. (2007). The global integration of diversity management: A longitudinal case study. *International Journal of Human Resource Management, 18*(11), 1895–1916.

Sonenshein, S. (2014). How organizations foster the creative use of resources. *Academy of Management Journal, 57*(3), 814–848.

Tajfel, H., & Turner, J. C. (1979). An integrative theory of intergroup conflict. *The Social Psychology of Intergroup Relations, 33*(47), 74.

Thomas, D. A. & Ely, R. J. (1996). Making differences matter. *Harvard Business Review, 74*(5), 79–90.

Visconti, L. (2011, September 28). Why multiculturalism fails and what it means to corporate America. DiversityInc. http://www.diversityinc.com/ask-the-white-guy/why-multiculturalism-fails-and-what-it-means-to-corporate-america/

Wrench, J. (2005). Diversity management can be bad for you. *Race & Class, 46*(3), 73–84.

3

SOURCES OF STRENGTH

Mobilizing Minority Racial, Ethnic, and Cultural Identities as Resources

Laura Morgan Roberts and Sandra Cha

In 1903, Dr. W.E.B. Du Bois identified the color line as the defining problem of the 20th century. Despite the election of a self-identified African American of multiracial and multicultural heritage as the 44th President of the United States of America, race continues to be an important analytical concept that explains systems of organizing, group differences in experiences, personal identities, and organizational outcomes in the 21st century (Proudford & Nkomo, 2006; Tesler & Sears, 2010). Scholars often portray the racial minority experience as a daunting series of attempts to navigate "everyday racism" (Essed, 1990), by coping with microaggressions such as discrimination, bias, stereotyping, racialized sexism, and gendered racism that shape and reinforce structural inequities.

We focus this chapter on the sources of strength that equip racial minorities in navigating racial dynamics in social systems. Specifically, we highlight the ways in which racial minorities mobilize racial, ethnic, and cultural identities as resources for personal and organizational effectiveness. We consider race to be "a social construction [rather than a biological fact] by which individuals and groups are classified by others, are assigned labels, and/or assign labels to themselves" (Proudford & Nkomo, 2006). We also recognize that "race is both an individual characteristic and a social/political issue with personal and collective meaning" (Ospina & Foldy, 2009). Our research on navigating race as a part of everyday work activity builds theoretical and practical bridges between diversity, inclusion, and positive organizational scholarship in important ways. Rather than study the sources or effects of bias per se, we have inquired into the experiences of racial minority professionals as they endeavor to handle complicated, and sometimes subtle or ambiguous, race-related dynamics that surface during everyday work activities.

A Resource Lens on Racial Identities at Work

While many of the racial minorities in our studies acknowledge the challenges of being racially underrepresented in their work groups, organizations, or professions, they also offer a resource view of how race-related experiences and social meanings about race can promote work effectiveness in racially diverse settings. Navigating race involves resourceful maneuvering among simultaneously occurring constraints and possibilities. In accordance with a burgeoning stream of research on positive identities at work (see Dutton, Roberts, & Bednar, 2010; Roberts & Dutton, 2009), our studies illuminate multiple pathways through which a minority racial identity may also be a source of strength that promotes favorable outcomes at work.

Sociologists and psychologists have established that identities are associated with resources. Sociocultural identities such as racial identity provide social status, relationships, and cultural experiences that generate "capital" in the sense that they provide access to opportunities and produce valuable insights that can equip people to interact effectively with social contexts (Bourdieu, 2001). The field of Positive Organizational Scholarship (POS) examines how organizations can discover and leverage this capital. Even so, with respect to race, researchers have typically classified dominant, majority cultural capital as being more desirable, valuable, and privileged than nondominant cultural capital, which is associated with minority and lower-status racial groups. Our research reveals several ways in which nondominant cultural capital also creates value for individuals who work in diverse organizations, through symbolism, relationship building, resilience, and creativity. This perspective is aligned with the research that supports that nondominant cultural capital is a valuable resource for building relationships and establishing legitimacy within one's own racial, ethnic, and/or cultural identity group (Carter, 2005). Nondominant cultural capital also equips leaders from racial minority groups—who may cultivate valuable leadership characteristics from their experiences as marginalized members of society, including self-reliance, creativity, diligence, perseverance, biculturalism, attunement to others' perceptions, and relationships with constituencies (Bell & Nkomo, 2001; Ospina & Foldy, 2009; Parker & Ogilvie, 1996; Thomas & Gabarro, 1999).

Toward a Typology of Nondominant Cultural Capital as a Resource

Our research on minority professionals (Cha & Roberts, 2014; Roberts, Cha, & Kim, 2014; Roberts, Settles, & Jellison, 2008) illuminates the resourcefulness of racial minorities as they navigate race in everyday work activities. The participants in our studies emphasized how the simultaneity of their race, gender, and age creates unique opportunities for engaging their nondominant cultural capital to increase personal and organizational effectiveness. The range of resources that are associated with nondominant cultural capital extends from surface-level

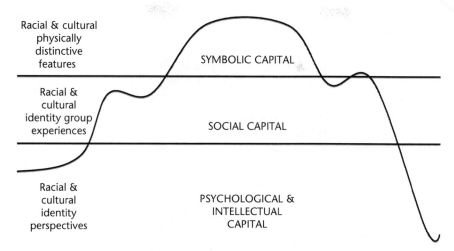

FIGURE 3.1 Types of nondominant cultural capital associated with minority racial identities.

characteristics to less visible yet still substantive sources of culturally based knowledge and insight (Figure 3.1).

Symbolic capital. Symbolic capital is a resource that minorities generate and mobilize via the power of their physical representation of diversity. While much has been written on tokenism and its deleterious effects on relationships and the well-being of minorities (e.g., Jackson, Thoits, & Taylor, 1995; Kanter, 1977; Yoder, 2002), it is important to acknowledge that some minorities empower themselves by increasing the salience of their distinctiveness in the workplace. For example, a young female Asian American journalist in one of our qualitative studies of identity remarked:

> [When] I got sent to [a particular] bureau, I think in terms of being young, Asian—you know, young, female, and ethnic, is that they were looking to brighten up the bureau and get some more personality. And I do, actually. I have a candy jar. Actually that's something that's . . . kind of apolitical but political . . . And the thing is it makes people come by your desk, they remember you, you have established a presence. And they think fondly of you.

Symbolic capital can also have deeper meanings that mobilize social change. The Rev. Dr. Martin Luther King, Jr., a symbolic leader of social justice and inclusion, embodied the power of nondominant symbolic capital. When Dr. King and other civil rights movement demonstrators were physically beaten by racist leaders and citizens during nonviolent protests, their struggle symbolized the hypocrisy between America's stated ideals and its legalized practices of brutal oppression (Roberts, Roberts, O'Neill, & Blake-Beard 2008).

Social capital. Social capital is a resource minorities can generate and mobilize via the power of building connections with members of their own identity groups by increasing the salience of their cultural backgrounds in the workplace. This way of engaging nondominant cultural capital was featured in Carter's (2005) foundational work on the topic; she examined how black adolescents used nondominant cultural capital to build relationships with one another. Subsequent research on racial minority professionals also illustrates the value of nondominant cultural capital in generating social capital with other racial minorities (Ely & Thomas, 2001). For example, we interviewed a 30-year-old African American female pediatrician who said, "If the patient is a minority, there is an automatic trust. It's a lot easier. I've had mothers and grandmothers say to me, 'I'm so proud of you.' I get that from the janitorial staff as well. I am always respectful."

Nondominant cultural capital also helps generate social capital in racially diverse situations. People who feel marginalized are more attuned to social cues (Frable, Blackstone, & Scherbaum, 1990). This social attunement equips minorities with cross-cultural competencies that promote relationship building across dimensions of difference. An example of social capital might be found in U.S. President Barack Obama's willingness to discuss aspects of his multi-faceted racial background as a way of connecting with other Americans through his public address ("A More Perfect Union") during the 2008 Presidential campaign.

Psychological capital. Nondominant cultural capital also generates psychological capital—through the benefits of group identification and self-esteem. Racial minority groups often serve as identity bases that provide belongingness and positive regard, both of which are valuable in fulfilling human needs and protecting people from psychologically threatening experiences. For example, Henderson and Bell's chapter in the current volume explains how racial pride fosters resilience and buffers the deleterious effects of racism on racial minorities.

Human/intellectual capital. Nondominant cultural capital also generates forms of human and intellectual capital (e.g., abilities and knowledge), particularly creativity. For example, minority scholars often draw upon nondominant cultural capital in multiple stages of the creative process of inquiry: building relationships with diverse colleagues and students (drawing on social capital), generating new research ideas (drawing on creativity), reviewing others' research (drawing on creativity), and obtaining access to research samples (drawing on social capital). These multiple forms of capital combined can be a source of strength for furthering creative research. (This book, *Positive Organizing in a Global Society*, is an example of such creative bridging. Our reexaminations of diversity-related phenomena through POS lenses have opened up new pathways of discovery and practice for those who study and shape 21st-century organizations.)

A Silver Lining

In sum, our research studies suggest that having a minority racial identity in the workplace—though it is often associated with significant stereotyping, bias, and discrimination—can have a silver lining for those who view that identity as a resource. Indeed, the very tokenism and marginalization that create challenges and stress for racial minorities can, paradoxically, also be sources of strength that empower minorities not only to navigate racism but also to make rich, unique, and powerful contributions to their work groups and organizations.

For Practitioners: Two Tips for Mobilizing Cultural Identities as Resources

1. **Take stock of your nondominant cultural capital.** Many of us belong, or have belonged in the past, to a nondominant identity group (e.g., being younger or older than one's teammates, holding a lower-status position in the organization, or being the token person from a country on a multinational team). If you revealed them, how could your nondominant identities serve as sources of strength in the workplace (e.g., as compelling symbols of the qualities you bring to a team or shared identities linking you to others)? Use this reflection to tap into the cross-cultural sensitivity, resilience, and creativity that are the unexpected fruits of having experienced marginalization.
2. **Seek to understand and support colleagues who draw on their nondominant cultural capital to benefit your organization.** Your support signals that colleagues can leverage their marginalized identities without fearing further marginalization at work. But don't pressure colleagues to do so: People's degree of comfort with their nondominant identities varies.

References

Bell, E.L.J.E., & Nkomo, S.M. (2001). *Our separate ways: Black and white women and the struggle for professional identity.* Boston, MA: Harvard Business School Press.

Bourdieu, P. (2001). The forms of capital. In M. Granovetter & R. Swedburg (Eds.), *The sociology of economic life* (pp. 96–111). Cambridge, MA: Westview Press.

Carter, P.L. (2005). *Keepin' it real: School success beyond Black and White.* New York: Oxford University Press.

Cha, S.E., & Roberts, L.M. (2014). *Engaging racial identity-related resources: A qualitative study of Asian Americans in journalism.* Manuscript in preparation, Brandeis University, Waltham, MA.

Dutton, J.E., Roberts, L.M., & Bednar, J. (2010). Pathways for positive identity construction at work: Four types of positive identity and the building of social resources. *Academy of Management Review, 35,* 265–293. doi:10.5465/AMR.2010.48463334

Ely, R.J., & Thomas, D.A. (2001). Cultural diversity at work: The effects of diversity perspectives on work group processes and outcomes. *Administrative Science Quarterly, 46*(2), 229–273.

Essed, P. (1990). *Everyday racism: Reports from women of two cultures.* Claremont, CA: Hunter House.

Frable, D. E., Blackstone, T., & Scherbaum, C. (1990). Marginal and mindful: Deviants in social interactions. *Journal of Personality and Social Psychology, 59*, 140–149. doi:10.1037/0022-3514.59.1.140

Jackson, P. B., Thoits, P. A., & Taylor, H. F. (1995). Composition of the workplace and psychological well-being: The effects of tokenism on America's black elite. *Social Forces, 74*, 543–557. doi:10.2307/2580491

Kanter, R. M. (1977). *Men and women of the corporation.* New York: Basic Books.

Ospina, S., & Foldy, E. (2009). A critical review of race and ethnicity in the leadership literature: Surfacing context, power, and the collective dimensions of leadership. *The Leadership Quarterly, 20*, 875–895. doi:10.1016/j.leaqua.2009.09.005

Parker, P. S., & ogilvie, dt (1996). Gender, culture and leadership: Toward a culturally distinct model of African-American women executives' leadership strategies. *The Leadership Quarterly, 7*, 189–214. doi:10.1016/S1048-9843(96)90040-5

Proudford, K., & Nkomo, S. (2006). Race and ethnicity in organizations. In A. Konrad, P. Prasad, & J. Pringle (Eds.), *Handbook of workplace diversity* (pp. 323–344). London: Sage.

Roberts, D. D., Roberts, L. M., O'Neill, R. M., & Blake-Beard, S. D., (2008). The invisible work of managing visibility for social change: Insights from the leadership of Reverend Dr. Martin Luther King Jr. *Business & Society, 47*, 425–456. doi:10.1177/0007650308323817

Roberts, L. M., Cha, S. E., & Kim, S. S. (2014). Strategies for managing impressions of racial identity in the workplace. *Cultural Diversity and Ethnic Minority Psychology, 20*, 529–540. doi:10.1037/a0037238

Roberts, L. M., & Dutton, J. E. (Eds.). (2009). *Exploring positive identities and organizations: Building a theoretical and research foundation.* New York: Routledge.

Roberts, L. M., Settles, I. H., & Jellison, W. A. (2008). Predicting the strategic identity management of gender and race. *Identity: An International Journal of Theory and Research, 8*, 269–306. doi:10.1080/15283480802365270

Tesler, M., & Sears, D. O. (2010). *Obama's race: The 2008 election and the dream of a post-racial America.* Chicago, IL: University of Chicago Press.

Thomas, D. A., & Gabarro, J. J. (1999). *Breaking through: The making of minority executives in corporate America.* Boston, MA: Harvard Business School Press.

Yoder, J. D. (2002). 2001 Division 35 Presidential Address: Context matters: Understanding tokenism processes and their impact on women's work. *Psychology of Women Quarterly, 26*, 1–8. doi:10.1111/1471-6402.00038

4

HOW IDENTITIES AND DISCRIMINATION CATALYZE GLOBAL ENTREPRENEURSHIP

Lakshmi Ramarajan and Emily LeRoux-Rutledge

In 2002, 21-year-old Christian Ngan left his home country of Cameroon to study in Paris. After 10 years in France, working in the financial sector, he made the life-changing decision to quit his job and move back to Cameroon to start a company. He founded a brand of natural cosmetics for black and mixed-race skin. "It seems a bit weird to say," he recalled,

> but I felt like I woke one morning and my vision changed. On one side, Europe was facing a financial crisis, and I did not have a social life. On the other side, Africa was booming and my dreams seemed more feasible over there.
>
> *(Douglas, 2014)*

Entrepreneurship plays a critical role in economic growth. Entrepreneurs in global contexts face a broad set of challenges. Research on diversity has emphasized that factors such as race, class, gender, and nationality can act as structural barriers to professional advancement (Ibarra, 1995; Thomas & Gabarro, 1999; Chugh & Brief, 2008) and to successful entrepreneurship (Essers & Benschop, 2007; Essers, Benschop & Dooreward, 2010). Positive Organizational Scholarship, on the other hand, focuses on facilitating favorable outcomes. From this perspective, factors such as identity and personal initiative serve as resources for professional advancement and entrepreneurial success (Frese & Fay, 2001; Roberts, 2005). This chapter integrates the two approaches, using the case studies of three African entrepreneurs to examine how identities and structural barriers can jointly act as catalysts for entrepreneurship in global contexts.

Three Entrepreneurs

The first case is that of Bimpe Nkontchou, a Nigerian woman in her late 40s. She trained as a lawyer in Nigeria at the University of Ife and also obtained a master's degree from University College, London. She then practiced as a lawyer for eight years for reputable Nigerian law firms. As a lawyer from an affluent background (both parents were medical doctors), she was well respected in Nigerian society. In 1995, for personal reasons, she moved to England. Initially, she believed she would be able to obtain a job at an English law firm of comparable prestige, but she quickly discovered that this was not the case, in part due to her gender, race, and nationality. As she put it,

> I soon realized that the opportunities in the legal services sector in the UK for an ethnic minority female were severely restricted and that my career would stagnate even if I was able to find a job in a prestigious English law firm in those conditions.

Unwilling to accept a lesser position, in 1998, she founded her own firm in England, Addie & Co. Solicitors, specializing in advising foreign investors doing business in sub-Saharan Africa. It also advised African entrepreneurs and companies doing business in both Africa and Europe.

The second case is that of Nimi Akinkugbe, a 53-year-old woman born and raised in Nigeria and East Africa. After obtaining a BSc in economics from the London School of Economics, she began her career as a treasury officer in a Nigerian bank and, over the course of 23 years, worked her way up to West African regional director in the wealth and investment management division of an international bank. Throughout her career, she demonstrated a deep personal commitment to promoting financial literacy, particularly among women. For many years, the Nigerian banking industry suited her well, providing the flexibility she needed to balance her professional life with her family life, even adjusting her work schedule when her children were young. In 2007, however, her bank merged with a multinational corporation, and she found her leverage considerably reduced. Corporate practices were being standardized across locations, and the influence of local Nigerian staff waned. She subsequently spent two years at another international bank, where she encountered common misconceptions and stereotypes about Africa. At this point, she decided to leave banking and become an entrepreneur. She obtained the African distribution rights to local editions of Hasbro's world-famous board game Monopoly. Founding a company called Bestman Games, she launched the City of Lagos Edition of Monopoly in 2012. More than just a board game, Akinkugbe believed, the product presented the idea of money management to Nigerians in a fun and nonthreatening format. It also presented Africa in a positive way on the international platform of Monopoly.

The third case is that of Claude Grunitzky, a 42-year-old Togolese man. Born to a diplomat father who was a member of the Togolese political elite, Grunitzky was partially raised in privileged circumstances. He spent part of his youth in Togo and part in diplomatic circles in Washington, DC. Although his father was wealthy, his mother was poor, so he experienced poverty when in his home country. At the age of 12, he was sent to an elite private school in France, and it was in this environment that he suddenly became conscious of having "outsider" status, particularly due to racial difference. This caused him to seek out and become part of a subculture in which that difference was celebrated: namely, the hip-hop culture in Paris. Later he moved to London, and then to New York, continuing his involvement in that community and founding two hip-hop magazines that featured established and rising stars such as Wu-Tang Clan and Alicia Keys. By the late 1990s, he was at the center of global hip-hop media. In his book, *Transculturalism*, Grunitzky explained his mission to bridge differences by promoting a global hip-hop culture: Central to this mission, he wrote, was his ability to connect the powerless to the powerful. He slowly built and expanded his businesses beyond print media to advertising and television. In 2010, he sold his businesses, and in 2012, he launched a new mobile venture in Togo to help poor business owners.

In all three cases, global entrepreneurial activity appears to have been stimulated by the experience of encountering structural barriers rooted in factors such as race, class, gender, and nationality in a global context. We identified three common catalysts.

Global transitions as jolts. First, all three individuals experienced a point of transition when they either physically or symbolically moved from a local to a global context. Bimpe Nkontchou became aware of the disadvantages of her gender, race, and nationality when she tried to get a job at a prestigious London law firm. Nimi Akinkugbe experienced disadvantage when her local bank merged with a multinational. This led to her categorization as a local, threatening her professional influence, and to the standardization of the bank's flexible work practices, threatening her family role. In the last case, Claude Grunitzky became aware of the disadvantages of his race and nationality when he enrolled at an elite French school. For each, a global transition acted as a jolt. Jolts are "discrepant events that cause people to pause and reflect on their experience" (Roberts, Dutton, Spreitzer, Heaphy, & Quinn, 2005). In all three cases, the jolts involved movement from a local to a global context. A jolt is not merely a shift in culture. Grunitzky's first global exposure in Washington, DC, was not a jolt, because there, his differences were accepted. Nor was it returning as a quasi-expat to his mother's modest home. It was his later global exposure that acted as a jolt because his differences put him at a disadvantage. Similarly, it was Akinkugbe's employment experience of stereotyping and discrimination as a local national in an international bank, rather than her earlier experience as a foreign student, that served as a jolt for her. Thus, discrimination may be a salient feature of global transitions that can act as jolts.

Prior status as a buffer. Note also that all three individuals had belonged to high-status groups in their local contexts. Nkontchou and Akinkugbe had successful, high-status professional careers; Grunitzky's status derived from his father's. This prior experience of high status may have acted as a buffer against the discrimination they encountered, helping them refuse to internalize their current disadvantage and maintain a critical distance. Research suggests that holding onto positive aspects of one's social identity may provide a counterbalance to negative experiences (Tajfel & Turner, 1987).

Combined identities as unique resources. Finally, all three individuals founded enterprises that leveraged the experiences and relationships from their supposedly subordinate identities together with their professional identities to create value. Nkontchou set up a law practice that served investors in sub-Saharan Africa and African entrepreneurs and companies. She thus turned her Nigerian and African identity into a strength in the global context where it was initially construed as a weakness. Akinkugbe chose the money-based game Monopoly for her entrepreneurial venture, which both built on and expressed her identity as a financially competent Nigerian woman, and fit with her commitment to helping Nigerian women learn to manage their personal finances. Lastly, Grunitzky used his chosen outsider identity to launch several media-based ventures to promote the world of black hip-hop, and later turned his national identity into strength when he launched a mobile-based venture to help small business owners in Togo. Indeed, Christian Ngan, in the opening example, stated that his dream was to create "a 100% African product that would make Africans proud" (Lyon, 2014). Combining and finding complementarities among their many identities proved to be a key resource for the global entrepreneurial activities of all these individuals.

Future scholarship can build on these ideas in several ways. First, these three points of commonality across our cases—experiencing a jolt, using previous status as a buffer, and drawing from intersecting identities—are by no means exhaustive. Future research should investigate more global entrepreneurs across countries and industries and to understand how identity and discrimination may catalyze global entrepreneurship. Second, our case studies illustrate that race, nationality, and gender identities may combine with professional identities to infuse how entrepreneurs design and form their organizations (Battilana, Leca, & Boxenbaum, 2009; Essers et al., 2010; Ramarajan, 2014). Future research could investigate the ways in which founders' multiple identities combine to define the existence and scope of new ventures. In particular, individuals who experience discrimination may create organizations in which social inclusion is part of their founding fabric. In this way, some kinds of global entrepreneurship may contain the seeds of resistance and social change (Golden-Biddle & Dutton, 2012).

Budding global entrepreneurs can also leverage the insights from our case studies. When confronted with structural barriers and discrimination in a global context, the pressures to conform can be great. Our cases illustrate that building a sense of agency, resilience, and awareness of what one will not compromise is critical to global entrepreneurship. Second, forging and maintaining close relationships with those that value one's unique identities can help buffer entrepreneurs when they face challenges in global contexts. Third, global entrepreneurs should search for complementarities between identities that have been marginalized and their professional skills and experiences. By embracing their own multiple perspectives and expertise, they can find insightful and creative ideas for their organizations in ways that will be personally fulfilling and will resonate with others. Our case studies suggest that when people choose to engage in entrepreneurial activities that resonate with marginalized identities in the face of discrimination, global entrepreneurship can become a form of resistance, and those identities can be a source of strength, giving the entrepreneur more power and passion to succeed in their ventures.

For Practitioners: Building a Foundation of Resilience, Relationships, and Resourcefulness

Structural barriers such as race, class, gender, and nationality are often obstacles to professional advancement. How can entrepreneurs in global contexts establish a foundation that will lead to successful professional outcomes?

- **Build resilience and self-awareness to resist and transform structural barriers.** When you confront your differences in a global context, notice how you respond; learn about yourself. What aspects of yourself are you unwilling to compromise?
- **Build relationships and community.** Seek out groups and communities that value your unique identities. They will help buffer you from the negative effects of the barriers you encounter.
- **Combine identities to create value.** Each of our identities gives us unique perspectives and experiences. By embracing your own multiple perspectives and expertise, you can find creative and purposeful ideas for your organization.

References

Battilana, J., Leca, B., & Boxenbaum, E. (2009). How actors change institutions: Towards a theory of institutional entrepreneurship. *Academy of Management Annals, 3*(1), 65–107.

Chugh, D., & Brief, A. P. (2008). 1964 was not that long ago: A story of gateways and pathways. In A. P. Brief (Ed.), *Diversity at work* (pp. 318–340). Cambridge: Cambridge University Press.

Douglas, K. (2014). Why an investment banker quit his job in Paris for a cosmetics firm in Cameroon. How we made it in Africa. http://www.howwemadeitinafrica.com/why-an-investment-banker-quit-his-job-in-paris-for-a-cosmetics-firm-in-cameroon/36140/2/?fullpost=1

EMLyon Business School (2014). Christian Ngan (M.S. 2010). Changing the world is resolving certain simple problems. *EMLyon Forever.* http://www.emlyonforever.com/s/groups/alumni-entrepreneurs-en/blog/christian_ngan_m.s._2010_changing_the_world_is_resolving_certain_simple_problems/7svp98dkOcrdp2F2utdF4w

Essers, C., & Benschop, Y. (2007). Enterprising identities: Female entrepreneurs of Moroccan or Turkish origin in the Netherlands. *Organization Studies, 28*(1), 49–69.

Essers, C., Benschop, Y., & Dooreward, J.A.C.M. (2010). Female ethnicity: Understanding Muslim immigrant businesswomen in the Netherlands. *Gender, Work & Organization, 17*(3), 320–339.

Frese, M., & Fay, D. (2001). Personal initiative: An active performance concept for work in the 21st century. *Research in Organizational Behavior, 23*, 133–187.

Golden-Biddle, K., & Dutton, J. E. (2012). *Using a positive lens to explore social change and organizations: Building a theoretical and research foundation.* New York: Routledge.

Ibarra, H. (1995). Race, opportunity, and diversity of social circles in managerial networks. *Academy of Management Journal, 38*(3), 673–703.

Ramarajan, L. (2014). Past, present and future research on multiple identities: Toward an intrapersonal network approach. *Academy of Management Annals, 8*(1), 1–71.

Roberts, L. M. (2005). Changing faces: Professional image construction in diverse organizational settings. *Academy of Management Review, 30*(4), 685–711.

Roberts, L. M., Dutton, J. E., Spreitzer, G. M., Heaphy, E. D., & Quinn, R. E. (2005). Composing the reflected best-self portrait: Building pathways for becoming extraordinary in work organizations. *Academy of Management Review, 30*(4), 712–736.

Tajfel, H., & Turner, J. C. (1987). The social identity theory of intergroup behavior. In S. Worchel & W. G. Austin (Eds.), *Psychology of intergroup relations* (pp. 7–24). Chicago, IL: Nelson-Hall.

Thomas, D. A., & Gabarro, J. J. (1999). *Breaking through: The making of minority executives in corporate America.* Boston, MA: Harvard Business Press.

5

INTERSECTIONAL IDENTITY SALIENCE AND POSITIVE IDENTITY CONSTRUCTION

Doyin Atewologun

Diversity research is touchy, difficult, and, for the socially privileged, potentially abstract and relatively unimportant (Chugh & Brief, 2008). But diversity can be beneficial and empowering for individuals and organizations, as new research is revealing (Ramarajan & Thomas, 2011). Historically, diversity scholarship and practice have highlighted the nonaffirming aspects of inequality and majority/minority group dynamics, seeking to "manage" diversity. Additionally, single identity groups (e.g., "women" and "minorities") are often the target of research and interventions. The salience of multiple, intersecting identities, facets of which are stigmatized and obscured, however, emerges from analyses of individuals' experiences. Insights from my work on gender, ethnic, and professional/managerial identities, suggest expanding diversity work's traditionally narrow focus to considering learning and constructive experiences prompted by identity multiplicity, experiences consistent with the Positive Organizational Scholarship (POS) approach.

In this chapter, I conceptualize identities as structured with multiple self-aspects (e.g., mother, professional, British) comprising separate facets in a constellation of identities. Identity salience refers to the temporary activation of an identity facet in response to contextual cues (Kenny & Briner, 2013; Rothbard & Ramarajan, 2009); it is a multilevel phenomenon—occurring in intrapersonal, interpersonal, and organizational domains (Atewologun, 2014). I demonstrate how multiple identities become simultaneously salient in everyday encounters and that there is generative potential therein. I seek to encourage readers (scholars, practitioners, and diverse professionals) to be mindful of everyday workplace encounters, even if ambiguous, which can be taken as opportunities for learning through self-insight or instrumental gains.

A promising development in diversity scholarship is the appreciation that a single-identity framework does not fully capture an individual's experiences, which occur at the confluence of multiple identities. Emphasizing the simultaneous and mutually constitutive nature of identity categories reflects an intersectionality perspective (e.g., Bowleg, 2008; Crenshaw, 1989). Individuals' intersecting identities are often presented as cumulative disadvantages, however; for example, the disabled Latina lesbian is assumed to be quadruply oppressed due to her ethnicity, sexual orientation, gender, and disability (e.g., Harley, Nowak, Gassaway, & Savage, 2002). The assumption is that intersecting identities, and the contexts in which they are marked, will be experienced as universally negative and disadvantaged. In contrast to this assumption, my research on black, Asian, and other minority ethnic male and female professionals indicated that experiences related to multiple intersecting identities could not be categorized so readily as nonaffirming (Atewologun, 2011; Atewologun, Sealy, & Vinnicombe, 2015). Indeed, professionals belonging to stigmatized groups do engage in proactive identity work to manage others' impressions of them (Roberts, 2005). Thus, a constellation of identities may expand the resources at minority professionals' disposal for engaging in external impression management and internal identity work.

My research on incidents that raised individuals' awareness of their genders, ethnic, and senior/managerial identities revealed that although it was sometimes easy to infer identity-affirming (e.g., pride at meeting a role model) versus identity-threatening (e.g., challenge to one's authority and expertise) experiences, responses were sometimes ambivalent (e.g., both pride and pressure at being labeled a role model) and at other times paradoxical (e.g., thriving at the opportunity to challenge negative stereotypes). In such encounters, some minority ethnic women and men agentically (as producers, rather than products of social systems) leveraged single, or a combination of, identities in their ensuing self-construction.

Other scholars have recognized the significance of multiple identities for positive and optimum functioning (e.g., Caza & Wilson, 2009; Rothbard & Ramarajan, 2009). My approach to multiple identities is similarly focused on identity structure; however, I emphasize identity dimensions experienced simultaneously, and in which the constellation of identities comprises a combination of advantaged (e.g., professional/manager) and disadvantaged (e.g., minority ethnic) identities. Next, I present exemplars to demonstrate how intersectional identity salience can lead to enhanced self-insight and subsequent identity reconfiguration and augmentation.

Consider the case of Trevor, a British citizen, second-generation Caribbean, and director in a professional services firm:

> I'm sitting in the first-class train carriage and I overhear this phone conversation. I can tell that the guy across the aisle is Caribbean; I could even guess which island. My first reaction: It's not very professional to speak to a stranger on the basis of his accent! It took me a while to work up to it, but then I thought, "We're stuck here for a while. How difficult can it be?" So I introduced myself, with a bit of Patois. We were strangers, but we just clicked. . . . We talked about our families, and then we started talking

about our professional networks. . . . I found out he sits on the same board as one of my key clients. . . . I realized later I was connecting with someone using something I would typically hide at work.

Overhearing the conversation raised the salience of Trevor's ethnic identity, but this conflicted with his professional identity. Having mustered the courage to reach out to his travel companion, he leveraged ethnic and cultural resources by communicating with Patois. This facilitated openness and self-disclosure, yielding social resources via the revelation of common professional networks. Ethnic and professional (and possibly gender) identities in combination enabled this interaction. A previously latent identity facet, one that Trevor typically hid as a senior professional, gained currency as a social resource, such that Trevor's professional identity was augmented by his ethnic identity. This encounter socially affirmed Trevor's intersecting identities and expanded his professional identity construction.

Trevor's experiences illustrate how everyday intersectional identity salience can occur indirectly, prompting self-reflection and identity growth toward integration and augmentation.

The case of Devi, an Indian woman on partner track at a professional services firm, depicts a more direct, jarring intersectional identity salience experience:

> I got the e-mail from the talent team, saying, "You've been recognized as a potential leader—we'd like to invite you to a leadership program for minority ethnic people." I admit, I didn't like it. But a couple of weeks before, my counselor had recommended me for the Women's Leadership Development Program, and I had been up for that. My reaction forced me to face assumptions I have about parts of myself, and aspects of my identity, I don't often think about. I find it easy to challenge feminine stereotypes: I'm as hungry, ambitious, aggressive, as my male colleagues. But I realized I wasn't as comfortable with facing up to changing the biases that people may have of my being a minority—and I hadn't acknowledged that fear in me. I am now learning to be comfortable with the fact that my ethnicity may mark me out and, unlike my gender, maybe there's relatively little I can do about it. Talking openly about my ethnicity is a new challenge . . . but I do want to be able to do it, and want to be a role model for younger Indian women in the firm.

Diversity initiatives such as minority leadership or professional network events may inadvertently unveil tensions at intersectional identity positions if individuals are forced to choose between multiple self-facets. This farcical choice, requiring Devi to decide which facet required greater remedial intervention, was probably invisible to her well-intentioned counselor and talent team; it offers a teachable moment for line managers and HR and leadership professionals who choose to view the opportunity through a POS lens. Notable too, however, is the mindful work that this tension prompted for Devi's leader identity construction: The e-mail raised awareness of differential responses to her "leader + woman" versus "leader + minority ethnic" identities. Devi felt less empowered to counter negative ethnic, compared to gender, stereotypes. Her conflicting responses to identity salience prompted awareness of a latent identity facet, thereby facilitating self-insight. Devi then opted to attend the minority development program to strengthen her ethnic + leader identity. She even anticipated further configuring her identities toward becoming a role model for younger Indian women, ultimately encompassing gender, ethnic, and leader facets into an enhanced self-construal.

Momentary encounters, although experienced initially with ambivalence and approached hesitantly, prompted mindful awareness, identity reconfiguration, and identity augmentation for Trevor and Devi. The exchanges prompted learning by raising self-awareness, triggering self-questioning, and offering self-insight into previously unactivated identity facets. The outcomes were private self-regard and social affirmation (momentarily with Trevor, potentially with Devi) and a sense of belonging in a space suited to multiple rather than single identity facets. Intersectional identity salience presented them with the opportunity to pull apart, reconfigure, and even strengthen the whole, of which constituted ethnic, gender, and professional/leader facets. Overall, identity construction (here, prompted by intersecting identity salience) can provide personal or social resources that can ultimately contribute to developing a positive self-concept (Ashforth, 2009).

Practically speaking, Devi's and Trevor's accounts are just two of myriad micro-episodes minority professionals probably face every day, some to negative effect (Cortina, 2008). Armed with an understanding of intersectional identities, diversity and inclusion professionals and business coaches could work with minority professionals to raise clients' attentiveness to situations (e.g., ambiguous events that trigger stereotype threat), with a view to managing this positively (e.g., via mindfulness techniques). Additionally, intersectional identity salience is relevant not only to stigmatized groups. We all simultaneously identify with multiple dimensions that, for better or worse, connect or differentiate us from others at work. This collective experience may provide diversity educators with inspiration for designing teaching and learning methods on privilege and disadvantage in which both majority and minority individuals can fully participate. Finally, the case examples may also encourage individuals to identify or create identity-enhancing environments, based on perceived alignment between their sociodemographic context and intersectional identities. The proposed outcome of this process is an expanded capability for managing contradictory and ambiguous identity experiences. Rather than self-defining as disadvantaged based on a single identity facet, intersectional identity encounters may expand individuals' possibilities for identifying positive experiences, self-defining in alternative ways to develop learning capacity through self-insight and potentially attain instrumental gains through extending social resources.

For Practitioners: The Positive Effects of Acknowledging Identity Intersections

What is the issue and why is it important?	We often associate multiple minority membership groups with nonaffirming assumptions. This limits professionals to having to choose which identities to display and which to hide, and downplays the fact that we are all privileged and disadvantaged to some degree in a given context. Paying attention to episodes that may be initially jarring or ambiguous because they draw attention to intersecting identities, however, offers opportunities for growth, through self-insight and identity augmentation.
What can we do about it?	Increase intersectional awareness and fluency by: • Acknowledging lived experiences at identity intersections and integrating this complexity and simultaneity into research designs • Adopting an integrated rather than strands-based approach to diversity and inclusion (e.g., implementing inclusive strategies that address privilege and disadvantage across the board; blending LGBT and race network social events) • Monitoring and maintaining quality data on multiple identities to identify subgroup patterns • Creating psychologically safe cultures that encourage dialogue about multiple identities
Useful exercises	• Integrating multiple identity facets into a holistic self-portrait through tools such as the Reflected Best Self Exercise™ • Learning mindfulness techniques to heighten personal awareness of responses to intersectional identity salient encounters and encourage constructive self-reflection and action

References

Ashforth, B. E. (2009). Commentary: Positive identities and the individual. In L. Roberts & J. Dutton (Eds.), *Exploring positive identities and organizations: Building a theoretical and research foundation* (pp. 171–187). New York: Psychology Press.

Atewologun, D. (2011). *An examination of senior black, Asian and minority ethnic women and men's identity work following episodes of identity salience at work* (Unpublished PhD thesis, Cranfield University, UK).

Atewologun, D. (2014). Sites of intersectional identity salience. *Gender in Management: An International Journal, 29*(5), 2.

Atewologun, D, Sealy, R., & Vinnicombe, S. V. (2015). Revealing intersectional dynamics in organisations: Introducing "intersectional identity work." *Gender, Work & Organization*. doi:10.1111/gwao.12082

Bowleg, L. (2008). When black + lesbian + woman ≠ black lesbian woman: The methodological challenges of qualitative and quantitative intersectionality research. *Sex Roles, 59*(5), 312–325.

Caza, B. B., & Wilson, M. G. (2009). Me, myself, and I: The benefits of work–identity complexity. In L. Roberts & J. Dutton (Eds.), *Exploring positive identities and organizations: Building a theoretical and research foundation* (pp. 99–124). New York: Psychology Press.

Chugh, D., & Brief, A. P. (2008). Introduction: Where the sweet spot is: Studying diversity in organizations. In A. P. Brief (Ed.), *Diversity at work* (pp. 1–10). Cambridge: Cambridge University Press.

Cortina, L. M. (2008). Unseen injustice: Incivility as modern discrimination in organizations. *Academy of Management Review, 33*(1), 55–75.

Crenshaw, K. (1989). Demarginalizing the intersection of race and sex: A black feminist critique of antidiscrimination doctrine, feminist theory and antiracist politics. *University of Chicago Legal Forum, 140*, 139–167.

Harley, D. A., Nowak, T. M., Gassaway, L. J., & Savage, T. A. (2002). Lesbian, gay, bisexual, and transgender college students with disabilities: A look at multiple cultural minorities. *Psychology in the Schools, 39*(5), 525–538.

Kenny, E. J., & Briner, R. B. (2013). Increases in salience of ethnic identity at work: The roles of ethnic assignation and ethnic identification. *Human Relations, 66*(5), 725–748.

Ramarajan, L., & Thomas, D. A. (2011). A positive approach to studying diversity in organizations. In K. Cameron & G. Spreitzer (Eds.), *Handbook of Positive Organizational Scholarship* (pp. 552–565). Oxford: Oxford University Press.

Roberts, L. M. (2005). Changing faces: Professional image construction in diverse organizational settings. *Academy of Management Review, 30*(4), 685–711.

Rothbard, N. P., & Ramarajan, L. (2009). Checking your identities at the door? Positive relationships between nonwork and work identities. In L. Roberts & J. Dutton (Eds.), *Exploring positive identities and organizations: Building a theoretical and research foundation* (pp. 125–148). New York: Psychology Press.

SECTION II

Authenticity

Section Introduction

Amy Lemley, Martin N. Davidson,
Laura Morgan Roberts, and Lynn Perry Wooten

What if we listened to each other's authentic voices? In the wake of the Ferguson, Missouri, police shooting of an unarmed black man named Michael Brown in the summer of 2014, U.S. cities had erupted in protest, and Starbucks CEO Howard Schultz decided there was "no ignoring it." With 60,000 minority employees in the United States—some 40% of its work force—the international coffeehouse chain had long been known as a diversity leader, publicly championing causes such as marriage equality and robust benefits packages for low-wage workers. As the protests raged on, Schultz, the company's white founder, extended an invitation to his employees to attend open forums in which all could speak freely on the subject of race. What role did skin color, race, and ethnic background play at work and in their lives?

Before a diverse group of hundreds assembled at each meeting, attendees took to the microphone to express their fears, concerns, and suggestions—but mostly to tell their stories. Schultz, too, shared his perspective during the three-hour gatherings, which included employees at all levels.

This invitation for authentic engagement opened the door for honest conversations and deeper understanding, even about potentially divisive issues. "In every city we've had these meetings, there has been a tremendous amount of learning," he told *USA Today*. "There's been a true level of compassion about what it's like to be in someone else's shoes" (Woodyard, 2015).

Be yourself. This oft-used expression can be harder to follow than it might seem. Where diversity exists, there are individuals making decisions about just how much "self" they can safely "be" around different others—in gender, race, style of dress, ways of speech, in personal values and beliefs, and so on. Diverging from the majority can feel risky; a positive organizational framework can make it rewarding both for the individual and for the enterprise. This section's first chapter, "Authenticity on One's Own Terms," explores how to begin creating a culture of authenticity, examining related scholarship with an eye toward future study. Hewlin proposes that core values alignment is a form of authentic expression that is critical for enhancing personal identities, relationships, performance, and well-being.

In "Authenticity and Organizational Norms: Through a Positive Organizational Scholarship Lens," we learn from a real-world example how standardization can marginalize a person or group, whether purposefully or not. Opie's chapter further develops the theme of this section by revealing the costs of inauthenticity—for the individual and the organization, specifically in regards to cultural displays. Opie explores the best ways to invite authenticity into a work culture, emphasizing that in the end, it is the individual, not the organization, who determines just how much of him- or herself to share.

Comfort level is intertwined with authenticity, perhaps paradoxically. Ferdman's chapter, "If I'm Comfortable Does That Mean I'm Included? And If I'm Included, Will I Now Be Comfortable?" argues that increasing inclusion may help members of one group to feel more connected or valued. But making room for differences may create discomfort in another group. It is also possible that neither group will feel entirely comfortable—which Ferdman suggests is not necessarily a problem, especially when members of the group, organization, or society are authentic about their discomfort and have opportunities to share those thoughts and feelings in constructive, productive, and authentic ways.

Accurate feedback is critical for development and growth, but too often there is an overreliance on feedback that highlights weakness, rather than leveraging strength. Roberts, Wooten, Davidson, and Lemley examine how culture influences authentic affirmation, which they describe as sincere expressions of praise, appreciation, or gratitude. After analyzing experiences using the Reflected Best Self Exercise™ in culturally diverse contexts, the authors propose mindful, culturally inclusive approaches toward strength-based leadership development and talent management.

The chapters in this section integrate diversity, inclusion, and positive organizational scholarship to highlight the delicate, yet generative possibilities for authentic engagement in diverse organizations. Being more authentic can strengthen identities, relationships, and organizations, as long as people are comfortable with being uncomfortable.

Reference

Woodyard, C. (2015, February 10). Starbucks CEO holds frank discussions about race. *USA Today*.

6

AUTHENTICITY ON ONE'S OWN TERMS

Patricia Faison Hewlin

> To be yourself in a world that is constantly trying to make you something else is the greatest accomplishment.
>
> —*Ralph Waldo Emerson*

This chapter joins a burgeoning conversation among scholars and practitioners regarding the expression of authenticity, with a particular focus on authentic engagement in environments where individuals bring divergent sets of values into the workplace. Broadly speaking, authenticity is behaving consistently with what one believes and how one feels. A core component of being authentic is upholding one's commitment to one's personal values (Erickson, 1995). Values are enduring beliefs that guide personally or socially acceptable modes of conduct (Rokeach, 1973). Our personal values drive our behavior, judgment, self-actualization, and presentation of self, and are typically associated with upbringing, socioeconomic status, and cultural background. In essence, personal values are central to how we define ourselves.

Given the importance of values, a central assertion in this chapter is that authenticity begins with an analysis of one's values, and is followed by the development of strategies for incorporating, versus shielding, the most important ones (i.e., one's core values) into work life. My emphasis on values contributes to existing thought on authenticity, which primarily centers on its individual-level outcomes, with a specific emphasis on well-being as the principal outcome (Ménard & Brunet, 2011), and within the organizational context, the impact of authentic leadership on follower outcomes (Ilies, Morgeson, & Nahrgang, 2005). Recent positive identities work that provides pathways for enhancing authenticity (Roberts et al., 2009) is consistent with the direction of this chapter. Bringing values to the forefront provides more specificity with respect to self-analysis, which is a critical component to enhancing one's authenticity and developing personal strategies for authentic engagement in daily work interactions.

This chapter speaks to positive organizational scholarship with respect to the well-being of an organization's members and how that affects the organization as a whole. Thus, positive organizational scholarship is a critical concept with respect to pushing forward research toward understanding the process of eliciting or supporting authenticity as well as how authentic engagement among organization members can serve as an avenue for enriching their well-being at work. Furthermore, given that managing authenticity can be a salient process for individuals who hold divergent values from the majority in the workplace, this chapter is relevant to diversity and inclusion scholars and practitioners. Addressing the question of how organizations can effectively facilitate authentic expression among all organization members could prompt a move toward leveraging and integrating diverse perspectives in the workplace.

Behaving in accordance with one's personal values offers a sense of authenticity that can lead to a wealth of benefits such as higher levels of personal vitality and lower levels of stress and anxiety (e.g., Lopez & Rice, 2006). For example, a man who values his family life and his role as a highly engaged father may find it very rewarding to share his children's accomplishments and talk about the time he spends with them in the evenings and weekends. Thus, authenticity for this person would include integrating aspects of his family life in workday conversations, which can enhance his level of personal satisfaction on the job. Given the benefits of authenticity, one would expect that authentic engagement in the workplace would be readily sought by all. Authentic engagement, however, can present itself with challenges for individuals who hold values that differ from the values of the majority in the workplace. For such individuals, integrating divergent values may be perceived as risky because their values may be looked upon unfavorably or may evoke stereotypes that highlight negatively the differences they bring to the environment (Roberts et al., 2009; Phillips, Rothbard, & Dumas, 2009). Indeed, inauthentic behaviors in which individuals suppress personal values and pretend to embrace organizational values with which they may not actually agree are positively associated with the degree to which members feel that they hold personal characteristics and values (e.g., physical appearance, gender, religious beliefs, etc.) different from those of the majority (Hewlin, 2009). Thus, for example, the family man described earlier might feel pressured to be inauthentic, "downplaying" this value in an organizational environment in which employees, especially men, are expected to hold their commitment to work as a paramount value.

For women, this pressure is salient in a wide range of organizational environments and careers (Blair-Loy, 2003). Thus, whereas a woman may highly value her family life, she may choose to avoid sharing this value at work in an effort to break the potential assumption that family life readily compromises a woman's ability to fulfill her work responsibilities. These and other strategies that can potentially compromise one's sense of authenticity, however, can be detrimental to personal well-being. Any behavior that is inconsistent with one's personal values or beliefs leaves one vulnerable to feelings of dissonance and emotional exhaustion (e.g., Hewlin, 2009; Meyerson & Scully, 1995).

How organization members can prompt increased authenticity and the potential challenges associated with displaying authenticity are therefore important issues to address for scholars and practitioners. One should bear in mind that well-meaning exhortations such as "be yourself" are abstract and fail to provide guidance for implementation. Moreover, such exhortations can potentially convey a narrow underlying message that one must display his or her "whole self" at all times, and anything less than that would be considered inauthentic. Such messages can actually hinder the degree to which a person engages in authenticity because bringing one's whole self may be a very difficult endeavor when one's whole self is different from the whole selves of the majority. As a result, full authentic engagement might seem like an impossible task. The view here is that authentic expression is a highly personal endeavor. It is defined and developed through the analysis of one's personal values and the subsequent development of strategies for authentic engagement at work. Individualized strategies developed on one's own terms can facilitate the development of quality relationships and a positive sense of self. The concept of authenticity on one's own terms is based on the assertion that authentic expression can be felt in a variety of ways. Whereas the delineation of a full range of authentic self-expression strategies one can employ is beyond the scope of this chapter, I will offer avenues for research and practitioner tool development.

An important facet of building authenticity begins with self-analysis (Roberts et al., 2009). In other words, to effectively engage in authenticity (i.e., being oneself), it is important to know oneself. For example, Roberts et al. (2009) suggest that a narrative approach in which an individual seeks to understand recurring internal experiences over the course of his or her life is an important step in self-analysis. This analysis should also include identifying and categorizing one's core and peripheral values (Lachman, 1988). Core values are particularly central, enduring, and generally resistant to change. They consist of values that are most important and dear to a person. Like core values, peripheral values can be linked to one's cultural background and socioeconomic and community environments, but they are less dominant and more pliable than core values. Simply put, core values are not negotiable, whereas peripheral values are. For example, not working on one's Sabbath can be a core value for some individuals whose religious practice forbids it. There may be others, however, who subscribe to the same religion but are more flexible on this issue because it is a peripheral value for them.

Once core versus peripheral values are identified, one can begin to consider the most important values to incorporate into one's work environment—those values that would lend themselves to the highest level of personal satisfaction. For example, a devout Muslim worker in a mainly conservative Christian environment might feel more authentic if he reveals his faith by perhaps sharing weekend activities associated with his mosque or other Islamic-based organization of which he is a member. Similarly, an African American might feel more authentic in the workplace when acknowledging in some way her cultural history and traditions from which she draws inner strength and pride; this acknowledgment might not be verbal, but rather, it could occur in the display of an artifact in her office.

Scholars can play important roles in building theory-driven models that illustrate the processes leading to the development of strategies people can employ for authentic engagement in the workplace. In future research, it will be critical to address interpersonal and work-related dynamics, as well as the perceived risk and other potential tensions that might arise when individuals choose to weave some of their core values into their work environments. Thus, it will be important for empirical research to capture the impact of varied levels of authentic engagement on performance, positive work relationships, and a positive sense of self. Additionally, the roles of practitioners in the positive organization as well as the diversity and inclusion arenas are critical. Collaborative approaches among practitioners in these fields will be beneficial with respect to guiding organization members toward identifying core values, and for helping diverse members devise strategies for authentic self-expression.

Along those lines, business coaching can involve not only determining ways in which one can incorporate personal values into the workplace, but also identifying the implications associated with selected strategies. Coaching should squarely address the potential risks and benefits of enhancing one's authenticity at work. Equally important is the development of tools for training organizations on how to foster safe environments in which members can honor their true selves. Such tools must center on facilitating authenticity among all organizational members, especially among those who bring divergent perspectives and values to the workplace.

This chapter highlights that although there are numerous benefits to authenticity, how one incorporates one's core, nonnegotiable values at work is a personal journey that involves discovering ways to honor those values. One size does not fit all, but rather, authenticity is highly individualized; it can be displayed and felt in a variety of ways. It is about developing a set of personal strategies that may require courage to implement; but the personal gratification of authenticity on one's own terms can foster positive work relationships that will benefit the overall work environment.

For Practitioners: Exuding Authenticity in the Workplace

- Authenticity is behaving consistently with what one believes and how one feels. A core component of being authentic is living up to one's personal values because values are central to how we define ourselves.
- Authentic self-expression can be a challenge for individuals with perspectives and characteristics (e.g. physical appearance, gender, religious beliefs, etc.) that are different from those of the majority. Even

well-intentioned exhortations to "be yourself" provide very little guidance on how individuals with divergent perspectives can effectively integrate their core values into the workplace.

Action Steps and Considerations

- Authentic expression is a highly personal endeavor that is defined and developed through the analysis of one's personal values and the subsequent development of strategies for authentic engagement at work.
- Collaborative approaches among scholars and practitioners can be useful in guiding organization members toward identifying core values and devising strategies for authentic self-expression.
- Training tools should center on how organizations can foster safe spaces in which members can honor their true selves.
- Business coaching should focus on identifying implications associated with selected self-expression strategies. Specifically, coaching should squarely address risks and benefits of enhancing one's authenticity at work.

References

Blair-Loy, M. (2003). *Competing devotions: Career and family among women executives.* Cambridge, MA: Harvard University Press.

Erickson, R. J. (1995). The importance of authenticity for self and society. *Symbolic Interaction, 18*(2), 121–144.

Hewlin, P. F. (2009). Wearing the cloak: Antecedents and consequences of creating facades of conformity. *Journal of Applied Psychology, 94,* 727–741.

Ilies, R., Morgeson, F. P., & Nahrgang, J. D. (2005). Authentic leadership and eudaemonic well-being: Understanding leader–follower outcomes. *Leadership Quarterly, 16,* 373–394.

Lachman, R. (1988). Factors influencing workers' orientations: A secondary analysis of Israeli data. *Organization Studies, 9,* 497–510.

Lopez, R., & Rice, K. (2006). Preliminary development and validation of a measure of relationship authenticity. *Journal of Counseling Psychology, 53,* 362–371.

Ménard, J., & Brunet, L. (2011). Authenticity and well-being in the workplace: A mediation model. *Journal of Managerial Psychology, 26,* 331–346.

Meyerson, D. E., & Scully, M. A. (1995). Tempered radicalism and the politics of ambivalence and change. *Organization Science, 5,* 585–600.

Phillips, K. W., Rothbard, N. P., & Dumas, T. L. (2009). To disclose or not to disclose? Status distance and self-disclosure in diverse environments. *Academy of Management Review, 34,* 710–732.

Roberts, L. M., Cha, S. E., Hewlin, P. F., & Settles, I. E. (2009). Bringing the inside out: Enhancing authenticity and positive identity in organizations. In L. M. Roberts & J. D. Dutton (Eds.), *Exploring positive identities and organizations: Building a theoretical and research foundation* (pp. 145–169). New York: Taylor & Francis Group.

Rokeach, M. (1973). *The nature of human values.* New York: Free Press.

7

AUTHENTICITY AND ORGANIZATIONAL NORMS

Through a Positive Organizational Scholarship Lens

Tina Opie

In May 2014, U.S. Defense Secretary Chuck Hagel reported to Congress that the Pentagon would review controversial new Army grooming guidelines that had enraged people both inside and outside the military. At issue were guidelines that banned hairstyles the Army viewed as "unkempt" or "matted." As a result, such natural hairstyles as dreadlocks and twists, styles almost exclusively worn by blacks and most often black women, were forbidden. The military was prohibiting black women from wearing hairstyles that embraced black hair in its natural state: groomed without chemical straightening or alteration.

Recent trends show more and more black women choose Afrocentric styles (Mintel, 2012). Yet black women may face organizational norms, shared expectations about group member behavior that indicate what is and is not acceptable (Levine & Moreland, 1990), that stunt this external expression, whether by regulation or by perceived social pressure. In this chapter, I investigate how the suppression of these hairstyle choices also suppresses authenticity and therefore damages black women's ability to be fully effective in the workplace. While I use black women to elucidate this topic, this is a potentially widespread issue given that most organizations have formal or informal expectations regarding employee appearance. Further, as organizations become more diverse, it is more likely that employees will possess identity traits that distinguish them from the majority in some noticeable way (wearing a head covering, for example).

To examine this issue, I first discuss the importance of authenticity and address how appearance norms may contribute to inauthenticity; I then consider its costs. After establishing this backdrop, I use a Positive Organizational Scholarship (POS) lens to explore how encouraging employees to express their authentic identities will benefit both individuals and organizations.

Authenticity refers to a state when one's internal experiences (e.g., thoughts, feelings, behavioral preferences) are consonant with external expressions (e.g., verbal disclosures, nonverbal displays, attire, grooming, etc.) (Robert et al., 2009). Authenticity contributes to positive self-regard (Roberts et al., 2009), adaptive functioning (Kernis & Goldman, 2006); well-being (Wood et al., 2008); and self-esteem (Kernis, 2003).

Yet authenticity sometimes seems impossible. For example, consider an organization dominated by Eurocentric and masculine norms (Bell & Nkomo, 2003; Combs, 2003). There, black women, given their double subordinate position, might perceive these norms as thwarting their authenticity. The military, with its hair grooming policies, is a blatant example. Here is the exact wording from Army regulation 670–1 "Uniform and Insignia: Wear and Appearance of Army Uniforms and Insignia":

(g) *Twists.* Twists are defined as twisting two distinct strands of hair around one another to create a twisted ropelike appearance. Although some twists may be temporary, and can be easily untwisted, they are unauthorized (except for French twists). This includes twists formed against the scalp or worn in a free-hanging style.

(h) *Dreadlocks.* Dreadlocks are defined as any matted, twisted, or locked coils or ropes of hair (or extensions). Any style of dreadlock (against the scalp or free-hanging) is not authorized. Braids or cornrows that are unkempt or matted are considered dreadlocks and are not authorized.

Ironically, these regulations prohibit Army women from wearing their hair shorter than a quarter-inch from the scalp, though men are allowed to. Women who would like to cut their hair very short to minimize hair-grooming challenges are unable to do so. This length is quite common among black women, particularly when they elect to cut off their chemically processed hair and start with a new hairstyle. In fact, this short hairstyle is so popular that it has its own moniker, the teeny weeny afro ("TWA"). Thus, when it comes to the Army, black women in particular are subjected to organizational appearance norms that suppress both ethnic expression and gender.

Such issues arise at various organizations. Consider a requirement that employees have "neatly groomed hair." That may seem simple. But what determines if a hairstyle is neatly groomed? Some might argue, for example, that black women's natural curly or kinky hair (even when tightly twisted or coiled) is not "neatly groomed." Perhaps this is why 80 percent of black women relax (i.e., chemically straighten) (Mintel, 2012) and spend significant amounts of time and money chemically altering their hair (Rosette & Dumas, 2007). Overall, natural hairstyles such as afros or dreadlocks are considered less professional (Opie & Phillips, 2015) and are worn less frequently than relaxed hairstyles (though natural hairstyles are growing in popularity among black women). This suggests they perceive Euro-centric hair to be normative. To be considered professional, many black women must suppress their authenticity or live in fear of negative ramifications. Further, grooming policies like the ones that require self-regulation based on others' expectations are associated with inauthentic functioning (Sheldon & Kasser, 1995). In sum, the suppression of Afrocentric hair among black women reflects a detrimental effect of white and gendered norms about hair in the workplace (Onwuachi-Willig, 2010).

Hair is a visible signifier of identity for women in many ways. Hair can be altered to conform to prevailing organizational norms; hence, hair conveys important messages about race and/or gender politics and stereotypes (Rollock et al., 2011). White women may cut their long hair so they will be perceived as more competent and mature; lesbian women may grow longer hair than they would prefer to be seen as less threatening; black women may straighten their hair to seem more professional; and the elderly may dye their gray hair to be viewed as more relevant (Weitz, 2001). Thus, examining hairstyle choices in the workplace explicates how mutable identity traits may be altered or suppressed in order to comply with organizational appearance norms.

Is such suppression costly? Unfortunately, evidence suggests it is. Conforming to organizational ideals that do not align with one's personal values is related to emotional exhaustion and the intention to quit (Hewlin, 2003, 2009). Further, when individuals alter their appearance in this way, they are more likely to feel alienated and less committed to the organization (Yoshino & Smith, 2013). Additionally, minorities and women likely bear cognitive and emotional burdens as they worry about how to navigate others' perceptions of their professionalism (Rosette & Dumas, 2007). Finally, inauthenticity is associated with a host of negative outcomes such as identity conflict, dissonance, low self-esteem, stress, and anxiety (White & Tracey, 2011; Wood et al., 2008). Thus, some organizational norms may directly or indirectly encourage employees to suppress identity traits that are important to the self. Given such potential harm, the benefit of such organizational norms is questionable.

Rather than merely trying to avoid these negative consequences, it is more helpful to consider the benefits of encouraging authenticity in the workplace—a perspective available through the POS lens. Given the opportunity, employees are likely to attribute the positive results they experience from authenticity (e.g., positive self-regard, adaptive functioning, and well-being) to their organizations. According to social exchange theory, employees would then positively recipro-cate (Cropanzano & Mitchell, 2005). In this way, organizations promote high quality connections (HQCs) with their employees. HQCs are more resilient and more likely to generate creative ideas. Further, individuals in HQCs experience a heightened sense of vitality and aliveness, positive regard from others (i.e., feeling known and appreciated), and engagement (Dutton & Heaphy, 2003). Employees and organizations benefit by both obtaining the positive benefits of authenticity and avoiding the costs of suppression. Black women, white women, lesbian women, and the elderly would feel free to display their authentic, natural hair if they chose to and contribute to a more liberated, visibly diverse workplace where individuals authentically express their identities.

Hair has served as the backdrop for this discussion, but in fact the current arguments apply to other identity displays (e.g., religious head coverings, makeup, tattoos, piercings). Not that organizations should eliminate performance norms such as etiquette and deadline adherence. Rather, they should consider which standards are truly task-relevant and which may have been established as though by default.

Broadening organizational norms benefits not only underrepresented minorities, but also people in the majority because of its ameliorative impact on perceived discrimination and its ability to unshackle majority members from norms that can ensnare them as well. When that majority accesses authenticity, a shift in perception becomes possible. Because perceived discrimination is most often associated with the majority, heightened majority authenticity in the workplace may provide individuating information that enhances workplace relationships for both majority and minority employees.

In the United States, white men are most prototypical of a leader, so they may be particularly pressured to conform to organizational norms and keenly denigrated when they deviate from norms. Research suggests that whiteness (Rosette & Dumas, 2007) and masculinity (Koenig, Eagly, Mitchell, & Risitkari, 2011) are attributes of the leadership prototype and that, in the United States, the leadership prototype is further characterized by being determined, goal-oriented, industrious, and persistent and possessing verbal skills (Gerstner & Day, 1994). Men in particular may be scrutinized if they violate norms of impersonality; therefore, men are encouraged to suppress emotional responses in the workplace (Greenberg, 1988; Rumens & Kerfoot, 2009).

Indeed, whenever individuals violate in-group prototypes, they are more likely to be denigrated (Hogg & Terry, 2000). But what if a white male is authentically expressive, if that is a key part of his self-conception and how he chooses to present himself? What if a white man wants to wear long hair or flamboyant clothes that violate norms of conservatism? What might organizations gain if rather than chastising a man for his long hair, they encouraged him to wear his hair however he chose? Again, research on authenticity suggests that both the organization and the individual will benefit. In essence, the benefits of authenticity are not limited to those who are traditionally identified as minorities.

Thus, broadening organizational norms so that all employees have the space to express their authentic identities stands to benefit both majority and minority employees. Finally, encouraging authenticity in the workplace could contribute to an organizational culture in which self-expression is valued and encouraged. A climate of authenticity has been found to alleviate emotional burnout, which has positive implications for employee absences, turnover, and performance decrements (Grandey et al., 2012).

For Further Study

Considering the benefits of authenticity, more attention should be given to the topic of authenticity in the workplace and its relation to organizational norms. In the United States, where people spend an average of 7.7 hours per day working (Bureau of Labor Statistics, 2013), the need for such research seems great. Organizations and employees stand to benefit if norms were broadened so that authenticity would be encouraged in the workplace. As the work force becomes increasingly diverse, employees will likely increasingly challenge the validity of organizational norms such as the Eurocentric, masculine norms typical of the American workplace. Organizations would do well to proactively encourage authenticity and ensure that norms are linked to job performance rather than culturally biased notions of what is and is not professional. A key goal of workplace diversity is to enhance work group effectiveness (Ely & Thomas, 2001); consequently, it makes sense for organizations to encourage employees to express their diverse, authentic identities rather than trying to match an outdated "ideal." In this way, authenticity in the workplace can help maximize the benefits of workplace diversity.

For Practitioners: Ways to Encourage Authenticity in the Workplace

1.   Notice your organization's appearance norms.

     a.   Examine which appearances strike you as professional and which appearances strike you as unprofessional.
     b.   Consider: What is it about the different appearances that led you to judge one as professional and another as unprofessional?

2.   Reflect.

     a.   Are your judgments/standards task-related or not?
     b.   Are particular demographic groups negatively impacted by such judgments?

3.   Evolve.

     a.   Given your unique context, how do you think your organization's norms might be adjusted so that they are task-related?
     b.   How might you ensure that norms are equally applied across demographic groups?
     c.   Involve employees.

          i.   Ask employees for feedback about organizational norms.
          ii.   Gather ideas on how to change norms if they seem inhibiting.

4. Model authentic behavior by expressing your authentic identity.

    a. Recognize that employees often mimic leader behavior.
    b. Identify elements of your authentic identity.

        i.   What elements of your identity matter most to you?
        ii. It may help to think about identity aspects that you express outside of work and conceal at work.

    c. Take the plunge: Express your authentic identity at work while being mindful of organizational culture and existing norms.
    d. Be prepared that you may need to reiterate the benefits of authentic identity expression to organizational leadership.

References

Bell, E. L., & Nkomo, S. (2003). *Our separate ways: Black and white women and the struggle for professional identity*. Boston, MA: Harvard Business School Press.

Bureau of Labor Statistics. (2013). American time use survey summary—2012 results. http://www.bls.gov/news.release/atus.nr0.htm

Combs, G. (2003). The duality of race and gender for managerial African American women: Implications of informal social networks on career advancement. *Human Resource Development Review, 2*, 385–405.

Cropanzano, R., & Mitchell, M. S. (2005). Social exchange theory: An interdisciplinary review. *Journal of Management, 31*, 874–900.

Dutton, J. E., & Heaphy, E. (2003). The power of high quality connections. In K. Cameron, J. E. Dutton, & R. E. Quinn (Eds.), *Positive organizational scholarship* (pp. 263–278). San Francisco, CA: Berrett-Koehler.

Ely, R. J., & Thomas, D. A. (2001). Cultural diversity at work: The effects of diversity perspectives on work group processes and outcomes. *Administrative Science Quarterly, 46*, 229–273.

Gerstner, C. R., & Day, D. V. (1994). Cross-cultural comparison of leadership prototypes. *The Leadership Quarterly, 5*(2), 121–134.

Grandey, A., Foo, S. C., Groth, M., & Goodwin, R. E. (2012). Free to be you and me: A climate of authenticity alleviates burnout from emotional labor. *Journal of Occupational Health Psychology, 17*, 1–14.

Greenberg, D. (1988). *The construction of homosexuality*. Chicago: The University of Chicago Press.

Hewlin, P. (2003). And the award for best actor goes to . . .: Facades of conformity in organizational settings. *Academy of Management Review, 28*, 633–642.

Hewlin, P. (2009). Wearing the cloak: Antecedents and consequences of creating facades of conformity. *Journal of Applied Psychology, 94*, 727–741.

Hogg, M. A., & Terry, D. I. (2000). Social identity and self-categorization processes in organizational contexts. *Academy of Management Review, 25*(1), 121–140.

Kernis, M. H. (2003). Toward a conceptualization of optimal self-esteem. *Psychological Inquiry, 14*(1), 1–26.

Kernis, M. H., & Goldman, B. M. (2006). A multicomponent conceptualization of authenticity: Theory and research. *Advances in Experimental Psychology, 38*, 283–356.

Koenig, A., Eagly, A., Mitchell, A., & Risitkari, T. (2011). Are leader stereotypes masculine? A meta-analysis of three research paradigms. *Psychological Bulletin, 137*, 616–642.

Levine, J. M., & Moreland, R. L. (1990). Progress in small group research. *Annual Review of Psychology, 41*, 585–634.

Mintel. (2012, August). Black hair care—US. http://www.mintel.com/

Onwuachi-Willig, A. (2010). Another hair piece: Exploring new strands of analysis under Title VII. *Georgetown Law Journal, 98*, 1079–1132.

Opie, T. R., & Phillips, K. (2015). *The impact of minority group member norm violation on perceived professionalism.* Manuscript in preparation, Management Division, Babson College, Babson Park, MA.

Roberts, L. M., Cha, S., Hewlin, P., & Settles, I. (2009). Bringing the inside out: Enhancing authenticity and positive identity in organizations. In L. M. Roberts & J. E. Dutton (Eds.), *Exploring positive identities and organizations: Building a theoretical and research foundation* (pp. 149–169). New York: Routledge.

Rollock, N., Gillborn, D., Vincent, C., & Ball, S. (2011). The public identities of the black middle classes: Managing race in public spaces. *Sociology, 45*, 1078–1093.

Rosette, A. S., & Dumas, T. L. (2007). The hair dilemma: Conform to mainstream expectations or emphasize racial identity. *Duke Journal of Gender Law and Policy, 14*, 407–421.

Rumens, N., & Kerfoot, D. (2009). Gay men at work: (Re)constructing the self as professional. *Human Relations, 62*(5), 763–786.

Sheldon, K. M., & Kasser, T. (1995). Coherence and congruence: Two aspects of personality integration. *Journal of Personality and Social Psychology, 68*(3), 531.

Weitz, R. (2001). Women and their hair: Seeking power through resistance and accommodation. *Gender & Society, 15*, 667–686.

White, N. J., & Tracey, T. J. (2011). An examination of career indecision and application to dispositional authenticity. *Journal of Vocational Behavior, 78*(2), 219–224.

Wood, A. M., Maltby, J., Caliousis, M., Linley, P. A., & Joseph, S. (2008). The authentic personality: A theoretical and empirical conceptualization and the development of the authenticity scale. *Journal of Counseling Psychology, 55*, 385–399.

Yoshino, K., & Smith, C. (2013). *Uncovering talent: A new model of inclusion.* Deloitte University Leadership Center for Inclusion.

8

IF I'M COMFORTABLE DOES THAT MEAN I'M INCLUDED?

And If I'm Included, Will I Now Be Comfortable?

Bernardo M. Ferdman

If being comfortable—at ease, without fear or stress, unconstrained, and relatively relaxed—is fundamental to the experience of inclusion, does that mean that when I am comfortable in particular social settings, including those in which people like me were previously uncomfortable because of their identities, beliefs, values, or styles—I am now included? And if I am included, isn't it reasonable to expect that I should be relatively comfortable and at ease? Most of us would answer affirmatively. But the relationship of comfort and inclusion is not as straightforward as it might initially seem.

As a diversity practitioner who greatly values the contributions of Positive Organizational Scholarship, I often highlight how focusing on inclusion provides an appealing way to advance diversity and derive its potential benefits. People typically resonate with the idea that inclusion involves increasing comfort and reducing discomfort for more people, especially those previously excluded or marginalized. In other words, the experience and benefits of inclusion—previously restricted to a few—should be extended to the many, eliminating barriers stemming from identity-based biases or invidious discrimination. From this perspective, inclusion in diverse groups and organizations requires people across a range of social identities to become more comfortable with each other and with themselves, in the process enabling smoother and more mutually supportive engagement and collaboration across all types of differences. Similarly, discomfort or conflict grounded in our social identities (e.g., Ruderman & Chrobot-Mason, 2010) may be taken as a signal that more work on inclusion is needed.

Yet this quite reasonable point of view tells only part of the story. A complementary and also vital way to think about inclusion—if it is to be the basis for truly reaping the benefits of diversity—is that it is not necessarily about making all of us fully comfortable, but rather that it involves more of us being *uncomfortable*—albeit with discomfort that is distributed more evenly and equitably. This is the perspective that I develop here.

Inclusion Does Involve More Comfort across Differences

First, it's important to acknowledge how inclusion does involve fostering more comfort for more people. To gain the full benefits of diversity, groups and organizations must take steps to become inclusive; they must proactively create, foster, and sustain "practices and conditions that encourage and allow each of us to be fully ourselves—with our differences from and similarities to those around us—as we work together" (Ferdman & Deane, 2014, p. xii). In this view, a key goal of inclusion is to maximize the degree to which individuals "feel safe, trusted, accepted, respected, supported, valued, fulfilled, engaged, and authentic in their working environment, both as individuals and as members of particular identity groups" (Ferdman, Barrera, Allen, & Vuong, 2009, p. 6)—in short, to increase experiences of inclusion that are positive and affirming.

There is much social psychology literature that speaks to the comfort felt by people when they are with others who are like them or who like them, or to the ways in which people are drawn to others who are similar to them. And work on prejudice and discrimination suggests that a foremost effect of exclusion is the sense of discomfort and of being undesired that is felt by those who are different. Inclusion involves reducing or eliminating this feeling. Thus, it is certainly apt to think about creating comfort as a core component of inclusion. At the individual level, inclusion involves a sense of belonging and participation, without having to give up or compromise valued aspects of oneself (Ferdman, 2014; Ferdman & Roberts, 2014). Similarly, members of an inclusive group or organization must develop mutual comfort with their differences and similarities.

For this reason, suggestions to increase inclusion by making room for differences often involve extending a sense of ease to more members of a group or organization and to reduce problematic conflicts associated with those differences. The Future Work Institute (quoted in Ferdman, 2014, p. 29), for example, in describing components of inclusion and the importance of how people and especially newcomers are treated, states that "a warm and welcoming atmosphere eases the process of 'learning the ropes' for the new member and aids in making the member comfortable in the new group environment." Hubbard (2004, p. 23), highlighting the importance of belonging, describes its two aspects as involving social connection or affiliation on one hand, and social acceptance on the other—the latter enabling people "to be with and among others with a sense of comfort and entitlement, or in short, a sense that she belongs and that she has a rightful place in the world." In my own work, I summarized this theme as follows: "Inclusion involves creating more comfort for more people, so that access, opportunity, and a sense of full participation and belonging are facilitated across a greater range of diversity than ever before, for the benefit of all" (Ferdman, 2014, p. 46).

Yet Inclusion Also Involves Discomfort

So inclusion certainly involves expanding people's sense of comfort. But, paradoxically, inclusion also involves creating more—and sometimes new types of—discomfort. Making space for and bringing out more differences in a diverse group or organization can often elicit discomfort and unease; it can be challenging for all involved. Comfort and inclusion do not necessarily go hand in hand; indeed, inclusion can sometimes lead to more, rather than less, discomfort—especially for those accustomed to prior ways of doing things. Importantly, this needn't be problematic, especially when members of the group, organization, or society learn to hold and address these differences and the associated discomfort in constructive, productive, and authentic ways. In contrast, it is to be expected and necessary.

When organizations and groups truly foster diversity and inclusion, differences among members in identities, values, ways of achieving goals, and preferences about both major and minor aspects of work and life become more salient. Rather than emphasize commonalities, inclusive groups and organizations work to incorporate both similarities *and* differences. And when the group or organization is truly inclusive, those previously in power should be less likely to impose their perspectives or ways of doing things. But these dynamics create stresses for the members and for the group as a whole with regard to managing the differences. And both the differences and these stresses create discomfort. This is how I have previously described the issue:

> Rather than treating membership and participation as a privilege granted by those traditionally in power to those previously excluded—often with assimilation to established norms as a condition of full acceptance—inclusive practices redefine who the "we" is in an organization or work group so that all have the right to be there and to have an equal voice, both in managing the boundary and in defining (and redefining) norms, values, and preferred styles for success (Ferdman & Davidson, 2002; Miller & Katz, 2002). This can be challenging because in many cases it requires ongoing reexamination of previously accepted or taken-for-granted ways of working and interacting. It means developing skills and practices for collectively reevaluating notions of what (and who) is "normal," appropriate, and expected in ways that incorporate more voices and perspectives, many of those unfamiliar or uncomfortable for those previously in power. *(Ferdman, 2014, pp. 12–13)*

Inclusion, then, can involve a good measure of discomfort, especially for those who were relatively comfortable with the previously less-inclusive system. The difference is that now, the discomfort is distributed more evenly and more equitably. Previously, discomfort was typically reserved for newcomers, for those with subordinated or marginalized identities, or for those seen to be deviant or different in ways judged to be inappropriate according to dominant norms. But in an inclusive group or organization, everyone must now experience some discomfort, in a milder form. This is particularly so for those who must shift their notions of what is correct or must incorporate these new and different—but now equal—participants. Many years ago, Miller (1994, p. 39) provocatively described the challenge this way: "*Inclusion* turns *comfortable* upside out and inside down" (italics in original). Inclusion requires all of us to engage in new and sometimes unfamiliar ways—necessarily moving us out of individual or collective comfort zones—while continuing to grow and learn for the benefit of all (Ferdman, 2014).

Toward Comfort with Discomfort

We need to think about creating inclusion not simply as being about the comfort or ease that we will all now experience when everyone is an "insider." Inclusion does not mean reproducing the dynamics of exclusive groups, except now with a greater diversity of members. Inclusion does not mean that everyone—both newcomers and old-timers alike—can simply relax, on the expectation that others in our group or organization will think and behave more or less like us.

Rather, to create inclusion, we must all become "outsiders" to some degree, expecting that others will not read our minds or agree with our perspectives. Inclusion requires expecting that the relative discomfort that comes from having to more regularly confront and engage with differences will be an everyday experience. In many ways, then, creating and engaging with inclusion "requires becoming more comfortable with discomfort, both individually and collectively" (Ferdman, 2014, p. 47). When we practice inclusion in a diverse group or organization, we are more likely to find ourselves in situations in which we do not fully understand our counterparts, and so must cultivate "the ability to not understand" (Gurevitch, 1989, p. 161) as well as to "lean into discomfort" (Katz & Miller, 2013, p. xi), which can facilitate learning and engagement, as well as trust (Katz & Miller, 2013).

Engaging effectively across differences requires us to be alert, attentive, and intentional. If being comfortable means feeling psychologically and physically safe, and trusting that one's contributions will be considered and valued, then this is certainly a critical part of inclusion. At the same time, inclusion means that we cannot assume that our way will be everyone's way, that others will easily understand us, or that we will easily understand them. To be attentive to and welcoming of diversity, we must effectively live with and even welcome the discomfort that comes from learning and growing, individually and collectively, when we engage with and truly face differences. As we expand our individual and collective comfort zones and experience the discomfort that comes with that type of stretching, we can also gain comfort from knowing that this will provide greater and more valuable benefits to us and to our groups and organizations.

Acknowledgments: I benefitted greatly from valuable comments, questions, and suggestions provided by Martin Davidson and Lauren Phillips on prior drafts, which helped me to improve this chapter.

For Practitioners: Becoming Comfortable with the Discomforts of Inclusion—Key Skills and Practices

To work and live inclusively in diverse groups, organizations, and societies, we need particular skills and practices to prepare us and those around us for the discomforts that inevitably arise when we must deal with differences. Here are a few:

- **Be fully alert, aware, and mindful.** Notice and take responsibility for your thoughts, feelings, and reactions, including those that are negative or possibly biased, especially about others who are different from you. Review and test your assumptions, especially about difference.
- **Learn about yourself and your identities in relationship to others.** Become familiar and conversant with your multiple identities and those of others, and with the complexity of those identities as they are expressed by individuals in their historical and social contexts. This includes learning about and acknowledging patterns of intergroup domination and subordination and our participation in those dynamics.
- **Expect and engage positively with differences.** Learn about and engage with others with a spirit of curiosity and appreciation. Be aware of and intentional with language. Invite dialogue and interaction across a range of differences. Understand that differences (and the associated discomfort) can be a source of growth and learning.
- **Learn to work with and skillfully manage differences, including those that are difficult or conflictual.** Develop your capacity to engage in conflict in ways that are effective, productive, and authentic. Recognize when the discomfort can or does become too difficult or intense and find ways to keep it productive and manageable, for yourself and for others.

References

Ferdman, B. M. (2014). The practice of inclusion in diverse organizations: Toward a systemic and inclusive framework. In B. M. Ferdman & B. R. Deane (Eds.). *Diversity at work: The practice of inclusion* (pp. 3–54). San Francisco, CA: Jossey-Bass.

Ferdman, B. M., Barrera, V., Allen, A., & Vuong, V. (2009, August 11). Inclusive behavior and the experience of inclusion. In B. G. Chung (Chair), *Inclusion in organizations:*

Measures, HR practices, and climate. Symposium presented at the Annual Meeting of the Academy of Management, Chicago, IL.

Ferdman, B. M., & Deane, B. R. (2014). Preface. In B. M. Ferdman & B. R. Deane (Eds.). *Diversity at work: The practice of inclusion* (pp. xxi–xxxii). San Francisco, CA: Jossey-Bass.

Ferdman, B. M., & Roberts, L. M. (2014). Creating inclusion for oneself: Knowing, accepting and expressing one's whole self at work. In B. M. Ferdman & B. R. Deane (Eds.). *Diversity at work: The practice of inclusion* (pp. 93–127). San Francisco, CA: Jossey-Bass.

Gurevitch, Z. D. (1989). The power of not understanding: The meeting of conflicting identities. *Journal of Applied Behavioral Science, 25,* 161–173.

Hubbard, A. (2004). The major life activity of belonging. *Wake Forest Law Review, 39,* 217–259.

Katz, J. H., & Miller, F. A. (2013). *Opening doors to teamwork and collaboration: 4 keys that change everything.* San Francisco, CA: Berrett-Koehler.

Miller, F. A. (1994). Forks in the road: Critical issues on the path to diversity. In E. Y. Cross, J. H. Katz, F. A. Miller, & E. W. Seashore (Eds.), *The promise of diversity: Over 40 voices discuss strategies for eliminating discrimination in organizations* (pp. 38–45). Burr Ridge, IL: Irwin.

Ruderman, M. N., & Chrobot-Mason, D. (2010). Triggers of social identity conflict. In K. Hannum, B. B. McFeeters, & L. Booysen (Eds.), *Leading across differences: Cases and perspectives* (pp. 81–86). San Francisco, CA: Pfeiffer.

9

AUTHENTIC AFFIRMATION?

Considering the Cultural Relevance of Strength-Based Practices in Global Organizations

Laura Morgan Roberts, Lynn Perry Wooten, Martin N. Davidson, and Amy Lemley

You are sitting in a private triage room in the ER of your local children's hospital, waiting for the on-call physician to arrive. On the shelf beneath the television, you notice a placard filled with comment cards that read, "Catch me at my best!" On each card, there is room to provide feedback about extraordinary caregiving encounters with any member of the hospital team. Fortunately, your child is only suffering from a virus, and you are discharged after a few hours. The care providers were gracious and considerate, but they entered and left the room so quickly that you never had time to develop a high-quality connection. Would it be presumptuous to tell someone you barely know that you caught them "at their best"? In the end, your hands were occupied with caring for your child, and you forgot to pick up the card on your way out.

You return to your hotel room after a long day of business meetings. It's late at night, and you just want to crawl into bed. As you pull back the covers, you notice the note card that falls onto the floor. "Over the top!" it reads, and cheerfully probes for examples of extraordinary service. You never had any serious problems with your room. In fact, you've scarcely been there during this trip. Check-in was smooth, and you haven't even interacted directly with the cleaning staff. As you rush off to your meeting the next morning, you forget to thank the hotel for its consistent service on your comment card.

After waiting several hours and spending more money than you anticipated on auto repairs, you are standing at the counter while your service attendant is finally closing out your paperwork. Before handing over your keys, he tells you that you will receive a customer service questionnaire via e-mail and hard copy. As he does at the close of every repair visit, the attendant requests that you choose all "5's" (the highest score) on the survey, if you were pleased with your service. "The company really wants our customers to rate us as a 5," he explains. "If you cannot rate us a 5, please give us one more chance to improve your service rating before you leave." You don't have any serious complaints (besides the amount of your bill). Should you comply with his request?

During new-employee orientation, you and your colleagues are invited to share your prior leadership successes with the entering cohort of 30 freshly minted MBAs. You take a deep breath and stammer through your introduction, trying to walk the delicate balance between projecting confidence and sounding arrogant. At the end of the exercise, you wonder how much all of you *really* learned about each person who spoke.

You receive your prework in the mail for an upcoming leadership development retreat. You are to complete what looks like a 360-degree feedback evaluation. You are already nervous about soliciting feedback from 10 to 20 people in your network. Then you realize that the questionnaire focuses only on your strengths! How are you going to find enough people who know you well enough to share detailed examples about your best qualities and valuable contributions?

These five scenarios demonstrate the groundswell of corporate interest and enthusiasm for "positive" approaches to leadership development and talent management, especially in U.S.-based companies. Everywhere we do business—online, by telephone, or in person—it seems we are being asked for compliments, almost before the transaction is completed: What are we good at? What did we do well? Executive leadership development programs, corporate culture change and diversity initiatives, and HR and career training programs, as well as schools ranging from elementary to postgraduate level use popular tools and frameworks, grounded in the principles of Appreciative Inquiry (AI) (Cooperrider & Sekerka, 2003; Cooperrider & Srivastva, 1987) (e.g., Gallup Strengthsfinder, the Values in Action inventory of character strengths and virtues, and the Reflected Best Self Exercise™). Yet these tools and frameworks are often met with skepticism. Consider the five scenarios above. Are these explicit requests for positive feedback an opportunity for customers, coworkers, or others to provide genuine, authentic affirmation? Or are they an orchestrated branding vehicle that pressures people to offer insincere praise?

These questions become even more complex when attending to Diversity and Inclusion (D&I) dynamics that affect the experience of *authentic affirmation*—sincere expressions of praise, appreciation, or gratitude for a person's, dyad's, group's, or organization's qualities and/or behaviors. As scholars, teachers, and developers of these "positive" approaches to leadership development and talent management, we have observed first-hand the implications of "difference blind" approaches to strengths-based paradigms. In this chapter, we will critically evaluate popular approaches to "positive" leadership development from a global diversity perspective, using the Reflected Best Self Exercise as a case example. We draw upon theory and practice to suggest mindful, culturally inclusive approaches toward strength-based leadership development and talent management.

Reframing Resistance toward the Reflected Best Self Exercise

Ten years ago, Roberts, Spreitzer et al. (2005) published an article in *Harvard Business Review* (*HBR*) entitled "How to Play to Your Strengths." The article featured the benefits of strengths-based development, as evidenced by the Reflected Best Self Exercise (RBSE). The RBSE is a tool developed by Quinn, Dutton, Spreitzer, and Roberts, available from the Center for Positive Organizations at the University of Michigan's Ross School of Business. The aim of the RBSE is to help people contribute maximally to their organizations and communities.

The Reflected Best Self Exercise is implemented through a multistep process. First, a participant submits a contact list of people who have seen them at their best—colleagues, clients, friends, and family. Those contacts receive a survey asking them to identify the qualities in that person that add value; they are then asked to write a story for each quality that illustrates how that quality allowed the participant to make a difference. This collection of stories allows people to enhance their understanding of their best selves as *reflected* by those who know them best. Thus, the RBSE is a holistic, strengths-based approach toward personal development in which people learn how to tap into their highest potential by analyzing their previous contributions.

"How to Play to Your Strengths" has been among the most widely read articles in *HBR* since it was published. Research articles have been published that further document the impact of the RBSE for adolescents and adults and uncover the mechanisms that create such a powerful impact from this unique feedback experience (Cable, Gino & Stats, 2013; Roberts, Dutton, Spreitzer, Heaphy, & Quinn, 2005; Spreitzer, Stephens, & Sweetman, 2009).

We (Roberts, Wooten, Davidson, & Lemley) have used the RBSE with thousands of clients and students globally in our corporate trainings, team-building exercises, executive leadership programs, executive coaching sessions, and in graduate and undergraduate courses in a variety of disciplines. This book on bridging Positive Organizational Scholarship (POS) with D&I affords us the opportunity to critically examine the global receptivity to "positive" leadership development practices, through the example of the RBSE.

In the remainder of our chapter, we identify the three most common forms of resistance against the RBSE that we have observed and locate their origins in divergent cultural value systems. After describing each form of resistance, we offer possibilities for reframing the RBSE that are culturally sensitive and inclusive.

Resistance against Hyperindividualism, Egoism, and Grandiosity

The premise of the RBSE is that individuals, through personal action, can make distinctive and valuable contributions to social systems. Yet this premise is often viewed as elevating an individualistic construction of the self, which contradicts the interdependent self-construals held by many cultural groups. What is embraced as self-actualization in some value systems is derogated as selfishness in others. In support of this view, Greenfield (1994) asserted the following:

> The independent individual is not a universal fact, but a culture-specific belief system about the development of a person. There is an important alternate belief system that is held by about 70 percent of the world's population (Triandis, 1989); it is called *interdependence or collectivism*.

Collectivistic belief systems can influence how people react to "positive" leadership development experiences such as the RBSE. While Laura was introducing the RBSE to a multicultural group of U.S. women senior executives, a Native American program participant expressed her concern and confusion with the exercise's standard instructions: *"Think of a time when you were at your best. . . ."* These instructions triggered in her a discomfort with the hyperindividualistic, self-centered orientation that is often associated with mainstream U.S. culture. An overemphasis on the self as an independent, distinctive contributor contradicts the collectivistic orientations of many cultures. From this Native American leader's vantage point, it was inconceivable to speak of herself as "object" separate from land, story, ancestors, and elders (Kenny & Fraser, 2013). Thus, she could not authentically engage with a process of reflecting on her *personal* best moments. The RBSE has presented similar cultural conflicts for other clients who hold stronger collectivistic orientations (e.g., participants from East Asian, African diasporic, Latin American, and Scandinavian cultures).

While some resist "positive" leadership due to the emphasis on the *self* as an independent actor, others resist the emphasis on *best*. Laura experienced this form of resistance from Danish executives when facilitating the RBSE. For many Danish executives, emphasizing one's *best* self was contrary to the law of *Jante*, or *Janteloven*. *Janteloven* originated from a 1933 novel *A Fugitive Crosses His Tracks (En Flyktning Krysser Sitt Spor)* by Aksel Sandemose, in which everyone in the Danish town of Jante abided by 10 laws against self-aggrandizement (e.g., "You're not to think you are anything special," "You're not to convince yourself that you are better than we are," "You're not to think you are good at anything"). These laws ensured harmony and stability in the fictitious town. Consequently, *Janteloven* has taken on a mythological status that guides social behavior in Denmark and Scandinavia. In light of the law of *Jante*, many Danish executives experience the RBSE as violating cultural principles.

These cultural concerns about egoism extend beyond Scandinavia. For instance, Latin American cultures emphasize the values of *humilidad* and *verguenza* (meaning interpersonal humility, shame, honor, and self-respect; Hill & Torres, 2010; Olmeda, 2003). Participants from the UK (i.e., London and Scotland) have expressed skepticism that the RBSE is too positive, and therefore inauthentic. In our sessions, many have shared that it is countercultural to provide positive feedback to coworkers, family members, or friends. Non-U.S. participants often respond to the RBSE with stereotypes of U.S. individualism and egoism (e.g., "Here we go with the overly positive, self-focused American idealism again!").

Similarly, when Lynn has worked with African American executives, their strong racial identity rooted in collectivism as represented by *Ubuntu*, an African word meaning "humanity to others" and associated with the expression, "I am what I am because of who we all are" has been a central point of tension (Allen & Bagozzi, 2001). They believe this is because the majority of their professional experiences honor individualism and do not reward or acknowledge that one's best self is the result of his or her interdependence with others in a community working together to create opportunities for all members to thrive. Interestingly, Lynn has coached women in certain professions who have also struggled with stereotypical notions of best self that ignore feministic principles of approaching work, such as, governing through egalitarian relationships, consensus decision making, and shared leadership responsibilities, and as a consequence their best selves emerge through "tempered radical" behavior (Wooten & Crane, 2004).

Despite the cultural contours of resistance, this discomfort with discovering best selves actually reflects global concerns. Research by the Gallup Institute shows that, when asked whether it's more important to focus on strengths or weaknesses, the majority of countries favor the weakness approach. U.S. survey respondents reported the strongest endorsement for strength-based approaches, but they were still a minority (41 percent favoring strengths vs. 59 percent favoring weaknesses). Other countries showed even stronger biases against strengths endorsement: Great Britain and Canada (38 percent strengths), France (29 percent strengths), Japan and China (24 percent) strengths. In every culture studied, the Gallup Institute also found that an overwhelming majority of parents believe that a student's lowest grades deserve the most attention (Hodges & Clifton, 2004).

In administering the survey that is prework for the RBSE, Amy sees the beginnings of such resistance, often weeks before the executive education classroom exercise occurs. After explaining the survey process via e-mail, she asks participants to submit 20 to 30 respondent names—with a maximum of seven nonwork contacts. Most comply easily. Some procrastinate. And some participants submit far fewer than the minimum and, when pressed, will say there simply are not that many people who know them well enough to have seen them at their best. Is this a tactic for avoiding an appearance of hyperindividualism, egoism, or grandiosity? Could this also be an indicator that the RBSE, like other 360-degree feedback exercises, is especially challenging for people with smaller, less diverse social networks?

Once people overcome their concerns with focusing on their personal strength-based development, many still experience an additional form of resistance. When asked to *"think about times in your life when you were at your best,"* many people struggle to recall examples, or at least any they think worthy of mentioning. A psychological barrier is feeding this form of selective amnesia about peak moments. In cultures that value grandiosity and instant gratification (e.g., big cars, big houses, celebrity lifestyles, rags-to-riches archetypes), participants often diminish the value of their own achievements, contributions, and interpersonal encounters. The Celebrity CEO culture of the United States (Khurana, 2004) may create idealized images of leadership as heroic, hypermasculine, and earth-shaking (Fletcher, 2002; Manz & Sims, 1991). Most people (male or female) will never experience this type of fame and notoriety. As a result, U.S. participants, and those who endorse similar belief systems, may hold unrealistic expectations regarding what constitutes a "best-self moment." This dynamic is an ironic effect of egoism; though cloaked in espoused humility (e.g., "I don't want to overstate my accomplishments"), these concerns are still driven by egoistic desires to "measure up" to societal expectations of so-called greatness.

Reframing the RBSE to Promote Authentic Affirmation That Is Relational, Developmental, and Meaningful

Those authenticity concerns about the RBSE are legitimate. To facilitate the process of strength-based development, we must develop inclusive, nuanced frameworks that are accessible to a broad range of cultural perspectives. Further, our POS-based tools and frameworks must be employed with cultural consciousness that will truly bring out the best in globally diverse individuals and groups.

First, we emphasize that *authentic affirmation is relational.* An important aspect of the RBSE that is often overlooked is its emphasis on interdependence in social systems. The state of being at one's best involves "actively employing strengths to create value, actualize one's potential, and fulfill one's sense of purpose, which generates a constructive experience (emotional, cognitive, or behavioral) for oneself and for others" (Roberts, Dutton et al., 2005, p. 714). Through the RBSE, participants gain a richer understanding of how they strengthen other people and social systems. In other words, when we are at our best, we bring out the best in others. *Every person matters* when actualizing human and organizational potential.

For example, the RBSE can be easily adapted to stimulate strength-based, interdependent reflections on peak experiences. In working with the Native American leaders we referenced earlier, Laura modified the exercise. Instead of asking them to think of times when they were at their *personal best*, she invited them to reflect upon times in which they felt most connected to their ancestors, elders, and land. This prompt resonated more strongly with their cultural value system, and thus created a more authentic experience of shared affirmation. The storytelling format of the RBSE also resonates with Native and African forms of co-creating identities and transmitting culture through narrative. Considering the cultural values of a minority group of participants allowed us to make the RBSE experience more robust for the entire group.

Second, we emphasize that *authentic affirmation is developmental*. Across the globe, emerging and accomplished leaders take the risk of completing the RBSE because they view it as a rare opportunity to learn, grow, and develop in new ways. Laura often tells her students that "the RBSE is not designed to be an ego boost, but . . . it will probably make you feel good!" One Danish student wrote in his final essay that the experience of completing the RBSE was like bungee jumping—frightening, exhilarating, and tremendously rewarding.

Research on cultivating and sustaining positive identities at work documents the value of using the RBSE as a platform for growth and development (Roberts, 2013). Through the exercise, participants anchor their idealized possible selves (i.e., who they hope to be) in the reality of their past contributions. They chart a path of personal development that is grounded in a realistic understanding of their potential. The exercise involves the co-creation of narratives that embody the personal and situational factors that support best-self engagement, and that enable people to articulate their vision and path toward progress more clearly. By (re)examining best selves, people are able to develop more robust action plans for being at their best more often, making their best selves even better, and bringing out the best in others. This action plan for best-self engagement is especially potent for marginalized members of organizations and communities, whose contributions often disappear (e.g., women's relational work in majority male contexts; Fletcher, 2001). Similarly, asset-based community development (ABCD; Green, Moore, & O'Brien, 2006) approaches toward social change are grounded in the understanding of how to strategically engage strengths and encourage positive deviance through the strengths of people who are structurally disempowered, but are powerful contributors to their communities (e.g., McIntosh, 2012).

Once people come face to face with their best selves and fully examine their own potential for extraordinary contributions, they can no longer blame their circumstances or surroundings for their limited contributions. The RBSE reveals people's capabilities for contributing in the workplace and beyond, and clarifies their commitment to value-creation in various domains of life. In other words, empowering best selves means raising the bar. The more people learn about their best selves, the more they expect of themselves. It's nearly impossible to take a "business as usual" approach to work after learning more about best-self empowerment. As people recognize the conscious and unconscious choices they are making in pursuit of best-self engagement vs. their comfort zone, they begin to empower themselves to reject the status quo and co-create the conditions in which their best selves can thrive and flourish (Quinn, 2004). Thus, developmental work to discover and enact one's best self is hard work, but rewarding as individuals create cycles of good to great by showcasing their values and identity to become results-oriented, purpose-centered, and receptive to feedback.

Third, we emphasize that *authentic affirmation is meaningful*. In contrast to people's self-conceived notions of heroic leadership, the RBSE illuminates the acts of "everyday greatness" that occur when people are leading where they are. The contribution stories that coworkers, friends, family, and mentors share are often based on micro-moments: seemingly insignificant encounters in which someone offered a word or deed that made a huge difference in how people experienced themselves and their situations (Roberts, Spreitzer et al., 2005). RBSE participants may not have catalogued this moment in their personal account of peak experiences, so getting this feedback helps them to discern which moments truly matter to the people and organizations that they value. They don't have to be celebrity CEOs to matter. With this insight about everyday greatness, people are able reframe the RBSE in terms of their larger goals for development and contribution. Focusing on the larger goals helps to liberate people from their egoistic desires to be *the* best, so that they can focus on learning and growing into their personal best (Crocker & Carnevale, 2013).

For Practitioners: How to Practice Authentic Affirmation

Cultural Consciousness

- Does the tool/framework/approach trigger cultural stereotypes? If so, discuss these explicitly with your clients, coworkers, and/or students.
- Does the tool/framework/approach incorporate inclusive cultural value systems? If not, how can you modify your approach so that it is better aligned with the cultural value system in which you are working?

Relational Affirmation

- Facilitate discussions of how people contribute to your team and/or community that highlights each person as a valuable and significant part of an interdependent social system. The more people know about each other's strengths, limitations, and values, the more effectively they can work together. Contribution conversations are positive and constructive ways to build mutual understanding within teams; they help people to be more honest about contributions and mistakes, and identify opportunities for value creation.

Developmental Affirmation

- Study your successes—and others' successes—with the sole intent of discovering how your strengths equip you to offer distinctive ideas, analyses, virtues, and connections that can improve the quality of your relationships and contributions. Use these insights about your contribution potential to enrich the functioning and productivity of organizations and communities. In other words, do more than play to your strengths. Keep asking yourself (and others) how you can be at your best more often.

Meaningful Affirmation

- Search for the small, yet powerful acts of everyday greatness around you. Look beyond the leaders who are in the spotlight to notice the larger, more diverse group of valuable contributors in your organization. Share your appreciation for generous, inspiring leadership moments that occur "on the sidelines" of organizational life. Affirm the interpersonal interactions that will bring out the best in others in the present and future.

References

Allen, R. L., & Bagozzi, R. R. (2001). Consequences of black sense of self. *Journal of Black Psychology, 27*, 3–28. doi:10.1177/009579840102700100

Cable, D. M., Gino, F., & Staats, B. R. (2013). Breaking them in or eliciting their best? Reframing socialization around newcomers' authentic self-expression. *Administrative Science Quarterly, 58*(1), 1–36.

Cooperrider, D., & Sekerka, L. (2003). Toward a theory of positive organizational change. In K. Cameron, J. Dutton, & R. E. Quinn (Eds.), *Positive organizational scholarship* (pp. 225–240). San Francisco, CA: Berrett-Koehler.

Cooperrider, D. L., & Srivastva, S. (1987). Appreciative inquiry in organizational life. *Research in Organizational Change and Development, 1*(1), 129–169.

Crocker, J., & Carnevale, J. J. (2013). Letting go of self-esteem. *Scientific American Mind, 24*(4), 26–33.

Fletcher, J. K. (2001). *Disappearing acts: Gender, power, and relational practice at work.* Cambridge, MA: MIT Press.

Fletcher, J. K. (2002). The greatly exaggerated demise of heroic leadership: Gender, power, and the myth of the female advantage. *CGO Insights, 13*, 1–4.

Green, M., Moore, H., & O'Brien, J. (2006). *Asset based community development: When people care enough to act.* Toronto: Inclusion Press.

Greenfield, P. M. (1994). Independence and interdependence as developmental scripts: Implications for theory, research and practice. In P. M. Greenfield & R. R. Cocking (Eds.), *Cross-cultural roots of minority child development* (pp. 1–37). Hillsdale, NJ: Erlbaum.

Hill, N. E., & Torres, K. (2010). Negotiating the American dream: The paradox of aspirations and achievement among Latino students and engagement between their families and schools. *Journal of Social Issues, 66*(1), 95–112.

Hodges, T., & Clifton, D. (2004). Strengths-based development in practice. In P. A. Linley & S. Joseph (Eds.), *International handbook of positive psychology in practice: From research to application*. Hoboken, NJ: Wiley and Sons.

Kenny, C. K., & Fraser, T. N. (2013). *Living indigenous leadership: Native narratives on building strong communities*. Seattle: University of Washington Press.

Khurana, R. (2004). *Searching for a corporate savior: The irrational quest for charismatic CEOs*. Princeton, NJ: Princeton University Press.

Manz, C. C., & Sims, H. P. (1991). Superleadership: Beyond the myth of heroic leadership. *Organizational Dynamics, 19*(4), 18–35.

McIntosh, P. (2012). Reflections and future directions for privilege studies. *Journal of Social Issues, 68*(1), 194–206.

Olmeda, I. (2003). Accommodation and resistance: Latinas' struggle for their children's education. *Anthropology of Education Quarterly, 34*, 373–375.

Quinn, R. E. (2004). Building the bridge as you walk on it: A guide for leading change. San Francisco, CA: Jossey-Bass.

Roberts, L. (2013). Reflected best self-engagement at work: Positive identity, alignment, and the pursuit of vitality and value Creation. In I. Boniwell & S. Davis (Eds.), *The Oxford handbook of happiness*. Oxford: Oxford University Press.

Roberts, L. M., Dutton, J. E., Spreitzer, G. M., Heaphy, E. D., & Quinn, R. E. (2005). Composing the reflected best-self portrait: Building pathways for becoming extraordinary in work organizations. *Academy of Management Review, 30*, 712–736.

Roberts, L. M., Spreitzer, G., Dutton, J., Quinn, R., Heaphy, E., & Barker, B. (2005). How to play to your strengths. *Harvard Business Review, 83*(1), 74–80.

Sandemose, A. (1933). A fugitive crosses his tracks. (*En Flyktning Krysser Sitt Spor*). New York: A. A. Knopf.

Spreitzer, G., Stephens, J. P., & Sweetman, D. (2009). The reflected best self field experiment with adolescent leaders: Exploring the psychological resources associated with feedback source and valence. *Journal of Positive Psychology, 4*, 331–348.

Triandis, H. C. (1989). Cross-cultural studies of individualism and collectivism. *Nebraska Symposium on Motivation, 37*, 41–133.

Wooten, L., & Crane, P. (2004). Generating dynamic capabilities through a humanistic work ideology: The case of a certified-nurse midwife practice in a professional bureaucracy. *American Behavioral Scientist, 47*(10), 848–866.

SECTION III
Resilience
Section Introduction

Amy Lemley, Laura Morgan Roberts,
Martin N. Davidson, and Lynn Perry Wooten

Ladda Tammy Duckworth's bio is a list of firsts. First Asian American woman elected to serve as a U.S. representative in Illinois. First disabled woman to be elected to the U.S. House of Representatives. First member of Congress born in Thailand. And first female double amputee from the Iraq War. As a U.S. Army helicopter pilot, Duckworth lost both legs and part of one arm in combat at the age of 36. Though she received a medical waiver, she fought hard to join the Illinois National Guard, serving as a lieutenant colonel. She worked in veterans affairs at the state and federal levels before running for Congress—and first losing, a defeat she took hard, famously recounting that she "sat in the bathtub and cried for two days." Finally elected in 2013 and reelected in 2014, Duckworth continues to champion the issues that gripped her during her years in veterans affairs and as a veteran herself, including medical benefits and employment incentives. The child of a vet whose family once needed food stamps, she supports effective social services programs. Facing tens of thousands of dollars in school loans, she advocates a service-for-scholarship exchange. Her strength, she says, "is in finding ways for the government to work for the people." Each November 11, she celebrates what she calls "Alive Day," the day she was shot down and survived. "Another year," she has said to herself. "What did I do this year to earn this?" (Riopel, 2014).

"That which does not kill us makes us stronger." In nine words, Friedrich Nietzsche aptly described the path to resilience. Positive Organizational Scholarship (POS) holds that resilience has a critical effect on individuals' well-being in organizations. Diversity and inclusion research has documented the barriers minorities face at work and their responses. The first chapter in this section, "Resilience and Failure," seeks to document just how resilience develops among marginalized groups and how POS principles might support that development. Giscombe emphasizes the importance of learning from and growing through failure; resilience is manifested through overcoming defensive and self-protective routines.

Turning specifically to the African American experience, Henderson and Bell's chapter, "Racial Socialization and Resilience of Minority Group Members," looks at positive ways minorities can handle and bounce back from instances of discrimination to achieve career success. The concept of racial socialization is introduced as a tool for developing resilience across the lifespan, which in turn helps potentially marginalized employees to achieve favorable work outcomes in diverse organizations.

"Social Resilience: Building Persistence in Interracial Relationships" introduces a new concept, social resilience, that describes a willingness to persist in the face of uncomfortable human interactions—such as those with people of other races. Menon and Chakravarti assert that social resilience means continuing to engage despite things such as damaging first impressions, unshared assumptions, awkward conversations, or even conflict. This willingness to be uncomfortable—something Ferdman's chapter in the Authenticity section also identified—is the key to connecting on a level that is meaningful and can be productive in the workplace.

These chapters bridge diversity, inclusion, and POS to probe into one of the hallmarks of capacity building in diverse societies—resilience. Diversity and inclusion are often met with unique challenges; individuals, identity groups, and organizations build capacity through cultivating resilience.

Reference

Riopel, M. (2014, November 14). Ten years after losing her legs, Duckworth returns to flying. *Daily Herald*.

10

RESILIENCE AND FAILURE

Katherine Giscombe

In a study that colleagues and I conducted on trust building in relationships between women of color and white male managers, we were struck by one extremely confident African American woman. She readily acknowledged to her boss that an assignment early in her tenure had gone poorly, and invited discussion. Her willingness to divulge subpar performance was, in her manager's words, "a milestone. She recognized this as an opportunity for me to coach her . . . she recognized that and leap-frogged past her peers." This stands in stark contrast to the accounts by many other women of color regarding their fear of revealing mistakes, and their practice of hiding vulnerabilities as a self-protective mechanism (Catalyst, 2004; Giscombe et al., 2011).

Diversity and Inclusion research on outsider or marginalized groups (that is, those who are disempowered in some way such as women, racial minorities, and lesbian, gay, bisexual, transgender, and queer or questioning [LGBTQ]) at work organizations is typically related to societal and cultural factors such as stereotyping, prejudice, complex intergroup relations, and discrimination (e.g., Bell & Nkomo, 2001; Heilman, 2001; Sidanius & Pratto, 1999). Research has found discrimination and prejudice to lead to negative outcomes for these groups such as compromised professional image and attributions of incompetence, which are deleterious to career advancement or even survival in a job.

Research has shown that not only is a minority member's performance viewed as less effective than a majority member's performance, but also that even when the performance is viewed as effective, it is less likely to be attributed to internal ability and competence. Greenhaus et al. (1990) found that the performance of highly successful black managers was attributed to help from others, rather than ability and effort.

Those from marginalized groups are also given less leeway regarding ambiguity. For example, in one study, men were viewed as highly competent *except* when information of failure was provided, but women tended to be viewed as highly competent only when *unambiguous* information of success was provided (Heilman et al., 1997). DiTomaso et al. (2007) showed that U.S.-born white men, as compared with nonmale, nonwhite, and/or non-U.S. born professionals, enjoyed greater access to favorable work experiences as well as the benefit of the doubt in the evaluation of their performance and promotability into management.

Given the enhanced stress of organizational life for those from outsider groups, it would seem that some degree of resilience would be helpful. How can members of these groups, already burdened by stigmatized identities, not just cope but succeed in what are sometimes exclusionary environments? The Positive Organizational Scholarship (POS) field has been investigating resilience as a key construct that affects individual well-being in organizations. At the same time, the Diversity and Inclusion (D&I) field has catalogued the many barriers facing minorities in organizations. By examining resilience with a D&I lens—that is, its development among marginalized groups—we should be able to enrich both disciplines' fields of inquiry and make positive change in organizations.

In the larger positive psychology field, "resilience" has been defined as the positive adaptation in the context of significant adversity (Masten et al., 2009). Thus, it can be developed over time, rather than being regarded as a fixed trait (Luthans & Youssef, 2009). More generally, resilience can be conceptualized as the capacity for adaptability, positive functioning, or enhanced proficiency following stressful events. Researchers of resilience also note that it can be enhanced by "mastery experiences." Such mastery experiences are more likely to occur when "individuals *have the ability to make and recover from mistakes* [emphasis author's] . . . Such individuals are more likely to regard mistakes as a natural part of competence-building" (Sutcliff & Vogus, 2003). Resilience, then, is acquired through a developmental process (Masten et al., 2009); given the right circumstances, organizational members are able to learn and perfect coping skills in the face of the ups and downs of organizational life.

Minority members may sometimes be even more cautious than most about making mistakes, given their concerns about disconfirming stereotypes of low competence. For example, research has found that "stereotype threat" (being at risk of confirming a negative stereotype about one's group) related positively to indirect feedback-seeking and discounting of performance feedback from superiors (Roberson, Deitch, & Block, 2003). Given biased attributions regarding skill, those from marginalized groups do not have as much leeway as those from majority groups to make and learn from mistakes. Marginalized group members are often keenly aware of others' perceptions of diminished competence, and are likely to be extremely cautious about making mistakes. These dynamics can make it quite difficult for the individual marginalized group member to develop resilience. And yet at least some clearly do, in spite of the intense scrutiny that can attend their presence in organizations.

On a broader level, the difficulty individual members of marginalized groups may have in building resilience has organizational ramifications. In taking pains to avoid mistakes, members of marginalized groups may contribute to less capacity for innovation in the organization. Alternatively, if norms exist allowing workers to make mistakes and learn from them, then individuals would feel freer to bring their "whole selves" to work and spend less time and energy in managing others' impressions of them. From an organizational perspective, companies would most likely develop greater success in innovation.

Acceptance of failure is critical for new knowledge creation—which seems especially important in a global, increasingly competitive, economy. In a study on adaptation to a new information system, it was shown that individuals working under the assumption that failures were inevitable, and that failures were appropriate to discuss, reported greater capacity to innovate than those individuals to whom it was communicated that failure was not acceptable (Lee et al., 2003).

An important question from a diversity and inclusion perspective is how is "failure as a learning opportunity" perceived when the actors are those from marginalized groups? Several lines of inquiry could follow:

- What types of impression management are most effective in ensuring that those in the organization make fair attributions of an individual's skill and worth? How does such impression management vary by a person's membership in a marginalized group?
- How does ambiguity of performance outcomes play a role? For example, would certain classes of failures be assigned relatively more negative, or positive, connotations depending on who commits the error? Is there a typology of failures that exist that are more, or less, negatively impactful on the individual committing the error? How do such typologies of failure vary by organizational culture?
- What are the characteristics of dyadic work relationships that nurture resilience? Is there a critical learning period that occurs early in the tenure of dissimilar pairs? Does a crisis and how it is dealt with at an early stage have a major effect (as it did in the example at the beginning of this chapter)? Longitudinal studies of dyads of managers and members of marginalized groups, especially using reciprocal methodologies, should shed some light on this. This would add complexity to the perspective that demographically dissimilar pairs take a longer time to develop closeness than more demographically similar pairs (Turban et al., 1999). Such a path of inquiry may also shift the conceptualization of resilience from its location in an individual to being a relationship dynamic.

Studying the role of failure in developing resilience at the individual level, concentrating on those from marginalized groups, is important from an epistemological perspective. Research in this area will contribute to enhanced knowledge and contextualization of two constructs important to social groupings and organizations. On a practical level, locating a study of these constructs within a diverse sample and delving into any extant gaps will deepen understanding of the work lives of those from marginalized identity groups, and help practitioners understand why some groups experience more positive outcomes than others and what can be done to enhance positive outcomes among a broader range of actors.

On a longer-term basis, this approach to research, which brings together the fields of D&I and POS, affords an opportunity to view failure from a fresh perspective: one that recognizes setbacks as growth opportunities for individuals, and a way forward toward greater innovation and success for the organization.

For Practitioners: Digging Deeper into Interpretations of Failure in Your Organization

- Overall, is the performance of those from marginalized groups examined on par with the performance of others? That is, are there any double standards for how performance is assessed?
- Examine recent "failures" within your organization, and examine the impact on the individuals responsible. Are some mistakes less impactful than others? What reasons might there be? Are certain kinds of mistakes more likely to be forgiven in your organization than others?
- What are the consequences of a mistake when the circumstances of the mistake are ambiguous? Do the consequences vary by groups of individuals (e.g., are women treated differently from men if they make the same mistake)?
- Examine performance reviews to see whether or not the way in which mistakes or setbacks are described vary by race, ethnic group, gender, or other minority status.
- Develop measures of innovation, relevant to your industry, to better understand which departments or divisions seem to do well in this area.
- Investigate the leadership, behavioral norms, and management styles of departments or divisions that seem to do well in innovating. Consider creating performance criteria based on innovation potential.
- In assessing the progress of marginalized groups in your organization, carefully examine the dynamics of the relationship between managers and direct reports, regarding trust, extent of feedback, fairness in assessing performance, and so on.

References

Bell, E., & Nkomo, S. 2001. *Our separate ways: Black and white women and the struggle for professional identity.* Boston, MA: Harvard Business School Press.
Catalyst. (2004). *Advancing African-American women in the workplace: What managers need to know.* New York: Author.

DiTomaso, N., Corinne Post, C., Smith, D. R., Farris, G. F., & Cordero, R. (2007). Effects of structural position on allocation and evaluation decisions for scientists and engineers in industrial R&D. *Administrative Science Quarterly, 52,* 175–207.

Giscombe, K., Agin, M., & Deva, V. (2011). *Building trust between managers and diverse women direct reports.* New York: Catalyst.

Greenhaus, J. H., Parasuraman, S., & Wormley, W. M. (1990). Effects of race on organizational experiences, job performance evaluations, and career outcomes. *Academy of Management Journal, 33,* 64–86.

Heilman, M. E. (2001). Description and prescription: How gender stereotypes prevent women's ascent up the organizational ladder, *Journal of Social Issues, 4,* 657–674.

Heilman, M. E., Block, C. J., & Stathatos, P. (1997). The affirmative action stigma of incompetence: Effects of performance information ambiguity. *Academy of Management Journal, 40*(3), 603–625.

Lee, F., Caza, A., Edmondson, A., & Thomke, S. (2003). New knowledge creation in organizations. In K. S. Cameron, J. E. Dutton, & R. E. Quinn (Eds.), *Positive organizational scholarship: Foundations of a new discipline* (pp. 194–206). San Francisco, CA: Berrett-Koehler.

Luthens, F., & Youssef, C. M. (2009). Positive workplaces. In S. J. Lopez & C. R. Snyder (Eds.), *The Oxford handbook of positive psychology* (pp. 579–588). New York: Oxford University Press.

Masten, A. S., Cutuli, J. J., Herbers, J. E., & Reed, M. J. (2009). Resilience in development. In S. J. Lopez & C. R. Snyder (Eds.), *The Oxford handbook of positive psychology* (pp. 117–132). New York: Oxford University Press.

Roberson, L., Deitch, E., Brief, A., & Block, C. (2003). Stereotype threat and feedback seeking in the workplace. *Journal of Vocational Behavior, 62,* 176–188.

Sidanius, J., & Pratto, F. (1999). *Social dominance: An intergroup theory of social hierarchy and oppression.* New York: Cambridge University Press.

Sutcliffe, K. M., & Vogus, T. J. (2003). Organizing for resilience. In K. S. Cameron, J. E. Dutton, & R. E. Quinn (Eds.), *Positive organizational scholarship: Foundations of a new discipline* (pp. 94–110). San Francisco, CA: Berrett-Koehler.

Turban, D. B., Dougherty, T. W., & Lee, F. K. (1999). The impact of demographic diversity and perceived similarity on mentoring outcomes: The moderating effect of time. *Academy of Management Proceedings,* E1–E6.

11

RACIAL SOCIALIZATION AND RESILIENCE OF MINORITY GROUP MEMBERS

Demetria Henderson and Myrtle Bell

Out of the huts of history's shame

I rise

Up from a past that's rooted in pain

I rise

—*Maya Angelou (1978)*

The history of blacks in America spans nearly 400 years and is full of examples of people achieving tremendous accomplishments in the face of insurmountable odds. What is it that led Harriet Tubman to escape slavery, and then, at the risk of losing her newfound freedom, venture back to the South more than a dozen times to guide hundreds of slaves to freedom? How does a community organizer of mixed race, who appears and identifies as black, become editor of the *Harvard Law Review* and later the 44th president of the United States? How do a people—in the face of immense adversity—manage not only to survive but to thrive and act with resilience?

Racial discrimination continues to factor into the lives of African Americans in the workplace, limiting career advancement opportunities, creating disengagement, and lowering satisfaction, which is related to decreased levels of job performance (Greenhaus, Parasuraman, & Wormley, 1990). Discrimination results in perceptions of isolation and alienation, which in turn often diminish self-esteem (Harris-Britt, Valrie, Kurtz-Costes, & Rowley, 2007), lowering an individual's capacity for resilience. Although overt discrimination still occurs, today, discrimination on the job is often demonstrated via racial microaggressions—subtle acts of aggressions or insults directed toward minorities (Solórzano, Ceja, & Yosso, 2000). We contend that minorities must circumvent or bounce back from acts of discrimination in positive ways to achieve career success. This chapter will explore how racial socialization, composed of messages about racial pride, identity, and preparation for bias, can cultivate a state of resilience, which helps to bring about positive work outcomes.

Resilience as a Positive State

One of the major goals of Positive Organizational Scholarship (POS) is to rigorously and systematically study positive states, such as resilience and meaningfulness, in an effort to understand how they influence both employees and the organization (Cameron, Dutton, & Quinn, 2003). Resilience is a "reduced vulnerability to environmental risk experiences, the overcoming of a stress or adversity, or a relatively good outcome despite risk experiences" (Rutter, 2012). Thus, resilience is a dynamic concept that is inferred based on judgments that an individual is performing *better* in comparison with others who have endured negative encounters. As such, resilience is a state (Cameron et al., 2003), as opposed to a trait, that ebbs and flows depending on personal circumstances and situations. For example, individuals may respond positively to a stressful event in one circumstance, but may react negatively to a different group of stressors in a different situation (Rutter, 1987).

The development of resilience encompasses two essential elements: risk factors and protective factors. Risk factors allow for an increase in an individual's susceptibility to negative outcomes, whereas protective factors counter negative outcomes (Masten, Cutuli, Herbers, & Reed, 2009). Protective factors include both internal and external variables (Wilson, Foster, Anderson, & Mance, 2009) and operate at three levels: (1) individual; (2) familial; and (3) societal (Rutter, 1987). For example, self-esteem at the individual level is a characteristic that serves as a protective buffer. Cohesive family units and strong external support systems also facilitate protection from hostile environments.

Research on African American children and adolescents has sought to answer the question as to why some individuals are capable of succeeding while others flounder in the face of adversity. Racial socialization and racial identity (Bennett, 2007) have each been found to demonstrate a buffering or mediating effect for African Americans when confronted with discrimination. Thus, we argue that resilience is an intangible positive force—a protective factor—that gives individuals the fortitude to persist in the face of obstacles such as discrimination.

A Model for Coping with Racial Discrimination

We propose that African Americans who have been exposed to racial socialization may have developed a strong racial identity that may more likely be linked to positive career outcomes. Racial socialization strengthens one's cultural values and enhances self-esteem by buffering the harmful effects of racial discrimination. As a result, the state of resilience for African Americans is maximized, which in turn increases the likelihood of positive work outcomes (Figure 11.1).

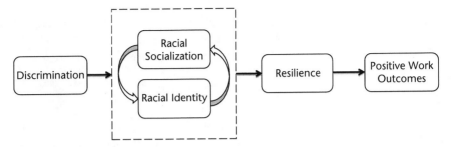

FIGURE 11.1 Model for coping with racial discrimination in the workplace. As defenses against discrimination, racial socialization and a strong racial identity give rise to a higher state of resilience, resulting in positive outcomes.

Racial Socialization

Racial socialization is an attempt to arm minority children with the protective skills and knowledge needed to overcome the discrimination they are likely to encounter due to their race (Stevenson, 1994). Specifically, racial socialization messages consist of (1) coping with prejudice; (2) acquiring pride in self; (3) acknowledging the need for a solid education; and (4) recognizing that fairness and the rules of the game are different for minorities (Thornton, Chatters, Taylor, & Allen, 1990). Researchers assert that through racial socialization, parents raise their children to have an awareness of the hurdles they will encounter in their lives and prepare them for how best to deal with these obstacles. In addition to the typical parental duties, African American adults have the additional role of ensuring their children are trained about the realities of the risk factors associated with being African American (such as racial profiling and employment discrimination). About two-thirds of black parents provide their children with racial socialization (Thornton et al., 1990). Thus, minority children are often taught to be resilient so that they may thrive and become productive adults, despite impediments over which they have no control.

In addition to the *protective* factor of racial socialization, Stevenson's (1994) research on African American adolescents also identified a *proactive* form of racial socialization. Proactive racial socialization consists of three factors—working in concert to promote cultural empowerment: (1) spiritual and religious coping, (2) extended family caring, and (3) cultural pride reinforcement. Together, these factors become the building blocks from which African Americans draw from an early age, and which help in shaping their identity by not only exposing children to the harsh realities of discrimination, but also giving messages of hope and opportunity. Although some racial socialization messages may engender higher levels of distrust, resulting in adverse behaviors (Wilson et al., 2009), research suggests that racial socialization messages can have a positive effect on the level of resilience exhibited by many African American children and adolescents, leading to higher levels of motivation and achievement (Bennett, 2007).

Racial/Ethnic Identity

Racial/ethnic identity is the close affiliation and kinship of ideas and feelings that an individual has with others of a similar racial or ethnic background (Bennett, 2007) and is one aspect of racial socialization (Harris-Britt et al., 2007). Similar to racial socialization, racial identity may provide minorities with a protective barrier against discrimination. A strong racial identity can assist members of minority groups in maintaining a positive perspective and cultivating higher levels of self-esteem (Crocker & Major, 1989) by focusing on the positive qualities of their racially identified groups (Sellers & Shelton, 2003). Thus, identification with one's race and culture establishes a set of principles that can be attributable to positive acts of behavior and interaction (Bennett, 2007; Ogbu, 1991). Moreover, a positive racial identity affords minorities the ability to work within various cultural contexts, which has been shown to be linked to increased opportunities and advancement (Bennett, 2007). Therefore, we posit that individuals conditioned from an early age to have a positive racial group identity are more likely to have higher self-esteem, leading to more positive outcomes when faced with adversity. We propose that a stronger self-identity leads to increased self-efficacy and positive outcomes in the workplace. It is those instances of racial pride and awareness that propel many to succeed when adversity arises.

Conclusion

Many African Americans believe they owe a great deal to those who came before them. There is a sense of pride and unmistakable reverence for those students who sat-in peacefully at a lunch counter in Greensboro, North Carolina, fighting for the same rights as whites; or those individuals who staged and participated in a march from Selma to Montgomery, Alabama, to gain the right to vote. Such events help to shape the lives of many African Americans and solidify their ethnic and racial identity. As a result, they often feel duty-bound to be nothing less than stellar, refusing to let their heroes' sacrifices be in vain.

An ample amount of research has investigated the negative consequences of racial discrimination. POS offers the ideal lens through which to examine the aspects of resilience that enable many African Americans to thrive in the business world in spite of discrimination. Social and familial support, as well as pride in one's race and culture, all serve as protective factors that can lead to forming a solid foundation from which African Americans can better position themselves to succeed in life and in their careers. Because resilience is viewed as a state, we have the ability to help individuals develop the strengths and aptitudes needed to cope with and overcome adversity by studying the positive effects of racial socialization. Our goal is to shed light on what we, as researchers, can glean by studying how those who have been socialized and have a strong sense of racial identity are better equipped to thwart the negative effects of racial discrimination and succeed.

Embedded in resilience are the coping mechanisms to which minorities subscribe when confronted with the stresses of discrimination.

There is far more research to be done on the relationship among racial socialization, racial identity, and resilience. Thus, for organizations to attract, recruit, and maintain a diverse workforce, POS research must continue searching for ways to diminish the negative effects of discrimination and foster success in spite of discrimination. Although we have focused on resilience as related to racial socialization of blacks, it is possible that socialization may help others who experience discrimination (e.g., people with disabilities) develop an awareness of the hurdles they may experience, prepare to deal with the obstacles they may face, and build resilience in a similar manner.

For Practitioners: What to Know about Resilience

- How do we engage our communities and organizations to advocate and promote familial and social support, along with the development of strong racial and cultural identities to mitigate the effects of racial discrimination?
- Resilience, as a state, may serve as the causal mechanism linking the attributes of racial socialization and racial identity with positive work outcomes. How then do we begin to educate minorities on how to increase resilience, individually and collectively?
- How might the protective factors of socialization and resilience against discrimination be applicable to other marginalized groups and individuals?

References

Angelou, M. (1978). Still I rise. In M. Angelou (Ed.), *And still I rise* (p. 41). New York: Random House.

Bennett, M. D. (2007). Racial socialization and ethnic identity: Do they offer protection against problem behaviors for African American youth? *Journal of Human Behavior in the Social Environment, 15*(2–3), 137–161.

Cameron, K. S., Dutton, J. E., & Quinn, R. E. (2003). Foundations of Positive Organizational Scholarship. In K. S. Cameron, J. E. Dutton, & R. E. Quinn (Eds.), *Positive organizational scholarship: Foundations of a new discipline* (pp. 3–13). San Francisco, CA: Berrett-Koehler.

Crocker, J., & Major, B. (1989). Social stigma and self-esteem: The self-protective properties of stigma. *Psychological Review, 96*(4), 608–630.

Greenhaus, J. H., Parasuraman, S., & Wormley, W. M. (1990). Effects of race on organizational experience, job performance evaluations, and career outcomes. *Academy of Management Journal, 33*(1), 64–86.

Harris-Britt, A., Valrie, C. R., Kurtz-Costes, B., & Rowley, S. J. (2007). Perceived racial discrimination and self-esteem in African American youth: Racial socialization as a protective factor. *Journal of Research on Adolescence, 17*(4), 669–682.

Masten, A. S., Cutuli, J. J., Herbers, J. E., & Reed, M.-G. J. (2009). Resilience in development. In S. J. Lopez & C. R. Snyder (Eds.), *The Oxford handbook of positive psychology* (2nd ed., pp. 117–131). New York: Oxford University Press.

Ogbu, J. U. (1991). Minority coping responses and school experience. *The Journal of Psychohistory, 18*(4), 433–456.

Rutter, M. (1987). Psychosocial resilience and protective mechanisms. *American Journal of Orthopsychiatry, 57*(3), 316–331.

Rutter, M. (2012). Resilience as a dynamic concept. *Development and Psychopathology, 24*(2), 335–344.

Sellers, R. M., & Shelton, J. N. (2003). The role of racial identity in perceived racial discrimination. *Journal of Personality & Social Psychology, 84*(5), 1079–1092.

Solórzano, D., Ceja, M., & Yosso, T. (2000). Critical race theory, racial microaggressions, and campus racial climate: The experiences of African American college students. *Journal of Negro Education, 69*(1–2), 60–73.

Stevenson, H. C. (1994). Validation of the scale of racial socialization for African American adolescents: Steps toward multidimensionality. *Journal of Black Psychology, 20*(4), 445–468.

Thornton, M. C., Chatters, L. M., Taylor, R. J., & Allen, W. R. (1990). Sociodemographic and environmental correlates of racial socialization by black parents. *Child Development, 61*(2), 401–409.

Wilson, D., Foster, J., Anderson, S., & Mance, G. (2009). Racial socialization's moderating effect between poverty stress and psychological symptoms for African American youth. *Journal of Black Psychology, 35*(1), 102–124.

12

SOCIAL RESILIENCE

Building Persistence in Interracial Relationships

Tanya Menon and Arjun Chakravarti

Organizations strive to construct diverse communities, but encouraging diverse interactions is the greater challenge (Marmaros & Sacerdote, 2006). For instance, the freshman rooming groups created by colleges such as Harvard University seem like a paradigm of perfect integration. The university administration ensures that most rooming groups contain people of different backgrounds, and few groups have clusters of the same minority.

Yet consider the fate of one such rooming group, a triad with an Asian American and two whites. They experienced no racial tension or even overt conflict, but stopped socializing together after a few weeks. Eventually, meaningful conversation ceased, and they simply engaged in superficial formalities. When it came time to choose sophomore roommates, the Asian lived with several other Asians, and the two whites lived with whites from other dorms. In contrast to the interracial harmony pictured in university brochures, diversity failed to persist for this group.

Diversity may certainly be a desirable social value, but the vast history of research on intergroup relationships predicts such difficulties in implementing it. The most recent trends in stereotyping and prejudice have focused on people's often aversive split-second first impressions towards those of other races. The results of these studies offer a depressing view of human decision-making, characterizing people as hopeless bigots who harbor secret prejudices.

Simply blaming people's racist motives offers a limited explanation for what happened in this specific case. Our quantitative case study at Harvard University focused on randomly assigned freshman roommates (class of 1995) who months later chose their own second-year roommates (Chakravarti, Menon, & Winship, 2014). In contrast to the two white–one minority triad, which was indeed significantly more likely to disband as compared with all other three- and two-person groups, we found that white–Asian dyads were no more likely to disband than white–white dyads. Because our research involved roommates randomly assigned to group structures, we can isolate group structure as the causal mechanism, ruling out other confounds such as the racial preferences of the roommates themselves (i.e., self-selection into diverse relationships), their personal characteristics, socioeconomic status, or idiosyncratic contextual features (e.g., the university's wealth, politics, or elite identity).

But why might these variations in group structure cause these differences in whether relationships survive? We suggest that the answer to this question lies in whether structures allow people to simply make an easy escape from an uncomfortable interaction or persist in that interaction.

Social Resilience

Beyond presenting a negative portrait of human decision-making, research that emphasizes split-second prejudice is also limited in its practical applications. The concern is that the psychological processes that emerge in what are typically hypothetical, short-term impressions do not generalize to actual organizations, where real people experience interdependence, expect future interactions, test first impressions, and develop longer-term relationships (Denrell, 2005). This short-term focus is prevalent in actual organizational settings as well, where managers often emphasize creating diversity (by selecting and hiring particular people) while ignoring the longer-term challenge of ensuring that that diversity survives and thrives. While people may have automatic, negative responses to people of other races, our starting point is the more positive and pragmatic question of how people can move beyond those impressions to form more inclusive social relationships and build better organizations. Our key point is that it is not merely having contact but persisting in it, even in the face of uncomfortable interaction, which allows organizations to realize diversity's potential to offer positive organizational environment that is fair and inclusive as well as its potential to yield strategic and financial value (Davidson, 2011).

To address these gaps in understanding how diversity persists, we draw upon resilience, a crucial organizing principle from positive psychology. According to Seligman (1990), resilience enables learning and growth in the face of failure. Resilience is the difference between the person who experiences learned helplessness in the face of failure and the one who persists and bounces back from that failure.

Building from this insight, we present the concept of *social resilience*. Social resilience refers to people's willingness to persist in the face of uncomfortable social interactions. Interactions with people of other races often involve discomfort: damaging first impressions, unshared assumptions, awkward conversation, and perhaps conflict. It is the process of continuing to interact with people even if initial first impressions are negative to retest and perhaps disconfirm those initial impressions. This persistence allows people to move beyond surface-level differences and appreciate deep-level commonalities (Phillips, Rothbard, & Dumas, 2008).

Social resilience is *not* a natural human tendency. The reason why automatic reactions persist is because of the natural human response to avoid aversive stimuli. If people have an initially unpleasant interaction with someone of a different race, they respond by reducing contact, thereby eliminating opportunities to revise initially negative impressions (Denrell, 2005). Thus, our starting point is the question: How can we ensure that people are resilient learners who are prepared to confront the discomforts of diversity without giving up on relationships and escaping to easier, more comfortable, and often less diverse social interactions?

Socially Resilient Structures

Certain individuals may be more socially resilient than others because of cognitive styles such as low need for closure. Some people are slower at forming definitive first impressions and may be more open to questioning and revising them. Such cognitive processes allow people to respond to negative behaviors by opening the channels of communications through questions and approaching others with a learning and forgiving orientation.

Because these individual differences reflect stable regularities and are therefore more resistant to change, our own research focuses on structures that facilitate social resilience. The natural experiment allowed us to assess which relationships persist and which disband after over a year of interaction. Rather than focusing on the more intransigent tasks of changing people's personalities or even their attitudes about diversity or people of other races, we simply sought to understand how particular structures either enhanced or impeded interpersonal discovery, mutual understanding, and liking.

Managerial Implications

We offer three design-related recommendations to facilitate persistence. Our first insight is that persisting in existing diverse relationships is easier than initiating new relationships. The second is to remove easy escape channels through which people can easily excuse themselves from initially uncomfortable relationships. The final insight focuses on creating dyadic spaces, which allows people to make and maintain interpersonal connections without the complications of coalitions.

1. Persistence is easier than initiation. One observation from the Harvard case was that it was easier to maintain diversity than to spontaneously initiate it. That is, most of the diversity that occurred in the second year was the product of administration-assigned roommates or dorm-mates who stayed together versus new diverse relationships. People were more likely to stay with a roommate of another race than to find different-race people without the benefit of that head start.

This finding underscores the simple power of behavioral channels. If it is effortful and uncomfortable to initiate interactions with people of other races, channels can remove those initial hurdles. When people are initially assigned to different-race roommates—or had easy channels to approach them—diversity has good chances of emerging.

2. Remove easy escape channels. In addition to facilitating behavioral channels for diverse people to interact, organizations might also consider ways to remove easy escape channels. Typically, if people find themselves in uncomfortable social interactions, they find ways to escape social contact even if they are in one another's physical presence on a regular basis as members of the same team or roommate group. For instance, once a roommate categorizes someone as "not a friend" early on, he or she is motivated to invest in other friendships and stop engaging with that roommate. Whereas dyads have no alternatives except each other, two whites in a two white–one minority triad can escape to each other. We found that two–one diverse groups were especially likely to disband when the minority had a cohesive group of same-race peers (e.g., students of Asian or African descent) who had readily available houses with those racial identities, as compared with minorities who lacked clear outside options.

3. There is power in dyads. A final finding highlights the dangers of coalitional dynamics. Same-race and diverse relationships were as likely to persist in two-person groups (two whites were no more likely to disband than whites grouped with students of Asian or African descent and other races). By contrast, in three-person groups with two whites and one minority, there were more challenges for diverse relationships. From a managerial viewpoint, managers might give diverse people more opportunities for dyadic interactions in which both races can experience numeric equality and do not have same-race options that present easy escape routes from the interaction.

Conclusion

In sum, we suggest that diversity research and practice might refocus on the persistence of diverse relationships, as compared with first impressions, attitudes, and beliefs, and simply hiring people of different races. By creating social situations that allow people to bounce back after negative or merely awkward first impressions, we can create organizations where people can experience meaningful, deep, long-term interaction with those who are somehow different from them.

For Practitioners: Building Social Resilience

Social resilience is *not* a natural human tendency. But it can be learned. People can overcome their negative initial impressions of dissimilar others and to persist in those relationships—despite some discomfort. The following design principles can guide leaders in building social resilience:

- Create dyadic interactions and also form triads in which no race is numerically dominant, minimizing coalitional dynamics.

(continued)

- When a task or group setting precludes dyads, expose individuals to one another dyadically before grouping to undermine spontaneous, race-based coalitions and first impressions.
- Encourage people to test automatic causal attributions (e.g., blaming people) with more charitable attributions (e.g., attributing to situations/ tasks) so that they become vigilant against the processes that could hijack their group processes.

References

Chakravarti, A., Menon, T, & Winship C. (2014). Contact and Group Structure: A Natural Experiment of Interracial College Roommate Groups. *Organizational Science, 25,* 1216–1233.

Davidson, M. N. (2011). *The end of diversity as we know it: Why diversity efforts fail and how leveraging difference can succeed.* San Francisco, CA: BK Business.

Denrell, J. (2005). Why most people disapprove of me: Experience sampling in impression formation. *Psychological Review, 112,* 951–978.

Marmaros, D. & Sacerdote, B. (2006). How do friendships form? *Quarterly Journal of Economics, 121, 79–119.*

Phillips, K. W., Rothbard, N., & Dumas, T. L. (2008). To disclose or not to disclose? Status distance and self-disclosure in diverse environments. *Academy of Management Review, 34,* 710–732.

Seligman, M.E.P. (1990). *Learned optimism.* New York: Knopf.

SECTION IV
Relating Across Differences
Section Introduction

Amy Lemley, Martin N. Davidson,
Laura Morgan Roberts, and Lynn Perry Wooten

In October 2013, the California Department of Social Services closed down Valley Manor Community Care Home in Alameda County after ongoing reports that it neglected its elderly patients. With no more paychecks coming, almost all the staff left. But because of an administrative error, 16 residents stayed behind, too frail, weak, confused, or isolated to do otherwise, some bedridden, some amputees, and some with dementia, all unable to fend for themselves or even place phone calls to family. As this terrible truth dawned on the facility cook Maurice Rowland and janitor Miguel Alvarez, they realized it was up to them: if they did not stay and care for these people—any one of whom could just as well have been a family member—who would? "I just couldn't see myself going home," Rowland said (Hamblin, 2014). Round-the-clock care for the facility's elderly patients—in need of food, medicine, hygiene, and companionship—all fell to them for two full days before Rowland and Alvarez decided to call the sheriff. They had no medical training, but they kept their residents healthy until help arrived. "Even though they wasn't (sic) our family, they were kind of like our family for that short period of time," said Alvarez, 34, who recalled his own parents having left him when he was a child. "Knowing how they are going to feel," he explained, "I didn't want them to go through that" (Hamblin, 2014).

Race, culture, age, educational level, and workplace role can be divisive. We are who we are. We spend time with whom we know. We do what we were hired to do. Collaboration seems natural when we're permitted to maintain these boundaries, often less so when we are asked to bridge them. This section explores connections—what they are, what they mean, and what possibilities emerge when we approach Diversity and Inclusion (D&I) from the Positive Organizational Scholarship (POS) standpoint.

Given the complex global nature of business in the 21st century, collaborating across cultures is a reality for many organizations. Decision making by divergent groups is a challenge that requires a multifaceted, boundary-spanning approach that weaves together a variety of perspectives. Chrobot-Mason, Yip, and Yu's chapter, "Leading beyond 'We': The Nature and Consequences of a Boundary Spanning Mindset" presents a framework for doing so, with examples of this concept in practice.

Next, shifting our focus from addressing diversity in groups, "Mentoring as a Connecting Competency Builder: Examining POS as a Catalyst for Mentoring across Dimensions of Diversity" zeroes in on one-to-one opportunities for personal and professional growth via diversity and inclusion. Blake-Beard, Murrell, Krothapalli, Halem, and Kweder argue that matching mentors and protégés who don't seem to "match" offers an opportunity not only for professional development and effectiveness but also less tangible benefits such as resourcefulness and resilience.

Throughout an organization, supportive and understanding relationships invite individuals and groups to embrace difference. Simola's chapter, "Fostering High-Quality Relationships across Difference: Exploring a Care-Based Approach to Life Story–Telling and Life Story–Receiving" explores what is possible within the framework of "high quality relationships." With opportunities available or programs in place, high quality connections (HQCs) enrich an organizational culture and create meaningful connections between individuals.

Dialogue is the key to inclusion from a POS standpoint. "Discursive Spaces That Foster Transformative Learning in the Engaging of Differences: Implications for Global Society" examines both academic research and practitioner experience to discover how engaging multiple dimensions of diversity promotes essential learning. In this chapter, Wasserman looks at how the engagement of multiple dimensions of diversity during a large-scale strategic planning process system enhanced the capacity for those involved to deal with the everyday complexities of their work through shared understanding.

Identity and relational complexities can make it difficult to shift from the "managing diversity" to a Leveraging Difference paradigm. Some individuals fear being lost, while others dread being singled out if their work world becomes one that emphasizes difference. How will everyone's needs be met? "Leveraging Difference in a 'Have Your Say' World" uses real dialogue from Wishik's consulting engagement to show how people talk through these concerns, moving from the negative to the positive once they are able to "have their say." Wishik offers suggestions for paired sharing and other activities designed to build high quality connections across difference.

We close this section with a concept born in sub-Saharan Africa, made famous by Desmond Tutu, and seen here as both helping and hindering inclusion. "The Two Faces of *Ubuntu*: An Inclusive Positive or Exclusive Parochial Leadership Perspective?" is a fascinating look at what is not just a simple word but an entire mindset that is accessible—and accessed—worldwide. Booysen presents Ubuntu as a model of inclusive leadership that bridges concern for "me" and "we" through relational practices.

The chapters in this section bridge diversity, inclusion, and POS to feature relational practices that forge connections across identity groups in diverse settings. As people expand their concern for others, and prioritize relational outcomes, they build capacity for leadership, mentoring, caregiving, strategic planning, and thriving in a global society.

Reference

Hamblin, J. (2014, November). The cook and the janitor. *The Atlantic.* http://www.theatlantic.com/health/archive/2014/11/when-the-home-closed/383075/

13

LEADING BEYOND "WE"

The Nature and Consequences of a Boundary Spanning Mindset

Donna Chrobot-Mason, Jeffrey Yip, and Alan James Yu

> Our mind is capable of passing beyond the dividing line we have drawn for it. Beyond the pairs of opposites of which the world consists, other, new insights begin.
>
> —*Herman Hesse,* Inside and Outside *(1920)*

In today's globalized and unstable economy, organizations are likely to encounter "wicked problems." Grint (2005) describes a wicked problem as one that is complex and novel, involving a great deal of uncertainty, having no apparent solution, and requiring a collaborative process to move forward. These problems require a multifaceted approach to decision making and an integration of perspectives across divergent groups using the principles of boundary spanning leadership (Ernst & Chrobot-Mason, 2010; Hogg, van Knippenberg, & Rast, 2012; Yip, Ernst, & Campbell, 2009).

In this chapter, we introduce the concept of a *boundary spanning mindset* using both theory and research. A boundary spanning mindset consists of (1) a cognitive capacity to mobilize the interaction of groups to resolve wicked problems, and (2) a motivation to improve intergroup interactions. Leaders who are capable of spanning boundaries seek to embrace and not overly simplify complexities, identify both differences and similarities across groups, and exercise authority while modeling collaboration. We extend perspectives on social identity theory to describe the characteristics and consequences of a boundary spanning mindset. From interviews conducted with organizational leaders, we present key elements of a boundary spanning mindset and how it differs from a bounded mindset. Finally, we offer implications for leadership development.

Elements of a Boundary Spanning Mindset

Our perspective on a boundary spanning mindset is derived from a longstanding body of research on social identity and intergroup relations in organizations (Ashforth & Mael, 1989; Hogg, van Knippenberg & Rast, 2012). A central tenet in intergroup and social identity theory is that people have a need for both inclusion and differentiation. Through identification with a social group, individuals are able to meet both needs; they experience a sense of belonging and affiliation with others in the group and also differentiate themselves based on group identity. Meeting both fundamental human needs contributes to a positive self-image. Unfortunately, decades of research have shown that this contributes to strong in-group bias as well (Gaerter & Dovidio, 2000). Thus, identity poses a challenge for leaders seeking to span boundaries to achieve intergroup collaboration.

Leadership may be defined as the creation of direction, alignment, and commitment (Drath et al., 2008). Thus, a key expectation of leaders is to create a shared vision or goal that unifies people under a common sense of "we." While this is indeed an important role that leaders play, creating a sense of "we" without recognition of unique intergroup differences is likely to backfire, causing increased conflict rather than cooperation. More specifically, in situations where the shared identity is amorphous, subgroup members might view this assimilation strategy as an identity threat when unique identities are ignored, or worse, marginalized (Hogg & Terry, 2000). We view this as a "bounded mindset" approach, where leaders are blinded to differences by bounding people under one common identity.

In contrast, leaders with a boundary spanning mindset identify with two or more groups and are motivated to establish linkages and manage interactions between the groups. It should be noted that the identity and motivation elements may not always coincide. A leader may identify with multiple groups but may not proactively work to establish linkages across groups. The basis, however, of a boundary spanning mindset is the dual identification with an in-group and an out-group. Leaders with a boundary spanning mindset are comfortable with the ambiguity of multiple identities *and* are motivated to establish linkages across different groups.

To better illustrate this mindset in action, we present findings from a research project conducted in partnership with colleagues at the Center for Creative Leadership (CCL). Thirty-seven interviews were conducted with mid- to senior-level managers participating in a CCL program entitled "Leading for Organizational Impact." During this weeklong program, participants were engaged in a simulation that might be classified as a wicked problem. In the simulation, participants were asked to make numerous organizational decisions involving diverse stakeholders, multiple groups, a large degree of ambiguity, and no apparent solutions. Following the program, interviewees were asked to describe the behaviors of participants who were influential in spanning boundaries during the simulation.

What emerged were examples of diverse ways to make sense of complex challenges. Based on the data, we identified three pairs of tendencies by which leaders might approach an organizational problem: *simplicity versus complexity, similarities versus differences, and authoritative versus collaborative.* Interviewees with a bounded mindset had a preference for one tendency in each pair. In contrast, interviewees who were effective boundary spanners displayed characteristics on both ends of each pair.

Simplicity versus complexity. Some interviewees attempted to simplify whatever challenges they were confronted with by distilling details to identify key issues or priorities. Typically this involved ignoring or minimizing the needs and priorities of multiple groups to focus on a core group or common set of priorities. One participant, feeling overwhelmed by competing demands and priorities in the simulation, provided his senior team a list of topics and asked them to vote on the top priorities. Others with positional authority in the simulation simply determined key priorities for all. In contrast, interviewees who focused on complexity attempted to uncover details and clarify multiple perspectives to view the problem more completely. For example, one participant met one on one with each division leader to better understand the full spectrum of competing demands from many positions before making a decision about how to act.

Similarities versus differences. Preferences also emerged during the simulation in attempting to manage the tension between integration and differentiation. For example, some participants called a meeting with various group leaders in the simulation to identify common issues. They then articulated a goal each group in the simulation could identify with and share, such as increasing market share. Others used meeting times to uncover differences across groups (i.e., unique challenges and opportunities not shared by all). They then attempted to negotiate a strategy to address as many of the groups' unique goals or needs as possible. One participant said that during the simulation, he "took time to interact with each of the individual members of the [executive] team, one on one, including the R&D person." This participant kept a list of individual participants and their top priorities.

Authoritative versus collaborative. Our data also revealed a noticeable difference in how decisions are made. Participants with positional authority in the simulation used an authoritative approach by articulating a strategy and a set of priorities for others to follow ("I recognized quickly what needed to get done and broke it down"). Other participants with less positional authority used personal influence, such as a charismatic personality, to gain support for their ideas. In contrast, participants who chose a more collaborative approach focused their attention on facilitating intergroup interactions to promote collective action. Rather than exercising authority on behalf of the entire organization, they chose to involve and engage others in the problem-solving process ("From the very beginning, when we went into the room, the four tables had been arranged in such a way that we would sit with our backs to one another. I suggested that the group turn the tables around and get them into a circular configuration. The idea resonated. It got us looking eye to eye and discussing the issues").

The interview data illustrate a *bounded* versus a *boundary spanning* mindset. Boundary spanning leaders approach wicked and ambiguous problems by engaging divergent groups using a variety of approaches with a lesser degree of bias than those with a bounded mindset. Rather than a tendency to act using just one side of the polarity, their tendency was to take actions that reflect both. For example, they attempt to approach organizational challenges by both identifying complex details *and* searching for simplicity as a way to provide clarity. They integrate both similarities *and* differences across groups. Finally, they know when to involve others in the process *and* when to provide authoritative direction and guidance. Focusing too intently on one way of making sense of complex challenges reveals a bounded approach, whereas a boundary spanning approach involves a combination of opposing tendencies.

How to Develop a Boundary Spanning Mindset

How then can leaders manage the tensions that exist when confronting complex organizational challenges? How can leaders develop a mindset that values a collective "we" as well as unique identities that distinguish between an "us" and a "them"? Leaders can develop a boundary spanning mindset by paying attention to distinct and complementary identities between diverse groups (Pittinsky, 2010). For example, in the debate on gun control and ownership, a boundary spanning mindset would entail an identification with and understanding of both groups—the unique and common concerns of each. Rather than ignore or play down identity dynamics, a person who identifies with the group that favors gun control, for example, could seek to actively talk with others who embrace gun ownership, seek to understand where they are coming from, and then help communicate the perspectives of both groups to each other in an attempt to work toward improved legislation.

While we may have certain preferences in how we approach wicked problems, we can improve our leadership capacity by embracing instead of retreating from intergroup differences. Leaders who have a tendency to seek simplicity in responding to organizational challenges could benefit by attempting to navigate complexity by engaging with others in a problem-solving process, and by leveraging differences of perspective. Similarly, leaders who typically value aligning groups over common concerns may step out of their comfort zones and attempt to negotiate over competing interests between groups. A boundary spanning mindset is one that goes beyond simplistic solutions in creating a common "we" identity and instead is attentive to intergroup differences to create an identity that values "we" as well as "me within we."

Acknowledgments

This research project was conducted in collaboration with Dr. John Fleenor, Stephanie Trovas, Richard Walsh from the Center for Creative Leadership (CCL), and Catie Wambaugh at the University of Cincinnati. We also wish to thank CCL faculty for conducting interviews.

For Practitioners: Tips for Developing a Boundary Spanning Mindset

- Embrace the complexity of the wicked problem, but be able to distill and simplify the problem in a way that is conducive to clear, decisive action that addresses multiple needs and concerns.
- Seek to understand what makes groups and individuals unique, but recognize and honor commonalities that unite groups in their intentions and actions.
- Identify both unique and common priorities, needs, and concerns across groups; then, communicate the unique perspectives of various groups to one another as well as a collective mission or set of objectives.
- Seek input from multiple groups and perspectives, and then act authoritatively to set clear direction.

References

Ashforth, B. E., & Mael, F. A. (1989). Social identity theory and the organization. *Academy of Management Review, 14*, 20–39.

Drath, W. H., McCauley, C. D., Palus, C. J., Van Velsor, E., O'Connor, P. M., & McGuire, J. B. (2008). Direction, alignment, commitment: Toward a more integrative ontology of leadership. *Leadership Quarterly, 19*(6), 635–653.

Ernst, C., & Chrobot-Mason, D. (2010). *Boundary spanning leadership: Six practices for solving problems, driving innovation and transforming organizations.* New York: McGraw-Hill.

Gaertner, S. L., & Dovidio, J. F. (2000). *Reducing intergroup bias: The common ingroup identity model.* Philadelphia, PA: Psychology Press.

Grint, K. (2005). Problems, problems, problems: The social construction of "leadership." *Human Relations, 58*, 1467–1494.

Hogg, M. A., & Terry, D. J. (2000). Social identity and self-categorization processes in organizational contexts. *Academy of Management Review, 25*, 121–140.

Hogg, M. A., van Knippenberg, D., & Rast, D. E. (2012). Intergroup leadership in organizations: Leading across group and organizational boundaries. *Academy of Management Review, 37*, 232–255.

Pittinsky, T. L. (2010). A two-dimensional model of intergroup leadership: The case of national diversity. *American Psychologist, 65*(3), 194.

Yip, J., Ernst, C., & Campbell, M. (2009). *Boundary spanning leadership: Perspectives from senior executives.* White Paper. Center for Creative Leadership.

14

MENTORING AS A CONNECTING COMPETENCY BUILDER

Examining POS as a Catalyst for Mentoring Across Dimensions of Diversity

Stacy Blake-Beard, Audrey Murrell, Vineetha Krothapalli, Jessica Halem, and Michelle Kweder

We are facing a number of changes in how we work. Thomas Friedman's critically acclaimed book *The World Is Flat* (2005) suggests that through globalization, a number of forces are shifting what is necessary for companies and individuals to become and remain competitive. These "flatteners," which include offshoring, outsourcing, and uploading, are indicators of the rapid pace of change we are encountering. These changes mean that, now more than ever, the strengths of our workforce are critical. The ability to connect with others across differences of all kinds is and will continue to be essential (Dutton & Heaphy, 2003).

Mentoring interactions develop and hone an invaluable and intangible asset—our ability to build relationships. But, there are a number of challenges with how mentoring has traditionally been conceptualized and enacted; the norms and practices of traditional mentoring may get in the way of meeting, and even seeing, the need to better understand the importance of quality in our relationships. In this chapter, we explore Positive Organizational Scholarship (POS) as a catalyst for better understanding mentoring across diversity by examining mentoring within the context of high quality interactions. We discuss several traditional assumptions about mentoring relationships and then view mentoring within three distinct lenses that are relevant to the POS construct. In closing, we pose questions for future research and practices that can leverage mentoring as a catalyst to building capacity for high-quality relationships across important dimensions of diversity.

Mentoring—Traditions and Assumptions

Mentoring has traditionally been defined as "a dynamic, reciprocal relationship between an advanced career incumbent (mentor) and a less experienced professional (protégé) aimed at promoting the development and fulfillment of both"

(Kram, 1985). Mentoring serves two basic functions—career and psychosocial. Professionally, mentoring helps the protégé learn the ropes and prepare for career advancement through sponsorship, exposure and visibility, coaching, protection, and challenging assignments. More personally, the mentoring relationship also enhances the protégé's sense of competence, clarity of identity, and effectiveness through activities such as role modeling, acceptance and confirmation, counseling, and friendship (Kram, 1985). The link between mentoring and positive identities at work, across both career and psychosocial functions, has been explored (Ragins & Cotton, 1999). Mentoring is a powerful tool for improving mentor and protégé job performance, helping socialize protégés, supporting long-range human resource planning, and promoting the development and support of organizational leaders (Allen et al., 2004; Blake-Beard, Murrell, & Thomas, 2007; Murrell, Crosby, & Ely, 1999; Wanberg, Welsh, & Hezlett, 2003).

While the qualities and benefits of mentoring are clear, the assumptions underlying these developmental relationships are still the subject of a great deal of research. Recently, Ragins (2012) stated that the field of mentoring, including academic research, has largely focused on "dysfunctional" and "traditional" mentoring while overlooking the possibility of a higher caliber of relational experiences. Mentoring is undergirded by a number of assumptions set in a traditional context: that mentoring partners will be similar to one another on key dimensions of identity (by virtues of forces of attraction); that the senior person is the source of knowledge and power; and that careers must proceed on an upward trajectory to be judged as successful. But these assumptions ignore the fact that we face "flattener"-induced changes, including increasing workforce diversity. This traditional perspective may be insufficient to understand the powerful nature of mentoring relationships as a catalyst for high-quality interactions at work. Using the POS framework to challenge these assumptions unleashes the power of mentoring to facilitate meaningful connections. Thus, we first draw from Quinn and Wellman's (2012) discussion on moving from traditional modes of change to POS-oriented modes of change; we then explore how viewing mentoring relationships as high quality interactions can provide insight into diversity at work.

Upending Traditional Assumptions of Mentoring— Adopting POS Strategies for Change

Quinn and Wellman (2012) describe several key forces that change the nature of the context in which we must examine diverse mentoring relationships. They remind us that while organizations are in a constant state of change, simply overcoming the obstacles the change process presents is not enough to ensure that people and their organizations flourish. Yielding positive outcomes means finding the properties for success in people and supporting initiatives that help them thrive through continual transformation and renewal. A POS-undergirded framework suggests that all who act as agents of change can move themselves and their organizations to positive states by leveraging processes to identify instances of "positive deviance." Drawing on positive deviance involves seeking out, sharing, and magnifying positive anomalies from traditional paradigms, processes, and—within the context of mentoring—relationships.

Identifying and then magnifying positive deviance means moving away from long-held understandings of work relationships. For example, we often presume mentoring relationships are rooted in the similarity and attraction paradigm (Byrne, 1971), which suggests that people are drawn to and connect with those who are similar to them. This conception of the social psychological forces that bring people together works fine—as long as we are similar to one another. What happens if an individual is not, on the face of things, similar to the person with whom she or he is trying to build a mentoring relationship? If building mentoring relationships is defined as seeking versions of yourself, then mentoring possibilities in the context of transformation and diversity may be quite limited. Presuming the existence of this traditional similarity-attraction self-selection requires us to assume assimilation is the only objective of interactions or connections through work, and that these interactions are driven exclusively by self-interest and dominant identities.

We also typically define mentoring as a one-to-one relationship of a senior/junior pair with the senior (older or more experienced) person mentoring "down" to a more junior individual. But changing organizational structures, expanding notions of influence, and shifting away from a definition of value based only on expertise means we must rethink how diverse mentoring relationships are formed, shaped, and developed. In addition, we must explore how they can be seen both as a source and an influence of positive deviance within the workplace. For example, what happens if the person from which you want to learn is not at a higher level than you in the organization? Can we assume that experience and age are synonymous with knowledge? What about other sources of power beyond those that are based on title or expertise alone?

Responding to these and similar questions means moving beyond traditional views of mentoring and diversity at work. Quinn and Wellman (2012) suggest we should "surrender control and begin to act 'with' others, co-creating trusting relationships and jointly constructed, attractive futures." Their framework suggests that our concept of mentoring must move from its traditional definition. Quinn and Wellman, applying the POS framework, push us to see outliers (or positive deviance) in practice and theory. Traditional assessments of value in relationships must move from a strictly instrumental definition of results (e.g., career mobility, individual satisfaction) to include a range of positive outcomes such as resourcefulness, organizational learning, and resilience (Quinn & Dutton, 2005). It also suggests that for diverse mentoring relationships, a shift from a strictly individual, need-based approach that follows principles of similarity-attraction must give way to a relational approach that takes into account multiple dimensions of developmental networks consistent with current thinking (Higgins, 2007; Higgins & Thomas, 2001).

Mentoring and POS: Avenue to High Quality Connections

Dutton and Heaphy (2003) note the importance of human connections in organizations, especially what they call "high quality connections" (HQCs)—short-term, dyadic, positive interactions at work (Stephens, Heaphy, & Dutton, 2012). POS is a call to better understand how to "build context that enables human flourishing by understanding the power of high quality interactions." The view that mentoring can be regarded as one of the best examples of positive interactions at work has been addressed previously (Ragins & Verbos, 2007) and defined from a relationship perspective (Higgins & Kram, 2001). Within the mentoring literature, quality has been characterized by terms including strength of ties, reciprocity, frequency of interaction, emotional exchange, satisfaction, mutual motivation, and interdependence (Wanberg et al., 2003). How to quantify the quality of high quality connections, however, is a complex task.

As we noted earlier, while traditional beliefs about growth and development are important, a view through this "old model" lens exclusively is limiting. Dutton and Heaphy (2003) present three POS concepts that we believe link HQCs with mentoring relationships quite clearly:

- Emotional carrying or the capacity to withstand the expression of emotion and the safety felt during emotion exchanges
- Tensility or the capacity of the relationship to withstand strain and to function in a variety of circumstances
- Degree of connectivity or openness to new ideas and influences.

As a result of these factors, people in HQCs feel a sense of vitality, positive regard, and mutuality—features that overlap substantially with mentoring relationships such as interdependence, capacity for mutual growth, and the exchange of emotion and identities at work (Ragins & Verbos, 2007).

A tremendous amount of research has sought to demonstrate the "return on investment" in mentoring relationships, including both career and psychosocial benefits. Some argue that this ROI focus reduces HQCs such as mentoring to a commodity and reinforces the avoidance and risk-averse behavior that has been documented in the case of mentoring and diversity (Thomas & Gabarro, 1999). For example, race differences in experienced conflict around diversity (Davidson, 2001) can interfere with the expectation of positive returns that are necessary through an exclusive use of the social exchange lens. It also ignores one of the benefits of diverse relationships: the transfer of knowledge and reciprocal learning that has been shown to take place in meaningful diverse relationships (Ely & Thomas, 2001). And it means that quality in mentoring relationships must be defined within the context of negotiated interactions over time that lead to resource enhancement. This focus ignores the more intangible benefits of HQCs such as trust, clarity of identity, and an overall sense of well-being that are central to the POS framework.

Factoring in Identity

We argue that understanding diverse mentoring relationships, especially within the dynamic and complex nature of global organizations, can most greatly benefit by bringing identity into the discussion. Dutton and Heaphy (2003) write that "other people are active players in the co-creation of who we are at work." This means that mentoring relationships not only provide opportunity for growth and development, and add value through resources and rewards, but can also define, shape, and transform co-constructed identities in the workplace. This can be seen in research that examines work identity and job crafting of one's career (Ibarra, 1992), the influence of role modeling on career and personal identity (Murrell & Zagenczyk, 2006), and the influence of identity-based mentoring relationships to both influence and affirm personal identity among high-potential managers (Murrell et al., 2008).

Within the context of mentoring, diversity is a powerful catalyst for future research. While there has traditionally been a focus on investigating developmental outcomes that represent a "return on investment" of mentoring, more can be done. We believe that deeper understanding of the quality in mentoring relationships may also stimulate inquiry into how identities at work are shaped, transformed, and yet sometimes devalued within the context of diversity. While a substantial amount of work has shown that issues of mentoring across diversity are both complex and mutually beneficial (Ely & Thomas, 2001), what constitutes "high quality" within diverse mentoring relationships has not yet been fully explored.

This new direction can pose some interesting questions that require us to better understand and measure "co-created" concepts of what determines high quality in mentoring relationships. Some would argue for a fundamental shift to weighting the views of protégés equal to those of mentors; or in the context of diversity, weighing the perspective of those from diverse, underrepresented, or lower-status groups equal to that of majority or higher-status organizational members. One-on-one or across an entire organization, the objective of mentoring must include attention to quality. This stance represents a shift from defining high quality connections externally to situating them within a range of different developmental networks that include greater attention to the role of network diversity.

For Practitioners: When High Quality Mentoring Relationships Succeed

High quality connections (HQCs) are critical to the development of successful mentoring. A shift from focusing these relationships predominantly on traditional goals, such as career mobility and compensation, allow different benefits to emerge, including resourcefulness, organizational learning, and resilience. With this shift, there is opportunity to introduce diversity of all kinds (race, gender, age, etc.) into these relationships to enhance these benefits for both the mentor and the protégé. Difference becomes a learning tool, even, or perhaps especially, when challenges arise.

HQCs through mentoring offer distinct benefits:

- They provide a chance for growth and development—on both sides.
- They add value through resources and rewards to/for both parties.
- They define, shape, and transform co-constructed identities in the workplace—especially within the context of global organizations.

References

Allen, T. D., Eby, L. T., Poteet, M. L., Lentz, E., & Lima, L. (2004). Career benefits associated with mentoring for protégés: A meta-analysis. *Journal of Applied Psychology, 89*, 127–136.

Blake-Beard, S., Murrell, A. J., & Thomas, D. A. (2007). Unfinished business: The impact of race on understanding mentoring relationships. In B. Rose-Ragins & K. Kram (Eds.), *Handbook on mentoring at work*. Thousand Oaks, CA: Sage.

Byrne, D. (1971). *The attraction paradigm*. New York: Academic Press.

Davidson, M. N. (2001). Know thine adversary: The impact of race on styles of dealing with conflict. *Sex Roles, 45*, 259–276.

Dutton, J. E., & Heaphy, E. D. (2003). The power of high quality connections. In K. S. Cameron, J. E. Dutton, & R. E. Quinn (Eds.), *Positive organizational scholarship* (pp. 263–278). San Francisco, CA: Berrett-Koehler.

Ely, R. J., & Thomas, D. A. (2001). Cultural diversity at work: The moderating effects of work group perspective on diversity. *Administrative Science Quarterly, 46*, 229–273.

Friedman, T. L. (2005). *The World is Flat: A Brief History of the Twenty-First Century*. New York: Farrar, Straus and Giroux.

Higgins, M. C. (2007). A contingency perspective on development networks. In J. E. Dutton & B. R. Ragins (Eds.), *Exploring positive relationships at work* (pp. 207–224). Mahwah, NJ: Lawrence Erlbaum.

Higgins, M. C., & Kram, K. E. (2001). Reconceptualizing mentoring at work: A developmental network perspective. *Academy of Management Review, 26*(2), 264–288.

Higgins, M. C., & Thomas, D. A. (2001). Constellations and careers: Toward understanding the effects of multiple developmental relationships. *Journal of Organizational Behavior, 22*, 223–247.

Ibarra, H. (1992). Homophily and differential returns: Sex differences in network structure and access in an advertising firm. *Administrative Science Quarterly, 37*, 422–447.

Kram, K. E. (1985). *Mentoring at work: Developmental relationships in organizational life*. Glenview, IL: Scott-Foresman.

Murrell, A. J., Blake-Beard, S., Porter, D. M., & Perkins-Williams, A. (2008). Inter-organizational formal mentoring: Breaking the concrete ceiling sometimes requires support from the outside. *Human Resource Management, 47*(2), 275–294.

Murrell, A. J., Crosby, F., & Ely, R. (1999). *Mentoring dilemmas: Developmental relationships within the multicultural organization*. Mahwah, NJ: Lawrence Erlbaum.

Murrell, A. J., & Zagenczyk, T. (2006). The gendered nature of role model status: An empirical study. *Career Development International, 11*(6), 560–578.

Quinn, R., & Dutton, J. E. (2005). Coordination as energy-in-conversation: A process theory of organizing. *Academy of Management Review, 30*(1), 36–57.

Quinn, R. E., & Wellman, N. (2012). Change the way you lead. Working Paper. Center for Positive Organizations, University of Michigan, Ann Arbor.

Ragins, B. R. (2012). Relational mentoring: A positive approach to mentoring at work. In K. S. Cameron & G. M. Spreitzer (Eds.), *The Oxford handbook of positive organizational scholarship* (pp. 519–536). New York: Oxford University Press.

Ragins, B. R., & Cotton, J. L. (1999). Mentor functions and outcomes: A comparison of men and women in formal and informal mentoring relationships. *Journal of Applied Psychology, 84,* 529–550.

Ragins, B. R., & Verbos, A. J. (2007). Positive relationships in action: Relational mentoring and mentoring schemas in the workplace. In J. E. Dutton & B. R. Ragins (Eds.), *Exploring positive relationship at work* (pp. 91–116). Mahwah, NJ: Lawrence Erlbaum.

Stephens, J. P., Heaphy, E., & Dutton, J. E. (2012). High-quality connections. In K. S. Cameron & G. M. Spreitzer (Eds.), *The Oxford handbook of Positive Organizational Scholarship* (pp. 385–399). New York: Oxford University Press.

Thomas, D. A. & Gabarro, J. J. (1999). *Breaking through: The making of minority executives in corporate America.* Boston, MA: Harvard Business School Press.

Wanberg, C. R., Welsh, E. T., & Hezlett, S. A. (2003). Mentoring research: A review and dynamic process model. *Research in Personnel and Human Resource Management, 22,* 39–124.

15

FOSTERING HIGH-QUALITY RELATIONSHIPS ACROSS DIFFERENCE

Exploring a Care Ethics Approach to Life Story–Telling and Life Story–Receiving

Sheldene Simola

One assumption inherent in much research on organizational diversity is that difference among individuals should be downplayed, because otherwise, it might lead to harmful conflict. In critique of this assumption, Ely and Roberts (2008) identified that negative outcomes tend to occur not as a consequence of difference or conflict per se, but rather, as a consequence of how individuals respond to them. When individuals have "inward-focused goals" aimed at protecting the image they hope others have of them, they respond defensively against threats of misinterpretation or devaluation of their social identity. This, in turn, limits effectiveness and performance. Conversely, when individuals have "outward-focused goals" aimed at constructively engaging and strengthening relationships and progressing toward other shared aspirations, possible threats to their identity become occasions for learning that can enhance both effectiveness and performance. Given the beneficial outcomes that outward-focused, relational goals can have for learning and performance, this chapter considers positive skills and tools that can be used to foster high-quality relationships across difference. It is argued that a care ethics approach to life story–telling and life story–receiving has significant potential in this regard.

Within the field of Positive Organizational Scholarship, Davidson and James (2007) defined high-quality relationships as those that demonstrate positive affect, regard, and rapport, while also being authentic, enduring, resilient, and effective. They argued that the critical factor for developing high-quality relationships across difference is the degree to which individuals are able to overcome previously held, stereotyped expectations in favor of a learning approach. Although inconsistency between stereotyped expectations and information arising from authentic engagement with diverse others will likely lead to conflict at times, such conflict is not necessarily negative. Rather, Davidson and James (2007) argued that it is through constructively engaging conflict rather than exiting relationships or enacting counterproductive behaviors that conflict is transformed into learning, and that high-quality relationships emerge. They identified five relevant skills, including managing emotion; recasting conflict in the context of overarching objectives; being inquisitive about others; providing and receiving accurate feedback; and promoting openness with and receptiveness to others through responsive self-disclosure.

An additional key perspective on the cultivation of high-quality relationships, including the central role of constructively engaging conflict as part of a learning orientation, is that of care ethics, understood as a type of "moral reasoning that derives from a concern for others and a desire to maintain thoughtful mutual relationships with those affected by one's actions" (Derry, 2005). Within a care perspective, a number of skills are identified as important to the learning orientation through which high-quality relationships emerge. These include skills associated with being willing and able to receive from diverse others information that might otherwise and erroneously be dismissed as disruptive, inflammatory, or irrelevant; facilitating voice among others by providing audibility for communication styles and ideas that do not necessarily conform to dominant norms; recognizing that resistance by diverse individuals to conventional ideas or approaches, though often construed as negative and obstructive, might well be positive and vital; engendering trust; and generating and integrating creative ideas into non–zero sum solutions responsive to the underlying interests and needs of a range of stakeholders (Gilligan, 1982; Simola, 2007). One tool with the potential to facilitate these approaches to learning and the development of high-quality relationships is the use of life story–telling.

Weischer, Weibler, and Petersen (2013) defined life story–telling as "a written or oral account of life, or a segment of life, told by the individual concerned . . . sharing one's life story with others." Within care ethics (Simola, 2007), as within positive approaches to learning and high quality relationships (Davidson & James, 2007), storytelling is seen as a potentially powerful way of facilitating openness, authenticity, and understanding among diverse individuals. In particular, we discovered that storytelling does not require individuals to communicate within the confines of socially dominant (i.e., formal, declarative, disembodied) or privileged forms of speech. Rather, all individuals can participate with equal authority, even when using more tentative or exploratory voices (Young, 1997). Additionally, storytelling can circumvent tendencies to become caught in counterproductive rationalizations or disagreements because participation typically involves a receptive and reflective stance, and creates a context for the emergence of empathy or other moral emotions that can facilitate greater sensitivity, openness, and commitment to responsive learning across difference. Moreover, storytelling offers specific paths through which both high-quality relationships and also enhanced organizational functioning and effectiveness can be achieved. In particular, storytelling averts predicaments associated with common advice to place ourselves in another's shoes and attempt to imagine that person's perspective. The assumption that one has sufficient similarity to another to be able to know the other's perspective is inaccurate, and risks the projection of one's self or sameness on others, thereby obscuring novel information, experiences, and ideas (Young, 1997). In contrast, "listening across the distance" (Young, 1997) through life story–receiving facilitates insights not only into the experiences, actions, and ideas of others, but also into one's own thoughts, feelings, and behaviors. When one listens across the distance, thereby taking diverse perspectives into account, each perspective is seen as irreplaceable in its own uniqueness and inimitability, and therefore requires creative integration resulting in non–zero sum (win–win) solutions versus compromise resulting in zero sum (win–lose) solutions.

Within businesses and organizations, the potential of life story–telling and receiving for developing positive, sustained, authentic, resilient, and effective relationships has been noted. For example, senior officials from Polaris Minerals Corporation and the Hupacasath First Nation spent innumerable hours without any formal agenda, fishing, hiking, eating, and talking not just with one another, but with one another's families in order to develop a stronger understanding of one another's cultures, values, and needs prior to negotiating a joint venture to develop a high-quality granite deposit on land claimed as Aboriginal territory (CBSR, 2005). The relational processes upon which the joint venture was established were seen as rare in many corporate endeavors. Yet it was these processes that ultimately allowed both parties to hear, engage, and learn from conflicting perspectives, to form high-quality relationships, and to resolve conflict not through compromise and therefore loss for one party, but rather, through non–zero sum integration of underlying interests and needs. They resulted in innovations that were not only profitable, but also environmentally and socially sustainable (CBSR, 2005). Similarly, life story–telling and receiving have been integral to the success of the UK-based "Seeing is Believing" program in which corporate executives receive guided support during facilitated visits with individuals from diverse communities to gain insight into significant social and environmental concerns and subsequently collaborate on sustainable solutions (BIC, 2013).

How then might leaders encourage and support the use of life story–telling and life story–receiving between or within organizations? One critical insight that emerged in our consideration of this question is that although life story–telling and receiving might well nurture relational processes and even facilitate the development of new collective identities, such activities cannot simply be imposed as specific and certain means to predetermined ends. Therefore, leaders should try to create a context conducive to storytelling activities, and allow the unfolding of potentially generative processes.

As we discovered through scholarly discussion and case example, a care ethics approach to life story–telling and receiving has significant potential. For scholar-practitioners of diversity, life story–telling might facilitate authorization of differences among individuals, thereby transforming the landscape of interaction from one that often reflects systemic power and privilege to one that reveals and supports a plurality of unique, inimitable, and irreplaceable voices. For positive organizational scholar-practitioners, life story–telling might heighten audibility of and attentiveness to what is often silent or unheard knowledge that can be gleaned only by "listening across the distance." Important areas for future research include detailed case studies and evaluations of life story–telling and receiving within organizations, as well as evaluation of alternate relational approaches such as play for their potential in building high-quality relationships and facilitating other positive outcomes.

For Practitioners: Bringing Life Story–Telling into Your Organization

- **Initiate and model life story–telling and receiving from the top down.** This will both demonstrate and invite participation by organizational members and other stakeholders. It will also reflect and begin to establish the scope and parameters within which the activities will occur (Chavez and Weisinger, 2008).
- **Remember that providing audibility through receiving the stories of others is critical.** Coach for authenticity and attentiveness. Technological and other distractions should be avoided. Otherwise, the message conveyed to coparticipants is one of disinterest and disconnection. Life story–telling and receiving are often intrinsically interesting, pleasurable, and rewarding and so they can be positioned and cultivated in these ways.
- **Create space and time for life story–telling and receiving.** Outside of organizations, particularly within executive levels, this might involve establishing blocks of unstructured time for conversation. This process is often aided by having relatively neutral focal activities (e.g., planting, building, hiking). Focal activities can provide comfortable starting points and also minimize pressure or expectation for specific outcomes, thereby engendering trust.
- **Within organizations or across employee groups, consider using a skilled external facilitator.** He or she can establish parameters, create predictability, support participants, facilitate discussion, and manage delicate or awkward moments. Establish regular and manageable timeframes (possibly tied to meetings) to stimulate interest and anticipation. Consider using extrinsic focal items such as self-selected food items, objects of interest or quotations for storytelling (Chavez & Weisinger, 2008). This can anchor storytelling in the everyday, thereby reducing pressure or expectation for "big" revelations while respecting individual choice in terms of type and level of disclosure. It can also avert predicaments associated with focusing directly on particular perceived differences or visual identities to the exclusion of unknown, nonvisible, or multiple simultaneously held identities of participants.

References

Business in the Community (BIC). (2013). The prince's seeing is believing. http://www.bitc.org.uk/programmes/princes-seeing-believing

Canadian Business for Social Responsibility (CBSR). (2005). *Synergy: A united perspective between the Hupacasath First Nation and Polaris Minerals Corporation*. Toronto, ON: CBSR.

Chavez, C. I., & Weisinger, J. V. (2008). Beyond diversity training: A social infusion for cultural inclusion. *Human Resource Management, 47*(2), 331–350.

Davidson, M. N. & James, E. H. (2007). The engines of positive relationships across difference: Conflict and learning. In J. E. Dutton & B. R. Ragins (Eds.), *Exploring positive relationships at work: Building a theoretical and research foundation* (pp. 137–158). New York: Psychology Press.

Derry, R. (2005). Care, ethics of. In P. H. Werhane & R. E. Freeman (Eds.), *The Blackwell encyclopedia of management, business ethics* (2nd ed., pp. 65–68). Malden, MA: Blackwell.

Ely, R. J. & Roberts, L. M. (2008). Shifting frames in team-diversity research: From difference to relationships. In G. Cooper & J. Pearce (Series Eds.) and A. P. Brief (Vol. Ed.), *Cambridge companions to management: Diversity at work* (pp. 175–201). Cambridge: Cambridge University Press.

Gilligan, C. (1982). *In a different voice*. Boston, MA: Harvard University Press.

Simola, S. (2007). Pragmatics of care in sustainable global enterprise. *Journal of Business Ethics, 74*(2), 131–147.

Weischer, A. E., Weibler, J., & Petersen, M. (2013). "To thine own self be true": The effects of enactment and life storytelling on perceived leadership authenticity. *The Leadership Quarterly, 24*(4), 477–495.

Young, I. M. (1997). *Intersecting voices: Dilemmas of gender, political philosophy, and policy*. Princeton, NJ: Princeton University Press.

16

DISCURSIVE SPACES THAT FOSTER TRANSFORMATIVE LEARNING IN THE ENGAGING OF DIFFERENCES

Implications for Global Society

Ilene C. Wasserman

If Diversity and Inclusion processes were a musical composition, minor chords would move into major chords with the occasional major seventh chords. The story this chapter tells is one of disappointments with moments of optimism and occasional high points where leveraging differences sparks energy and hope.

Potential moments of optimism resounded in my research as I looked at what forms of discursive processes—or, said another way, what patterns people were making as they were communicating—fostered transformative learning in the engagement of complex dimensions of diversity: the personal, positional/ professional, and cultural aspects of diversity, in dialogic encounters (Wasserman, 2004). My research was motivated by contradictions I heard from—on the one hand—the minor notes expressing the dominant public discourse of discouragement and diversity fatigue, and—on the other hand—what I heard from my clients who said they came alive when they had the opportunity to sit with and engage with others whose narratives were so different from their own. I wondered: How might we broaden this experience of diversity such that diversity among people is viewed as essential to rich and creative outcomes?

In this chapter, I pursue this question by looking at how the engagement of multiple dimensions of diversity in a strategic planning process with a large health care system enhanced the capacity for those involved to deal with the everyday complexities of their work lives. Two viewpoints informed the design of the strategic planning approach: the SOAR process, an appreciative approach to strategic planning where the focus is on Strengths, Opportunities, Aspirations, and Results (Stavros, Cooperrider, & Kelley, 2006); and the relational communication perspective (Wasserman & Gallegos, in press). The relational communication perspective incorporates the models of human development (Kegan, 1994, 2000), integral theory (Wilber, 2000), social identity (Gallegos & Ferdman, 2012; Wijeyesinghe &

Jackson, 2012), transformative learning (Mezirow, 1978, 1991, 2000), the Coordinated Management of Meaning (CMM) (Pearce, 2004), and Positive Organizational Scholarship (Cameron & Spreitzer, 2010). The relational communication perspective guides the work my colleagues and I do to foster inclusive cultures at work: cultures that seek out and invite different perspectives and acknowledge the richness beyond the challenges of engaging those whose ways of seeing, being, and experiencing shared moments are different.

The articulation of the relational communication perspective emerged from a critical moment and a turning point in my work in the mid-1990s. At that time, I had been working with the thought leaders in the field of culture change and diversity and saw an opportunity for this focus to become more a part of the everyday work experience rather than a separate and distinct initiative. Further, I questioned whether having such separate and distinct diversity initiatives so clearly defined in their focus had the potentially paradoxical effect of marginalizing the very process intended to affect the ability of historically marginalized people to contribute and advance. As I recalled:

> Imagine my surprise when, while working with a group selecting steering team members for a strategic planning process for a large health system, the focus turned to assuring representation from different groups by: race, gender, culture, sexual orientation, nationality, different abilities, tenure, discipline, etc.
>
> *(Wasserman & Durishin, 2014)*

This passage speaks to the heart of how I felt seeing the group I was working with spontaneously enact a form of integral diversity maturity; that is, seek out diversity as a taken-for-granted criterion for better outcomes (Gregory & Raffanti, 2009). This chapter reveals the fuller story of what preceded and followed this moment.

The Story of Good Health Network

The Good Health Network (GHN) prides itself on developing its own internal change agents (CEs). In the last two years, these CEs have focused on building strategic capacity, aligning the organization's internal resources, and strengthening working alliances across other support functions. In keeping with GHN's approach to continual learning and development, our role as external consultants was to support and coach the internal resources, enabling them to take the lead in incorporating the principles of Appreciative Inquiry with the work of the organization. The internal consultants translated this approach into both a language and a process consistent with the health care system's evolving cultural transformation strategy.

We launched with three-day SOAR training for a group of 40 representatives from eight departments. This multidisciplinary team became the staff for this change initiative. The next step was for this staff team to create a steering team intentionally recruited for its multiple dimensions of diversity. The 45 people representing different departments, levels, disciplines, generations, time with the organization, and culturally diverse backgrounds, along with the staff team, signed on to meet monthly to help devise the next steps of the strategic planning and culture change process.

Passion was seeded at this initial orientation and training to involve as many people as possible using meetings and events that were already planned. Building on an existing schedule of large employee meetings, the format was revised from the CEO making a speech to the CEO introducing a conversation designed to have people in the organization talk with one another about how what they did every day connected with the mission of the health care system. After the CEO presented information about the status of the network, he asked each person to pair with someone he or she did not know and:

1. Tell a story about a time when you were at your best at GHN.
2. Explore the conditions that made this possible.
3. Imagine what would support those conditions more often for you and others.

The paired conversations stimulated lively discussions among the larger group of employees. After the exercise, participants filled out evaluation forms. The research and evaluation team, led by colleagues from health systems research, analyzed the feedback to identify themes in the conditions present when people are at their best. Results were used to guide a strategic planning summit that involved 10 percent of the whole network.

The design of the conversational spaces or dialogic spaces enabled people to build relationships across multiple dimensions of differences in generative conversations. In one segment, everyone was asked to pair with someone he or she did not know and who was different from him or her on as many dimensions as possible (e.g., culture, gender, position, age, profession, etc.) In another, people were asked to share their beginnings with health care and talk about what inspires their passion to do what they do. Then, they asked to suspend their humility for a moment and share a story that epitomizes how their unique contribution shows up in their daily work. These questions were designed to elicit story sharing—one of the discursive processes found to foster transformative learning in the engagement of social identity groups in dialogue (Wasserman, 2004). They were also designed to emphasize strengths and possibilities.

The energy from these conversations went viral: evidence of conversations about "reframing opportunities," shifting problem statements to exploring possibilities, the valuing of storytelling, sharing different perspectives and experiences, and crucial conversations continued to be evident across the system. As one leader stated, "The team is laughing more, learning more, and increasing the inquiry process to better work through challenges. They are working more collaboratively across boundaries." The boundary crossing described included professional and positional as well as cultural and other social identities. Further, some shared stories about how these qualities of conversations have spilled over to colleagues' personal lives.

Relational theory highlights the value and importance of high-quality connections and engagement in the process of diversity maturity. For each of the stages of integral diversity maturity—rewiring, or heightened awareness; clarifying, or the engagement of new perspectives; mastering, where new understandings emerge and are applied; and transcending, when one opens to new meaning-making possibilities—the argument is made that growth is enhanced in the process of relating. The strategic planning effort introduced discursive processes that fostered a culture of curiosity and generativity.

Changing our frames of reference, particularly in relationship with others who are different from us, requires a particular set of skills for engagement. First, it requires relational agility, or the capacity to move from *talking at* to dialogic engaging or *being with*. Second, it calls for the ability to critically reflect on one's taken-for-granted assumptions or frameworks and to view them as one of many possibilities. Third, it requires one to hold one's own perspective at risk of being changed as a result of a relationship with others (Buber & Smilly, 1959; Wasserman, 2004). The benefits of this high engagement process continues to be evident in departmental meetings, where people now ask probing questions of one another and suggest opportunities to reframe vicious cycles into virtuous, generative ones.

Relational eloquence (Wasserman, 2005), the capacity to shift our attention from the individualistic cognitive perspective to the relational arena, requires a deep capacity for attending to others. Self-awareness and relational eloquence are like muscles. They need to be exercised. We enhance our self-awareness and relational eloquence by looking at what we are making together: noticing how our past experiences influence interpretations we make in the moment, noting how we are framing the beginning, middle, and end of the stories we tell, and what contexts we highlight as we are making meaning. While our stories are not likely to be the same, our lives are enriched by the many stories we encounter.

Conclusion

The chords of the sound of engagement of multiple dimensions of diversity are complex (Holvino, 2010). They vary in cycles of tones, resonance, and dissonance. Potentiality lives in those cycles. Just as the members of the health care system became more fully engaged when they had the opportunity to sit with and engage with the social worlds of others whose narratives were so different from their own, intentionally considering who is in the room, and assuring the conditions for meaningful engagement, is essential to rich and creative outcomes.

For Practitioners: How to Begin the Dialogue

To begin a fruitful dialogue among the members of your organization, consider the framework that worked so well for GHN. Story sharing has been found to foster transformative learning in the engagement of social identity groups in dialogue. These exercises are also designed with an emphasis on strengths and possibilities.

Begin with pairs. Encourage participants to seek out a partner who is least like them (e.g., of another gender, race, generation, etc.—the more variation, the better). Then ask them to take turns responding to the following:

- Provide a conversation guide.
- Ask people to take turns so that each person has the experience of being the full focus of the other.
- Invite people to begin by sharing their beginnings with your organization or area of specialty and talk about what inspired their initial passions to do what they do.
- Then, ask them to go deeper, describing their unique experiences with the particular topic at hand.

Engaging in this dialogue will leave participants with a number of valuable skills and experiences:

- Having a sense of value and greater clarity of one's own story
- Relational agility—holding the story of the other and one's own side by side
- Being at risk of having your story be influenced by the story of the other
- Learning the skill of reframing and using it as an opportunity

References

Buber, M., & Smilly, R. G. (Trans.). (1959). *Between man and man*. Boston: Beacon Press.

Cameron, K. S., & Spreitzer, G. M. (Eds.). (2010), What is positive about positive organizational scholarship? *The Oxford handbook of positive organizational scholarship* (pp. 1–14). New York: Oxford University Press.

Gallegos, P. V., & Ferdman, B. M. (2012). Latina and Latino ethnoracial identity orientations: A dynamic and developmental perspective. In C. L. Wijeyesinghe & B. W. Jackson (Eds.). *New perspectives on racial identity development: Integrating emerging paradigms into racial identity models* (pp. 51–80). New York: New York University Press.

Gregory, T., & Raffanti, M. (2009). Integral diversity maturity: Toward a postconventional understanding of diversity dynamics. *Journal of Integral Theory and Practice, 4*(3), 41–58.

Holvino, E. (2010). Intersections: The simultaneity of race, gender, and class in organization studies [Special issue]. *Gender, Work and Organization, 17*, 248–277.

Kegan, R. (1994). *In over our heads: The mental demands of modern life*. Cambridge. MA: Harvard University Press.

Kegan, R. (2000). What forms transforms? In J. A. Mezirow (Ed.), *Learning as transformation: Critical perspectives on a theory in progress* (pp. 35–70). San Francisco, CA: Jossey-Bass.

Mezirow, J. (1978). Perspective transformation. *Adult Education Quarterly, 28*(2), 100–110.

Mezirow, J. A. (1991). *Transformative dimensions of adult learning*. San Francisco, CA: Jossey-Bass.

Mezirow, J. A. (2000). *Learning as transformation: Critical perspectives on a theory in progress*. San Francisco, CA: Jossey-Bass.

Pearce, W. B. (2004). The coordinated management of meaning. In W. Gudykunst (Ed.), *Theorizing communication and culture* (pp. 35–54). Thousand Oaks, CA: Sage.

Stavros, J., Cooperrider, D., & Kelly, D. L. (2006). SOAR, a new approach to strategic planning. In P. Holman, T. Devane, S. Cady, & Associates (Eds.), *The change handbook* (pp. 375–380). San Francisco, CA: Berrett-Koehler.

Wasserman, I. C. (2004). *Discursive processes that foster dialogic moments: Transformation in the engagement of social identity differences in dialogue* (Doctoral dissertation). Retrieved from ProQuest Dissertations and Theses database. (UMI No. 3168530).

Wasserman, I. C. (2005). Appreciative inquiry and diversity: The path to relational eloquence. *AI Practitioner: International Journal of Appreciative Inquiry, 8*, 36–43.

Wasserman, I. C., & Durishin, L. (2014). Culture change and strategic conversations: Adaptive leadership in action. *AI Practitioner: International Journal of Appreciative Inquiry, 16*(1), 37–41.

Wasserman, I. C., & Gallegos, P. V. (in press). Enacting integral diversity: A relational communication approach.

Wijeyesinghe, C. L., & Jackson, B. W. (Eds.). (2012). *New perspectives on racial identity development: Integrating emerging frameworks*. New York, NY: NYU Press.

Wilber, K. (2000). *Integral psychology: Consciousness, spirit, psychology, theory*. Boston: Shambhala Press.

17

LEVERAGING DIFFERENCE IN A "HAVE YOUR SAY" WORLD

Heather Wishik

> There is a Talmudic story about two first-century rabbis, Hillel, the "tolerant and liberal 'loose constructionist' of the Law," and Shammai, "the exacting and inflexible 'strict constructionist.'" A Christian tried to provoke them by asking them to teach him the entire Torah while he stood on one leg. It is said that Shammai, angered, hit the man with a stick. Hillel responded by saying, "That which is hateful to you, do not unto another: This is the whole Torah. The rest is commentary—[and now] go study."
>
> —*Philologos, 2008*

Lately, I have encountered challenges to the Leveraging Difference paradigm about Diversity and Inclusion that I offer when consulting about diversity (Davidson, 2011). This paradigm positions differences as strategic opportunities to drive desired results, in contrast to the traditional U.S. "managing diversity" paradigm, which has usually positioned diversity as a problem to be managed.

In the past, my consulting colleagues and I might have labeled as resistance client comments that rejected core premises made at the outset of a workshop or design meeting. Now, I am considering other interpretations. This new perspective may support more sustainable learning relationships, communities of peer learners among colleagues in client organizations and a multitude of "high quality connections" (Dutton & Heaphy, 2003).

These challenging behaviors suggest a need for nuanced customization that involves and is transparent to the client. Such client involvement may offer increased self-agency and empowerment as the clients themselves co-create the interventions and learning designs (Shor, 2012), and may help further organizational empowerment (Peterson & Zimmerman, 2004).

Because the Leveraging Difference model invites entertaining *any* relevant difference, members of groups that have nominally benefited from traditional managing diversity sometimes express concerns that they may lose ground when new groups are singled out for attention. These concerns in part grow out of managing diversity's scarcity approach, where traditionally excluded groups fight for small amounts of organizational resources. Once the impacts of having everyone in the organization engaged in driving strategic results through difference become clear, scarcity-related concerns tend to dissolve. The isolation of managing diversity efforts in the HR and marketing departments also ends, as operational leaders discover effective ways to drive results through Leveraging Difference (Davidson, 2011).

Other concerns relate to fear that considering any relevant difference will allow the group to avoid acknowledging the most tenacious differences, such as race in the U.S., gender in Bahrain, and religion in Northern Ireland. Instead, we find Leveraging Difference aids in a more nuanced consideration of these tenacious differences. For instance, Leveraging Difference helped a U.S. Northwest organization stop trying to imitate its Northeastern branches in hiring African Americans, and to recognize their race/culture issue was Asian American attrition due to lack of promotion into management, based on unexamined biases about leadership style (Davidson, 2011).

Despite what is possible with this new framework, organization members are tentative. It is shortsighted, however, to presume that pushback in workshops or design meetings is pushback against the model itself. Rather than being resistance, or only resistance, it seems equally possible that the apparently rejecting statements I am getting from clients at the outset are a contemporary form of conversation through statement and comment, one that mirrors what is routine in social media, blogging, and comment options in online news sites.

Challenging comments come before I have a chance to explain why and how a paradigm shift could be useful and what Leveraging Difference means. In response to my saying, for example, "I would like to explore with you what differences matter to your work, and suggest we use an approach called Leveraging Difference to do so," I have immediately gotten "I don't think this 'Leveraging Difference' language will fly here" and "I don't see any reason to change from our 'managing diversity' approach." Others say things like "We are just sales guys. This Leveraging Difference thing sounds too complicated"; "We've only collected data on race and gender, so those are the only differences we should focus on"; "Our customers are watching what we do on diversity, so diversity is what we have to call this work"; "In Brazil, the only difference that matters is economic class"; "In the Netherlands our issue is immigrants—otherwise, we are very tolerant."

These comments could be resistance. They are also clues about which differences are relevant. The clients are telling me what matters, what differences are making a difference, even as they appear to reactively reject my suggested approach.

Contemporary media formats invite, legitimize, and empower individuals to offer immediate expression of opinion in statement form in response to any content. At its worst, rather than involving study and learning, this form of commentary-laden conversation may help individuals feel authorized to dismiss anything not aligned with their existing views. At best, an ongoing variety of responsive comments could be a means of opening up possibilities of meaning and peer learning.

Recently, I offered a webex about mitigating bias to a hiring committee from the Southern United States. I used a scenario about a candidate with a strong Boston accent. "Actually," said one participant, whose name was Bill,[1] "I would ask the candidate how *they* feel about Southern accents." This comment elicited knowing laughter from the group. Without deflecting, I modified my scenario, asking about an Asian candidate who spoke strongly accented English.

Maya: "I think this version of the mini-case isn't useful. We are a global organization. We don't have biases about accents or language. Let's move on."

Les: "I disagree. I hate this scenario because it pushes me to admit something I am ashamed of—I often cannot understand Chinese speakers' English and I get frustrated and stop trying."

Ken: "I agree—actually when I see an Asian name on a resume I hesitate to bring the candidate forward for consideration."

Marc to Les: "Have you ever spent time outside the U.S. for more than two weeks as a tourist?"

Les: "No actually, I haven't."

Marc: "I once worked for several months in Indonesia. My livelihood depended on understanding the English spoken by Indonesian colleagues. After a week or two, I got better at understanding them."

Julie: "I agree. I was in the Peace Corps and it got easier to understand accented English over time."

Les: "That's really interesting. I guess I need to be more patient and give it more time. Thanks."

This is an example of a moment when an apparently challenging first comment led to group learning through dialogue. As the consultant, I just needed to stay out of the way.

"Total Noise"

David Foster Wallace named the current interactive media environment "the tsunami of available fact, context, and perspective that constitutes Total Noise" (Wallace, 2007). Thomas Friedman calls it "the digital river," an onslaught of inputs and communication channels that arrive, largely unedited, "judgment not included" (Friedman, 2013). The normalization of expression of personal opinion without prior information gathering or reflection, the blurring of opinion, fact and fiction, and the rhetoric of customization and individual truths may challenge practitioners like me to be radically more inclusive about who plans and designs our work.

Changing the dialogue requires changing how participants are empowered to participate and the forms of conversation we expect and facilitate. Simultaneously, participants need support toward openness, resilience, and respectfulness in the face of difference and revelation of their own unconscious biases. They need more confidence in their ability to learn and change (Dweck, 2006), more skills for reflection and skills for making judgments about information and opinion.

Interestingly, conversation through statement or comment, sometimes called debate or argument, is central to the Jewish tradition of studying in pairs (*havruta* or fellowship). In this tradition, pairs of students, as different from each other as were Hillel and Shammai, listen to rabbinical presentations and study Torah and Talmudic texts. Through dialogue, debate, comments, applications, and stories drawn from their lives, the pair helps each other understand the rabbi's meaning and discover textual meanings. Perhaps an updated, more inclusive version of the paired learning practices of the *bet midrash*, the Jewish study hall, offers a useful analogy to forms of conversation for use in Leveraging Difference work.

Constructivist Listening

One approach to shifting conversational form might be to use "constructivist listening" (Weinglass, 1990; also called "attentive listening"). This practice involves pairs taking turns being speaker and listener, to address a given topic or question. The speaker has a specified time for speaking, during which the listener does not speak and minimizes nonverbal responses. This practice gives the speaker 100 percent of the power to construct the story or response he or she wishes to tell, without interruptions or redirections from his or her listener, verbal or nonverbal.

Constructivist listening may short circuit the rapid-fire, reactive, commentary type of communication typical of the digital river. A topic or query is posed, and then, instead of instantaneous reactivity, the structure offers each person extended space to construct his or her own commentary, with time for thought and silence from the listener. If the speaker runs out of things to say and needs to reflect, the listener remains silent since the speaker's time is his or her own. While these silences feel awkward to many people, the speaker often finds something he or she had not yet thought of to add. Such additions are often more thoughtful than reactive.

Constructivist listening requires that listeners only listen. They are constrained from expressing their reactivity, if any, to what the speaker says, to focus on holding the space open for the speaker to speak. During listening, listeners often discover that their assumptions about what the speaker meant, or where the speaker was heading, were in error. Thus listeners often learn about the benefit of slowing down reactivity and commentary, to give time to discover what a speaker actually means.

While clients could certainly challenge the constructivist listening structure itself, I find usually they are curious and willing to try it, since it is so different from the active listening they have been taught.

Recently, I had the opportunity to explain the Leveraging Difference paradigm to two client groups. I decided to try attending to the need for early comment and dialogue. I gave each person a paper copy of the Leveraging Difference diagram. After introducing myself and providing a few sentences of context and explanation about the model, I asked pairs to discuss "seeing difference," the first step in the model, before explaining the rest. I asked the pairs to use constructivist listening and gave each speaker two minutes. The structure of constructivist listening requires, as explained above, that speakers take turns. It is not dialogue, not yet.

The request: Tell one mini story about a difference that mattered in your family, and tell one difference about you that has mattered at work.

The sample response provided: My father was Jewish, my mother was Christian; neither family would give them a wedding so they had to elope. I learned early that religion mattered. At work, my legal training matters: I analyze in a way that isn't shared by my consulting colleagues, so I need to slow down and explain my conclusions.

After both speakers in the pairs finished, I asked the pairs to chat with each other before we debriefed. Interestingly, after listening in this structured way, the discussion between the two people tended to be interpersonally warm and deep. A level of "swift trust" (Meyerson, Weick, & Kramer, 1996) was built in four minutes. This trust carried over; the members of each pair were more mutually supportive, open, curious, self-disclosing, and willing to enjoy their multiple differences of experience. These are some of the characteristics of good dialogue (Bohm, 2004).

Positive psychology suggests that "high quality connections" can support a variety of positive workplace outcomes (Dutton & Heaphy, 2003). Diversity and Inclusion consultants might put facilitation of high quality connections among members of client organizations at the center of the design of any Leveraging Difference intervention. Constructivist listening and pair chats are a part of such design. Group comment forums, electronically mediated or in other forms, could also work well.

I am still exploring the possibilities. My clients are pushing me to innovate and to remember that if their connection with me is not also of high quality, constantly renewed, they will push back. One of the reasons I work from the Leveraging Difference paradigm is that I believe it to be radically more inclusive than was much of "managing diversity" work. Working from Leveraging Difference approaches, any difference relevant to the client group's desired outcomes is legitimate to address. Everyone's identity and story are possibly relevant for seeing, learning, engaging, and leveraging.

Improving the paradigm only gets me in the door, however. I still have to enact consultation in ways that are actively inclusive of everyone in the room. In this communication, technology, and media environment, this means in particular empowering co-creation from the outset, constant attention to appropriate customization, and peer learning through comment forums, dialogue pairs, and other ways for giving voice at each step.

Hillel, I hope, is smiling.

For Practitioners: Pushing through Pushback to Spark Meaningful Dialogue

Pushback in initial stages of consultation may have to do with the client member's desire to assure services will be customized. Deeper fears may also be at play: What if my underrepresented group loses our hard-won attention if everyone's differences matter? What if my difference involves unearned status or privilege? What if I discover I don't know as much as I think I know? What if this work hurts my work relationships?

As practitioners, we need to honor the client's need for reassurance, hold back our own reactivity when there's pushback and still move learning forward. Here are some ideas:

Give up the role of "expert." Instead, slow down during the early design, listen longer and more quietly, ask open-ended questions, use strategic self-disclosure, and design early interactions that can lead to high quality connections.

Don't be afraid to disrupt things a bit. Clients may want to stay comfortable about ways of interacting, the workplace climate, and so on. Be willing—even when they don't want you to—to take clients into unfamiliar situations where basic assumptions, values and behaviors are revealed as less universal and more contingent.

Stay open to possibilities as clients engage—help clients explore why an idea might or might not work to accomplish their goal, particularly when clients make a design suggestion that raises initial concerns for you as consultant, or triggers your own assumptive fast reactivity.

Note

1. Pseudonyms are used throughout.

References

Bohm, D. (2004). *On dialogue* (2nd ed.). Oxford: Routledge.

Davidson, M. N. (2011). *The end of diversity as we know it: Why diversity efforts fail and leveraging difference can succeed.* San Francisco, CA: Berrett-Koehler.

Dutton, J. E., & Heaphy, E. D. (2003). The power of high-quality connections. In K. S. Cameron, J. E. Dutton, & R. E. Quinn (Eds.), *Positive organizational scholarship* (pp. 263–278). San Francisco, CA: Berrett-Koehler.

Dweck, C. S. (2006). *Mindset: The new psychology of success.* New York: Random House.

Friedman, T. (2013, April 27). Judgment not included. *New York Times.* http://www.nytimes.com/2013/04/28/opinion/sunday/friedman-judgment-not-included.html?hp

Meyerson, D., Weick, K. E., & Kramer, R. M. (1996). Swift trust and temporary groups. In R. M. Kramer & T. R. Tyler (Eds.), *Trust in organizations: Frontiers of theory and research.* Thousand Oaks, CA: Sage.

Peterson, A. P., & Zimmerman, M. A. (2004). Beyond the individual: Nomological network of organizational empowerment. *American Journal of Community Psychology, 34*(1,2), 129–145.

Philologos. (2008, September 24). The rest of the rest is commentary. *Forward.* http://forward.com/articles/14250/the-rest-of-the-rest-is-commentary-/

Shor, I. (2012). *Empowering education: Critical teaching for social change.* Chicago, IL: University of Chicago Press.

Wallace, D. W. (Ed.). (2007). Introduction. *The best American essays 2007.* New York: Mariner Books.

Weinglass, J. (1990). Constructivist listening for empowerment and change. *Educational Forum, 54*(4), 351–370.

18

THE TWO FACES OF *UBUNTU*

An Inclusive Positive or Exclusive Parochial Leadership Perspective?

Lize A. E. Booysen[1]

In this chapter, we explore *Ubuntu*, a philosophical thought system conceived in sub-Saharan[2] Africa, where it influences work practices as well as community life. *Ubuntu* is a positive, inclusive, and relational-enabling cultural construct that has a favorable, generative impact on how organizations are managed. Although it can devolve into an exclusive parochial practice, *Ubuntu* can be practiced in an inclusive nonexclusionary manner that optimizes its enabling potential, as this chapter will demonstrate.

A Positive Cultural Generative Mechanism

Ubuntu, a Nguni word that literally translates to "I am because of others," was popularized by Desmond Tutu and Nelson Mandela in the 1990s with the downfall of Apartheid in South Africa. There is a diverse cross-section of literature on the term, but the common understanding is that it means fundamental respect and compassion for others. *Ubuntu* is an expression of collective personhood, interconnectedness, and collective morality. It implies encouraging individuals to express themselves through the group—through group support and commitment, acceptance and respect, cooperation and consensus, caring, sharing, and solidarity (Malunga, 2006).

Roberts (2006) emphasized the importance of identifying generative enablers across cultures, since culture plays a role in shaping perceptions of positivity, and Luthans, van Wyk, and Walumba (2004) identified *Ubuntu* as a possible "positive strength-based perspective" in South African organizations. I seek to extend this notion and show that *Ubuntu* is also (1) inclusive and relational in nature and (2) extends beyond South Africa to encompass other parts of the world where organizations take a relational view of leadership, even if they don't know that it is very similar to *Ubuntu*—for instance, in Native American and Aboriginal cultures.

Bolden and Kirk (2009) pointed out that the relational view of leadership relates well to the collectivistic and humanist values of *Ubuntu*, stating that *Ubuntu* "bridges the 'individual' and the 'collective.'" Inclusive leadership, similar to *Ubuntu*, involves relational practice, collaboration, consensus building, true engagement, and creating inclusive work cultures. The major focus of both *Ubuntu* and inclusive leadership is on collective relational practice, the entwined nature of our relationships, and increased inclusion of interconnected systems. *Ubuntu* can thus be considered not only relational but also inclusive in nature and centers on the interdependence of the individual and collective (Booysen, 2012).

Ubuntu as an organizational leadership approach generated mostly conceptual and anecdotal publications in the 1990s equating "African Leadership"[3] with *Ubuntu* (Nkomo, 2011). Walumba, Avolio, and Aryee (2011) claimed that although the nations of Africa are not a homogenous group, and indeed are widely diverse, research is beginning to show that there might be commonalities across sub-Saharan African cultures aligned with *Ubuntu*. These include hospitality, mutuality, solidarity, and emphasis on harmony, compassion, humaneness, acceptance, relational practice, respect and dignity, a collective interdependent ethos, extended family obligations, shared responsibility, filial piety, deference to authority, and paternalism. Muchiri (2011) found that various sub-Saharan African cultures do indeed demonstrate compassion and generosity, respect for the dignity and welfare of others, and mutuality: values similar to those of *Ubuntu*. Wanasika, Howell, Littrell, and Dorfman (2011) concurred that sub-Saharan African cultures focus heavily on extended family and group obligations or in-group collectivism, which also spills over into institutional collectivism. Walumba et al. (2011) linked this emphasis on human interdependence and striving for harmony in social relations to a high level of humane orientation, where self-interest is seen as second to helping another.

Caveats to *Ubuntu:* Its Possible Exclusive Nature

While *Ubuntu* can be seen as a positive generative mechanism for organizations, it can lead to discriminatory practices: It is heavily focused on extended family and group obligations, conformity and compliance with group norms and regulations, paternalism, and deference to authority and status, which can culminate in in-group favoritism, oppression, sexism, ageism, high levels of power stratification, and stifling of individual aspirations. Muchiri (2011) asserted that the close-knit social framework influenced by family ties, ethnicity, and religion can culminate in in-group favoritism and oppression of the other. The way leadership is viewed will also be swayed by how the group perceives the leader's ability to safeguard it. This in-group loyalty to kinship may develop into parochialism, exclusion, tribalism, and nepotism (Malunga, 2006).

Organizational structures in sub-Saharan Africa have been characterized as paternalistic, with high gender differentiation and management systems permeated by patrimonial behaviors characterized by sexism and patriarchal power structures. While consensus is highly valued for decision making within levels, it is hierarchical between levels, and age groups, and leaders are expected to be paternalistic and authoritative (Wanasika et al., 2011). The undertones of power stratification, deference to authority, and status based on age and wisdom, paternalism and patrilineal values embedded in *Ubuntu* may lead to lifelong rule and dictatorship, gender and age inequality, and skewed privileges and discrimination (Muchiri, 2011).

Ubuntu's Inclusive Intent

We want to argue that *Ubuntu* practiced in an inclusive manner is indeed a positive generative and relational leadership practice. Khoza (2011) and Malunga (2006) argued that the intention of *Ubuntu* is to be inclusive and to respect diversity. Therefore, true *Ubuntu* is practiced in a humane way that furthers social justice, equality, social responsibility, and sustainability (Table 18.1). Key values are trust, fairness, openness, reconciliation, and peacemaking through the principles of reciprocity, relational practice, participatory practices, inclusivity, and a sense of shared destiny. Of course, leaders must be aware of the downside of *Ubuntu* so that it can be practiced in a way that diminishes the potential for exclusion.

TABLE 18.1 Examples of Inclusive Qualities and Exclusive Potential of *Ubuntu*

Leadership Assumption	Leadership Practice and African Proverb	Leadership Implications

Sharing and collective ownership of opportunities, responsibilities, and challenges	Sharing of responsibilities: *"Your friend's child is your own child."*
	
	Sharing of privilege: *"A lit candle loses nothing by lighting another candle."*
	
	Collaboration: *"United, the ants can take a dead elephant to their cave."*
		• Both leaders and followers need to take responsibility—no blaming
		• Fair distribution of benefits and efforts to everyone
		• Work load, resources, and remuneration are equitable
		• Collaboration and teamwork are important
		• Collective shared responsibility: All must pull their weight
		• Participatory decision making and leadership
		• Individual leaders should not be allowed to become too powerful
		
		Downside:
		  • May stifle individual efforts
		  • Social loafing may occur
		  • Nonperformers may be protected

(*Continued*)

TABLE 18.1 (Continued)

Leadership Assumption	Leadership Practice and African Proverb	Leadership Implications
Importance of people and relationships over things	Loyalty to family and in-group relationships: *"Kinship is like a bone: It does not decay."* Understanding of and respect for a common bond for survival: *"A river that forgets its source will soon dry up."*	• Organization is seen as extended family • Work and family life are intertwined and have blurred boundaries • Strong in-group cohesion and support; loyalty to own group • Organizational interest more important than personal interest • Leaders must be in service to the organization rather than accumulating personal wealth and power • Rituals celebrating success, growth, and loss connect people to one another and their cultural values *Downside:* • In-groups are protected at all costs • Blind loyalty to the group and especially older leaders • Inward looking and complacent

Sources: Booysen (2012) and Malunga (2009).

Concluding Thoughts

In summary, *Ubuntu*, "Africa's gift to the world," according to Desmond Tutu, is a relational inclusive construct focusing on interrelationships, interconnectedness, and social collectivism that focuses on both the social and individual units: *Our (individual) humanity is inextricably bound to the humanity of others (the collective).*

Ubuntu is a philosophical thought system, and like many other philosophies (and religions), how it gets translated is context-bound: It is practiced by people with specific group-belonging who have varying power differentials, which oftentimes further their own agendas. For *Ubuntu* to be practiced in an inclusive way, it should focus not only on "own preservation" (own collective), excluding others, but also on "other preservation"—thus inclusion for the common good of all (larger collectives). *Ubuntu* is a tolerant and accepting way of being that extends beyond own-group belonging.

Ubuntu is a promising indigenous, inclusive, and relational generative mechanism that is under-researched. Future research could focus on how these Positive Organizational Scholarship principles, inherent in *Ubuntu*, can be integrated in leadership practices across cultures.

For Practitioners: An *Ubuntu* Primer

Ubuntu:

- Can be seen as a positive sub-Saharan African cultural generative mechanism, affirming interconnectedness, inclusion, and relational practice
- Can also be discriminatory due to its focus on extended family and group obligations, paternalism, and deference to authority and status, which can culminate in in-group favoritism, oppression, and sexism
- Is not intended to be parochial, exclusive, or discriminatory in nature; its essence is to be inclusive—to respect and value own and other collectives; the challenge is to capitalize and to build on the inherent inclusive nondiscriminatory positive practices of *Ubuntu*, while minimizing the possible exclusionary practices
- Is not a panacea, but a promising indigenous, under-researched inclusive and relational cultural generative mechanism, which is underutilized in leadership practice, with potential to be implemented across cultures

Notes

1. Up front, I need to make my own subjective positionality and insider/outsider status clear. My identity as a white South African holds its own biases and tensions in terms of my voice. Like Nkomo (2011), I can also ask "Should I speak and can I speak unproblematically about 'African' leadership and management given my identities?" and "Can a privileged White Afrikaner (or so called Afropean or Eurokaner) female academic who grew up in Apartheid South Africa, now living in diaspora in the United States, speak about *Ubuntu*?"
2. Although some authors claim Ubuntu is peculiar to South Africa (Nkomo, 2011), others assert that it is a general African philosophy prevalent in Eastern, Central, and Southern Africa (Malunga, 2006) and even across the continent (Khoza, 2011). Most consensus is, however, that Ubuntu pertains to sub-Saharan African countries; similar expressions exist in most Nguni sub-Saharan African languages (Bolden & Kirk, 2009; Muchiri, 2011; Walumba, Avolio & Aryee, 2011).
3. Africa is a complex continent comprising 54 countries and diverse populations that are divided along cultural, linguistic, and ethnic lines, all with different realities. Therefore, any scholarly quest for a distinctive "African" leadership style would be essentialist in nature.

References

Bolden, R., & Kirk, P. (2009). African leadership surfacing new understandings through leadership development. *International Journal of Cross cultural Management, 9*(1), 69–86.

Booysen, L.A.E. (2012, July 23–25). *The application of "African" leadership principles and practices in inclusive leadership.* The 5th Equality, Diversity and Inclusion International Conference, Toulouse Business School, Toulouse, France.

Khoza, R.J. (2011). *Attuned leadership African humanism as compass.* Johannesburg, South Africa: Penguin Books.

Luthans, F., van Wyk, R., & Walumba, F.O. (2004). Recognition and development of hope for South-African organizational leaders. *Leadership and Organization Development Journal, 25*(6), 512–527.

Malunga, C. (2006). Learning leadership development from African cultures: A personal perspective. INTRAC PraxisNote 25.

Malunga, C. (2009). *Making strategic plans work: Insights from African indigenous wisdom.* London: Adonis & Abbey.

Muchiri, M.K. (2011). Leadership in context: A review and research agenda for sub-Saharan Africa. *Journal of Occupational and Organizational Psychology, 84*, 440–452.

Nkomo, S. M. (2011). A postcolonial and anti-colonial reading of "African" leadership and management in organization studies: Tensions, contradictions and possibilities. *Organization, 18*(3), 365–386.

Roberts, L. M. (2006). Shifting the lens on organizational life: The added value of positive scholarship. *Academy of Management Review, 31*(2), 292–305.

Walumba, F.O., Avolio, J. W., & Aryee, S. (2011). Leadership and management research in Africa: A synthesis and suggestions for future research. *Journal of Occupational Organizational Psychology, 84*, 425–439.

Wanasika, I., Howell, J.P., Littrell, R., & Dorfman, P. (2011). Managerial leadership and culture in sub-Saharan Africa. *Journal of World Business, 46*, 234–243.

SECTION V

Inclusive and Equitable Systems

Section Introduction

Amy Lemley, Lynn Perry Wooten, Martin N. Davidson, and Laura Morgan Roberts

In 1912, Girl Scouts founder Juliette Gordon Low took a strong stand that all girls of all races and classes, U.S. natives or immigrants, rural or urban, could be part of the club. Today, the organization is 2.8 million members strong, and inclusivity remains at the forefront of its programming innovations. Girl Scouts of Northern California, for example, assessed its population and created three innovative programs: Daughters of Farm Workers for migrant children; the Hispanic Initiative, which inspired one Latina scout to found a 100-girl troop; and Got Choices, for at-risk girls, including those in the juvenile justice system. These programs are designed to teach positive decision making, healthy lifestyles, and beneficial relationships with peers, families, and communities. To strengthen its network, these outreach programs "connects Girl Scout community organizers with parents, community members, school districts, and local, knowledgeable Girl Scout volunteers to deliver innovative programs and build sustainable volunteer-led troops" (Girl Scouts of Northern California, 2012).

Across the country, the Maryland State Boychoir, a soprano singing group, initiated organizational changes to be more inclusive of boys' gender identity development. The boychoir saw its members begin to lose confidence as their high, clear voices of childhood were overtaken by the croaks of puberty. Leaving this elite group after years of intense work together (some join as third graders) means saying goodbye to a significant part of their lives. The choir director understood. To accommodate their lower registers, the organization formed the Changed Voice Choir, extending young men's singing careers—and sense of belonging—as they await the smooth bass and tenor of adulthood (Tucker, 2007).

It comes down to culture. For meaningful and lasting change to take place, Diversity and Inclusion efforts are best accomplished in an organization with a stated—and demonstrated—commitment to positive leadership. According to this section's first chapter, "Diversity Management as a Generative Strategic Process: When the Business Case Meets Positive Organizational Scholarship," the key is to weave learning with specific actions that prompt the positively deviant behavior that become part of the fabric of the organization. Wooten, Parsons, Griswold, and Welch examine the intersection of diversity management and Positive Organizational Scholarship (POS) against a backdrop of Competing Values, and show how certain processes, techniques and practices net extraordinary results and create lasting value.

Canham's chapter, "From Exclusion to Inclusion: Inclusion and Empowerment in a South African Organization" examines the shift in thinking required for a large South African bank to stop viewing diversity efforts as a mandated burden and instead see them as an opportunity for all individuals and the organization to flourish. Interviews with bank employees reveal a degree of empowerment, particularly among black employees, that has prompted positive deviance and transformed the organizational culture.

"Assessing Organizational Culture and Engaging Faculty Diversity in Higher Education" discusses how diversity efforts at the higher education level can net a richer reward through the introduction of formal initiatives that draw on POS principles. Flowers, Moore, Flowers, and Flowers argue that, after an assessment of the existing culture, colleges and universities should develop comprehensive plans for engaging and supporting underrepresented faculty in leadership roles. A human-centered approach is critical to ensure individual and organizational achievement.

Turning to the philanthropic sector, "Learning Together: A Positive Approach to Diversity and Inclusion Education" demonstrates how the tools of Appreciative Inquiry can help bridge difference. Rosenberg asserts that an organization's success relies in part on laying the groundwork beforehand: A positive framing of Diversity and Inclusion that elucidates individual as well as organizational benefit inspires upfront commitment to the effort. This chapter emphasizes the essential role that inclusive cultures and appreciative inquiry play in stimulating philanthropy.

Reminding us that a diverse employee base necessarily means diverse work–life balance preferences, Kossek invites readers to consider the effectiveness of an organization's work–life balance programs and policies in her chapter, "Organizational Support and Empowerment of Diversity in Work–Life Identities." Do they cover a range of options so that all types of workers can make use of them? An executive choosing to work from home with a laptop is deemed acceptable, but is a last minute shift swap possible for a factory worker? Do work–life options exist in name only (never used, used by only high-level employees, or their use is frowned upon) or are they accessible (used by employees at all levels without judgment)?

These chapters bridge diversity, inclusion, and POS to show that, with the right foundation, Diversity and Inclusion programs and policies can have a galvanizing effect for teams and organizations and an empowering effect on individuals. A POS outlook from an initiative's inception helps create a culture in which difference is valued as something to enhance the growth of both employee and employer.

References

Girl Scouts of Northern California. (2012). *The campaign for girls: 100th anniversary campaign goals of Northern California.*

Tucker, A. (2007, December 7). Harmony in puberty. *Baltimore Sun.* http://articles.baltimoresun.com/2007-12-09/news/0712090109_1_state-boychoir-voice-choir-boy-choirs

19

DIVERSITY MANAGEMENT AS A GENERATIVE STRATEGIC PROCESS

When the Business Case Meets Positive Organizational Scholarship

Lynn Perry Wooten, Kelle Parsons, Robby Griswold, and Skot Welch

The management of diversity entails actions that are designed to create greater inclusion of stakeholders from various backgrounds into both the formal and informal organizational structures through deliberate policies, programs, and practices (Barak, 2013). Many organizations invest their time, resources, and energy in managing diversity because of the business case for organizational diversity, which is based on the premise that diversity can be leveraged through effective inclusion practices that lead to an increase in the total human energy available to the organization (Miller & Katz, 2002). This process results in a more capable workforce to achieve performance goals, serve diverse customers, and harness the collective knowledge of its employees for innovation; and the alignment of organizational values with corporate social responsibility (Richard, 2000; Slater, Weigand, & Zwirlein, 2008; Deloitte, 2011). But, this does not happen magically. Instead, it is ingrained in a systematic approach that entails understanding how an organization's culture facilitates or prohibits its capacity to leverage diversity and establish a rationale and practices for diversity management that are consistent with the organization's mission and goals (Maltbia & Power, 2009).

Positive Organizational Scholarship (POS) offers a complementary perspective to the business case of diversity management. POS is inspired by identifying, understanding, and enacting the generative mechanisms that create positive deviance in people, groups, and organizations (Cameron, Dutton, & Quinn, 2003; Dutton & Glynn, 2008; Roberts, 2006). A POS perspective enables us to unpack the processes of constructive change by exploring how organizations conceptualize, learn, engage partners, and deploy energy for the management of diversity and inclusion. Based on our experiences, we propose two key practices that empower leaders and their organizations to engage in positive deviant behavior that produce collective resourcefulness and generative dynamics when managing diversity: (1) a commitment to organizational learning and (2) the capacity to strategically leverage resources to create value for organizational stakeholders.

Diversity Management and the Learning Organization

Learning organizations are described as work environments where organizational members collectively build the capacity to create, share, acquire, reconfigure, transfer, and leverage knowledge for the purpose of creating desired results (Garvin, 1993; Senge, 1990). The essence of a learning organization is a culture where people are continuously learning how to learn by working toward a shared vision, engaging in systems thinking, and employing mental models. This entails the commitment of individual organizational members to learning and the investment of teams working together to discover insights that are not attainable at the individual level of learning.

In the context of managing diversity, we have concluded that learning organizations are better positioned to engage in practices that focus their energies on producing positive deviant behavior. We believe this is because learning is anchored in a shared vision that serves as an aspirational compass for directing behavior (Stavros & Wooten, 2011). A shared vision for diversity is an explicit verbal and symbolic expression that not only defines the organization's commitment, but also serves as a frame of reference for the present and envisioned future. Moreover, a shared vision creates purpose, promotes the integration of organizational values, and channels resources toward opportunities where the organization can use diversity and inclusive practices as a vehicle to realize positive outcomes.

Complementing this shared vision for the management of diversity is the organization's ability to engage in systems thinking and have a set of mental models to guide its behavior. System thinking is grounded in inquiry that explores the interrelated factors of diversity and the ecosystem with which the organization interacts, including external factors such as demographic, economic, and social trends as well as internal factors such as leadership, organizational culture, strategic priorities, power structures, and employee identities.

The value of systems thinking is reaped through the process that equips organizations with a cognitive map for understanding how stakeholders, institutions, and individuals influence the management of diversity, and, when coupled with mental models, leads to conceptual clarity. Organizations interested in uncovering their mental models related to diversity management explore the best of their past behaviors for envisioning a better future while recognizing their blind spots, biases, and tendencies for the exclusion of differences (Maltbia & Power, 2009). Also, we believe an essential mental model for embracing diversity management is an understanding of individuals, groups, and organizations as cultural beings, a complexity of identities, perspectives, and experiences that influence actions (Williams, 2001).

Digging deep to understand the mental models that govern diversity management practices can be challenging for many organizations, but it is also an opportunity to create generative dynamics, the ability of an organization to develop, expand, reconfigure, and transform resources to achieve organizational goals as a result of its diversity. For learning organizations, the work of managing diversity is embedded in both the personal mastery and team mastery of its members. In our opinion, personal mastery for diversity management emerges as individual organizational members invest in practices for improving their actions through acquiring knowledge and applying this knowledge to opportunities and challenges in their work environments (Mosher, 2010). This personal mastery can manifest in several forms as organizational members demonstrate mental agility—the ability to critically think about the possibility associated with the management of diversity and draw connections; people agility—skills for working with people from diverse backgrounds and creating high-quality relationships; innovation agility—a passion to seek and experiment with diverse ideas and endeavors to find solutions and develop new practices, products, and services; self-awareness agility—the extent to which an individual has knowledge of his or her identity, values, and competencies and can present the best self; and results agility—the ability to envision what successful diversity management practices are and act purposely to achieve these outcomes (DeRue, Ashford, & Myers, 2012; Lombardo & Eichinger, 2000; Mitchinson & Morris, 2014).

In learning organizations, personal mastery becomes more powerful when it transcends from the individual to interpersonal relationships and team mastery. Team mastery occurs when diverse individuals work together as a team to accomplish organizational goals and transform their knowledge into collective work products desired by their stakeholders (Katzenbach & Smith, 1993). During the process of team mastery, mutual trust and respect are essential as team members learn how to think together and develop routines for constructively managing conflict and valuing differences (Cropper, 2014).

Enabling Diversity Management Practices to Create Value

In our opinion, when learning is coupled with specific actions, diversity management evolves into positively deviant behaviors that become institutionalized. For this to transpire, we contend that positively deviant behaviors are grounded in specific "enablers": processes, techniques, or practices that organizations use to produce extraordinary results and create value (Cameron & Lavine, 2006; Wooten & Cameron, 2010). As illustrated in Figure 19.1, we believe extraordinary diversity management outcomes are associated with organizational learning and enablers that focus on four competencies associated with the Competing Values Framework and represent the competing tensions of managing the external environment versus internal environment and focused versus flexibility: (1) collaborate—investing in inclusive cultures; (2) control—designing systems for measuring diversity; (3) create—leveraging diversity for product and service

- Development of
  Human Capital
- Inclusive
  Organizational
  Culture
- Diversity of
  Partnerships

- Entrepreneurial
  Work Practices
- Innovation as
  a Value
- Flexible Organizing
  of Work

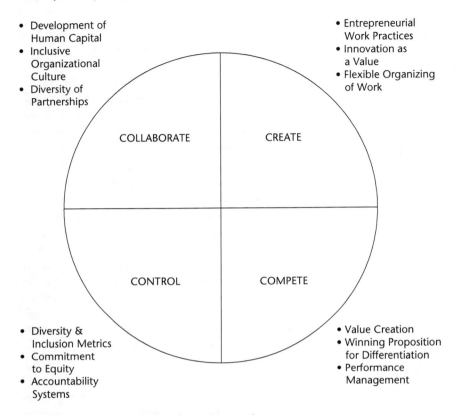

- Diversity &
  Inclusion Metrics
- Commitment
  to Equity
- Accountability
  Systems

- Value Creation
- Winning Proposition
  for Differentiation
- Performance
  Management

FIGURE 19.1 The Competing Values Framework

innovation and (4) compete—leveraging diversity for performance goals (Cameron, Quinn, DeGraff, & Thakor, 2006).

From our work with organizations, we have observed that *collaboration* is a core component of diversity management practices. Behaviors focusing on the management of human capital, inclusive organizational cultures, and a web of partnerships are practices supporting the collaborate enabler. But the management of human capital goes beyond the status quo of hiring diverse individuals for "certain positions" because it is the right thing to do to achieve or maintain demographic diversity at all levels (Jackson & Holvino, 1988). Inclusivity is indicated by the organization embedding the contributions of diversity into its vision, mission, strategy, and as a way of operating (Maltbia & Power, 2009). This inclusion extends beyond the boundaries of the organization through a diversity of partnerships that form a nexus effect by working with suppliers, customers, community stakeholders, and even competitors to solve problems or seize opportunities (Yip, Wong, & Ernst, 2008).

The *control* competencies support collaborative practices by emphasizing equity and measurement systems for diversity management. The systems in these organizations support equity in the workplace by ensuring all organizational members receive fair treatment. Also, there is a culture where the expected behaviors are defined and rewarded, and consequences are associated with dysfunctional behaviors. As a result, these organizations have level playing fields because the association between a favored status group and "special" access to resources and opportunities has been eradicated (Nishii & Rich, 2014). In reality, managing notions of equity is complex. But a commitment to equitable systems helps employees recognize that marginalization is not tolerated and, therefore, they are more willing to bring their authentic selves to the workplace and constructively contribute to the organization's goals (Ely & Thomas, 2001). In addition to equitable systems, organizations striving to achieve positive deviance have set up diversity management accountability systems for goal setting and measuring performances (Hubbard, 2004: Myers & Wooten, 2009).

In contrast to the control enabler, integrating diversity management with an organization's *creative* capabilities entails a culture where a diversity of voices is heard, regardless of who or what rank they are (DeGraff & Quinn, 2007). This diversity of voices is input for the creation of innovative management practices, products, and services. Furthermore, innovation from diversity is a byproduct of an environment that encourages entrepreneurship and the flexible organizing of work so that all employees feel empowered to scan for opportunities and experiment.

Lastly, we propose that for an organization to create value from diversity management it has to embrace a mindset that the practices will yield a *competitive* advantage. Thus, focusing on competing as a competency is the conscientious identification that the management of diversity should be linked to the performance of individuals, groups, and the organization. This comprises connecting the winning proposition, the points of differentiation that provide value for the organization's stakeholders with its myriad of activities, such as being the employer of choice, providing excellent customer service, achieving high profit margins, holding the dominant market share in certain sector, or solving a societal problem (Pietersen, 2002). We avow that when this is accomplished, organizations are at their best because they are "broadening and building" upon the generative potential of diversity management.

A Case in Point: Zingerman's Community of Businesses[1]

Zingerman's Community of Businesses is an organization that exemplifies this effort to engage in positive deviant behavior to intentionally grow collective resourcefulness and generative dynamics related to diversity and inclusion. From its start as a delicatessen in Ann Arbor, Michigan, in 1982, Zingerman's has become an Ann Arbor institution by pursuing deep growth and vertical integration, rather than scaling beyond the city. Zingerman's generates approximately $56 million in revenue and now includes nine individual businesses in a broad range of areas including a creamery, a coffee company, and a leadership and employee training organization.

In 2010, Zingerman's formalized its commitment to diversity and inclusion by creating a diversity and inclusion team to implement practices and processes that would yield better decisions and business results. The organization was well situated to pursue this effort to leverage diversity to achieve performance goals because of its focus on organizational learning and creating value for its stakeholders.

A Learning Organization

Zingerman's has a long commitment to cultivating a learning organization culture. Since 1994, the organization has developed time-limited vision statements about its desired future state. Their current document, Vision 2020, articulates a clear, shared central identity for the organization and provides direction for all staff members (Zingerman's, 2007). While the overall vision includes elements of diversity and inclusion, a newly formed team also maintains a shared model for how the organization will achieve its vision for diversity and inclusion and how doing so will help the organization flourish. In practice, these clear vision statements provide space for Zingerman's staff to learn, grow, and develop in ways that serve to move the organization toward that vision, and they articulate the shared values to which Zingerman's is willing to dedicate resources, including training time. In each case, the "what" and "how" of the vision are descriptive but do not explicitly articulate the steps for how the organization will achieve this vision; instead, those decisions are left to the daily work of staff to create, learn, and develop through actions and idea sharing. One common example is "open book finance," a practice in which Zingerman's staff members take responsibility for tracking and reporting on a particular metric for the company aligned with the Vision 2020, which allows staff to learn about the business, take ownership of affecting that metric, and innovate to improve.

Vision 2020 also points to mental models and the ways Zingerman's engages in systems thinking. It articulates the importance of both internal and external contexts, including the global food industry, the local business community, and demographics, along with the internal context of longstanding leadership and advancement structures and practices and employee training programs. As one of its first tasks, the Diversity and Inclusion Committee scanned the internal environment for the assumptions the organization makes about topics like leadership, advancement, decision making, and training, with the goal of intentionally considering how these assumptions affect the climate for inclusion and diversity in the organization. These actions serve as opportunities for individual staff members, as well as teams, to critically evaluate their own assumptions, consider new and better ways to achieve the organizations' goals, and understand how diversity and inclusion interplay with these practices.

Value Creation through Strategically Leveraging Resources

In an effort to develop sustainable processes related to managing diversity, Zingerman's engaged Global Bridgebuilders as a partner to learn about their five-step process for leveraging diversity to create value and explore ways to deploy elements that were congruent with work that already had been done (Global Bridgebuilders, 2014). The collaboration integrates elements of Global Bridgebuilders' four competencies of the Competing Values Framework: *control, collaborate, create,* and *compete*. The first three steps in the process involve the *control* quadrant: The organization undergoes an "inclusion systems assessment," in which an organization measures and analyzes its current diversity management practices. The questions in this assessment address systems such as leadership, communication, organizational development, external relationships, and process improvement/systems criteria. After the completion of the assessment, the organization conducts focus groups and produces a strategic gap analysis report to further analyze diversity management practices and outcomes. The fourth step relates to the *collaborate* quadrant: employee advisory councils, along with a professional development curriculum, equip staff to jointly identify, discuss, and solve problems related to diversity and inclusion. This step intentionally creates a structure that is inclusive of different ideas and perspectives and provides the data from the analysis steps to uncover issues. The fifth step, which includes ongoing reassessment of diversity and inclusion metrics, involves the *create* and *compete* quadrants: the organization expects to realize new venues for leveraging their diversity for product and service innovation as well as enhanced performance goals. In practice, Zingerman's is already a leader in this area, providing a work environment that explicitly invites all employees to bring their "whole selves" to work, trains managers in inclusive management practices, and encourages them to create and share ideas to improve service, products, and processes.

By employing many elements of these positively deviant behaviors to intentionally grow collective resourcefulness and deploy energy for managing diversity and inclusion, Zingerman's seems well positioned to reap the benefits of diversity and inclusion through greater innovation and organizational performance.

Conclusion

This chapter advances the idea that diversity management can be incorporated into an organization's strategy for achieving positive deviance. To accomplish this, we advocate that organizations commit to continuously learning and building the capacity to align diversity management practices with their strategies to create value for organizational stakeholders. The Zingerman's case study in this chapter is illustrative of this behavior. Zingerman's is an organization that is committed to learning as it assesses, conceives of, and enacts diversity management practices. Moreover, for Zingerman's, diversity management is not behind the scenes as the organization engages in strategic visioning and actions. Instead, diversity management is on the stage and fueling the organization "to a better tomorrow than today." Similar to Zingerman's, it is our desire that in the future, research and organizational practices will integrate "positively deviant" diversity management into the mainstream of its thoughts and actions.

For Practitioners: Generative Practices in Action for Diversity Management

Capacity Building as a Learning Organization

Shared Vision	Systems Thinking	Mental Modeling	Team Mastery	Personal Mastery
The organization has a shared vision for diversity that is aligned with its current strategy and future positioning.	The organization has developed contextual awareness to understand how the macro-environment influences diversity management practices.	The organization has conversations to identify the assumptions that influence its diversity management practices.	Team members invest energy in learning from each other.	Individuals invest energy in thinking about the management of diversity.
The vision outlines the purpose of why the organization manages diversity.	The organization has mapped its ecosystem to take into account external and internal factors for managing diversity.	The organization is aware of its blind spots, biases, and tendencies for inclusion and exclusion of stakeholders.	Team members value differences.	Individuals are skilled at working with people from diverse backgrounds.
The vision for diversity management is consistent with the organization's values.		The organization comprehends that individuals and groups are complex cultural beings.	Teams have routines for constructively managing conflict.	Individuals experiment with diverse ideas as a practice for innovating.
			Trust and mutual respect are hallmarks of teamwork.	

Enabling Value Creation

Collaborate	Control	Create	Compete
The organization's culture is inclusive of differences.	The organization has systems to ensure equity and equal treatment.	The organization has a culture that recognizes and values a diversity of voices as input for innovation.	The management of diversity is employed as an asset to broaden and build the organization's core competencies.
Diversity management is a core aspect of the organization's human resource management practices.	The culture rewards inclusive practices and there are consequences for exclusion.	The work environment encourages entrepreneurship and experimentation.	The management of diversity is viewed as a source of competitive advantage.
To achieve its goals, the organization has a diversity of partnerships.	There is a diversity management scorecard for goal setting and measuring performance.	Employees are empowered to scan the environment for opportunities.	Diversity is connected to the organization's "winning proposition" for its value-creating activities.

Note

1. The composing of the Zingerman's case study was a collaborative effort with Robby Griswold, who is the community partnerships coordinator and chair of the Diversity and Inclusion Committee at Zingerman's, and Skot Welch, principal bridgebuilder, Global Bridgebuilders.

References

Barak, M.E.M. (2013). *Managing diversity: Toward a globally inclusive workplace.* Thousand Oaks, CA: Sage.

Cameron, K. S., & Lavine, M. (2006). *Making the impossible possible: Leading extraordinary performance—the Rocky Flats story.* San Francisco, CA: Berrett-Koehler.

Cameron, K., Dutton, J., & Quinn, R. E. (Eds.). (2003). Foundations of positive organizational scholarship. *Positive organizational scholarship* (pp. 3–13). San Francisco, CA: Berrett-Koehler.

Cameron, K. S., Quinn, R. E., DeGraff, J., & Thakor, A. V. (2006). *Competing values leadership.* Cheltenham: Edward Elgar.

Cropper, B. (2014). Five Learning Disciplines. *Change Forum.* http://www.thechangeforum.com/Learning_Disciplines.htm

DeGraff, J. T., & Quinn, S. E. (2007). *Leading innovation: How to jump start your organization's growth engine.* New York: McGraw-Hill.

Deloitte. (2011, September). Only skin deep? Re-examining the business case for diversity. Deloitte Point of View.

DeRue, D. S., Ashford, S. J., & Myers, C. G. (2012). Learning agility: In search of conceptual clarity and theoretical grounding. *Industrial and Organizational Psychology, 5*(3), 258–279.

Dutton, J. E., & Glynn, M. (2008). Positive Organizational Scholarship. In C. Cooper & J. Barling (Eds.), *Handbook of organizational behavior* (pp. 693–711). Los Angeles, CA: Sage.

Ely, R. J., & Thomas, D. A. (2001). Cultural diversity at work: The effects of diversity perspectives on work group processes and outcomes. *Administrative Science Quarterly, 46*(2), 229–273.

Garvin, D. A. (1993). Building a learning organization. *Harvard Business Review, 71*(July–August), 78–91.

Global Bridgebuilders. (2014). Case study: City of Dallas, Texas. *Global Bridgebuilders,* 1–5.

Hubbard, E. E. (2004). *The diversity scorecard: Evaluating the impact of diversity on organizational performance.* Oxford: Routledge.

Jackson, B. W., & Holvino, E. V. (1988). Developing multicultural organizations. *Journal of Religion and Applied Behavioral Science (Association for Creative Change), Fall,* 14–19.

Katzenbach, J. R., & Smith, D. K. (1993). *The discipline of teams.* Boston, MA: Harvard Business Press.

Lombardo, M. M., & Eichinger, R. W. (2000). High potentials as high learners. *Human Resource Management, 39*(4), 321–329.

Maltbia, T. E., & Power, A. (2009). *A leader's guide to leveraging diversity: Strategic learning capabilities for breakthrough performance.* Oxford: Butterworth-Heinemann.

Miller, F., & Katz, J. (2002). *Inclusion breakthrough: Unleashing the real power of diversity.* San Francisco, CA: Berrett-Koehler.

Mitchinson, A., & Morris, R. (2014). Learning about learning agility. Center for Creative Leadership.

Mosher, B. (2010, June 27). Embedded learning. *Chief Learning Officer*. http://www.clomedia.com/articles/embedded_learning

Myers, V., & Wooten, L. P. (2009). The transformational power of a mission-driven strategy: Extraordinary diversity management practices and quality of care. *Organizational Dynamics, 38*(4), 297–304.

Nishii, L. H., & Rich, R. E. (2014). Creating inclusive climates in diverse organizations. *Diversity at work: The practice of inclusion* (pp. 330–363). San Francisco, CA: Jossey-Bass.

Pietersen, W. G. (2002). Reinventing strategy: Using strategic learning to create and sustain breakthrough performance. New York: John Wiley & Sons.

Richard, O. C. (2000). Racial diversity, business strategy, and firm performance: A resource-based view. *Academy of Management Journal, 43*(2), 164–177.

Roberts, L. M. (2006). Shifting the lens on organizational life: The added value of positive scholarship. *Academy of Management Review,* 31(2), 292–305.

Senge, P. (1990). The leader's new work: Building learning organizations. *Sloan Management Review, 32*(1), 7–23.

Slater, S., Weigand, R., & Zwirlein, T. (2008). The business case for commitment to diversity. *Harvard Business Review case study*, 51.

Stavros, J., & Wooten, L. (2011). Positive strategy: Creating and sustaining strengths-based strategy that SOARs and performs. In K. Cameron & G. Spreitzer (Eds.), *The Oxford handbook of positive organizational scholarship* (pp. 825–839). Oxford: Oxford University Press.

Williams, A. P. O. (2001). A belief-focused process model of organizational learning. *Journal of Management Studies, 38*, 67–85. doi:10.1111/1467-6486.00228

Wooten, L. P., & Cameron, K. S. (2010). Enablers of a positive strategy: Positively deviant leadership. In P. Linley, S. Harrington, & N. Garcea (Eds.), *Oxford handbook of positive psychology and work* (pp. 53–65). New York: Oxford University Press.

Yip, J., Wong, S., & Ernst, C. (2008). The nexus effect: When leaders span group boundaries. *Leadership in Action, 28*(4), 13–17.

Zingerman's. (2007). Vision 2020. http://www.zingtrain.com/node/304

20

FROM EXCLUSION TO INCLUSION

Inclusion and Empowerment in a South African Organization

Hugo Canham

April 2014 marked the 20th anniversary of the watershed year that ushered in the first all-inclusive multiparty elections that signified the beginning of the democratic era in South Africa. Bolstered by newly open markets and equity policies, those two decades saw the rapid growth of a black middle class with a significant corporate presence. In addition to having the largest economy in Africa, South Africa has one of the most racially, culturally, and linguistically diverse populations on the continent. This poses significant challenges and possibilities for the nation's organizations. To date, much of the related organizational research has focused on and documented the challenges of access, while the benefits of equity policies in the South African workplace remain understudied. For this reason, this chapter examines the positive attributes of psychological empowerment that have accrued from access and inclusion, drawing on interviews with managers employed by a major South African bank.

Background

Faced with extreme economic and social inequality at the dawn of democracy, South Africa enacted measures intended to create social stability and prevent anarchy (Ramphele, 2008). Moreover, to bolster the new democracy, a range of laws was promulgated to ensure access to employment opportunities and skills development for the millions of South Africans who had hitherto been excluded from meaningful formal employment (in particular, the Employment Equity Act, No. 55 [Republic of South Africa, 1998a] and the Skills Development Act, No. 97 [Republic of South Africa, 1998b]). Until the early 1990s, black South Africans (nearly 90 percent of the population) were denied access to such employment. Patriarchy intersected with racism and ensured that women, people with disabilities, and black people were barred from substantive employment opportunities (Ramphele, 2008). These three groups of people, termed "designated groups," were targeted for redress in light of past discrimination, inclusion, and training interventions.

In some settings, positive outcomes accrue from equitable access and inclusion (Crenshaw, 2000; Guinier, 2003). In the South African context, documentation of such outcomes is sparse. Since 2000, successive Commission for Employment Equity (CEE) reports have lamented the slow pace of change related to the representation goals and inclusion of designated groups. A number of researchers have documented the challenges and obstacles in the way of desired changes (Bezuidenhout et al., 2008; Habib & Bentley, 2008; Modisha, 2007; Nkomo, 2011). But little research has documented or analyzed the nature of positive change and the evolving workplace as it relates to the inclusion of traditionally marginalized groups. In fact, however, the South African workplace of today is a far cry from that of 1994 (Commission for Employment Equity, 2007, 2012; Modisha, 2007).

A Different Lens: Positive Organizational Scholarship

A Positive Organizational Scholarship (POS) lens can help create a vision of what equitable access and inclusion would look like in South Africa. Cameron (2005) says POS is primarily focused on the study of organizations' positive outcomes, attributes, and processes. The bias of this scholarship is toward the generative, life giving, and ennobling human states of being. POS can be applied to both the micro- and macro-organizational levels. (Dutton, Glynn, & Spreitzer, 2006). Following Luthens's (2002) and Cilliers & May (2010) insistence that POS should be theoretically informed, this chapter draws on the theory of psychological empowerment, exploring the degree to which access has provided empowerment and how much value it has for individuals and the organizations in which they are employed.

Following Conger and Kanungo (1988), Spreitzer (1995) defined psychological empowerment as "increased intrinsic task motivation manifested in a set of four cognitions reflecting on an individual's orientation to his or her work role: meaning, competence . . . , self-determination, and impact." *Meaning* is defined as the value of a work goal judged against the individual's own ideals and standards. *Competence* (or self-efficacy) is the person's belief that he or she has the capability to competently carry out a work task. *Self-determination* refers to the individual's sense of having choice in initiating and regulating behavior while carrying out that job. Finally, *impact* is the degree to which an individual can influence strategic, operating, or administrative outcomes at work (Spreitzer, 1995). Psychological empowerment is contextual, dynamic, and may fluctuate over time (Menon, 1999; Zimmerman, 1995). Psychological empowerment as espoused in empowerment literature (Spreitzer, 1995; Zimmerman, 1995; Rappaport, 1987) is an ideal that moves us closer to the realization of a more humane and equitable society as well as more fulfilled employees.

This orientation is adopted here to engage the data emanating from a study on empowerment in a single large bank in Johannesburg, South Africa. This research project sought to understand patterns of inclusion and psychological empowerment within the context of the existence of a policy framework of inclusion. While much of the data presented a negative picture of empowerment, there was significant recognition of the positive attributes that have come with access.

Access to Opportunity

The existence of a strong discourse against affirmative action (Nkomo, 2011) does not preclude a significant number of managers from recognizing the benefits of affirmative action and employment equity initiatives within the bank. Nearly all 30 black managers who participated in the study spoke highly of employment equity; some argued that they might not have had access to meaningful employment without the legislation.

> I would never get a chance if there was no employment equity; if affirmative action was not there, I would have not been given a chance.
>
> *(Participant 51, 88)*[1]

For Participant 16, employment equity has been important in making her voice heard:

> Well, I am very comfortable with being an employment equity candidate. If it's going to give me a voice to be heard and a face in the corporate industry, why not?
>
> *(Participant 16, 211)*

According to Participant 14:

> When you empower people it actually creates a level of trust and growth in people.
>
> *(Participant 14, 14)*

Access also provides social empowerment. Friedman (1992) views social empowerment as access to the basis of household reproduction, such as supportive living and work space, surplus time, knowledge and skills, social organization, social networks, instruments of work and livelihood, and financial resources. Within an organization, access should lead to inclusion such that one is involved in the distribution of scarce resources such as prestige and status, knowledge, identity, and membership. Modisha (2008) notes that there have been real leaps into black middle-class identities, access to power, and new ways of imagining radically different futures and identities where choice is a real possibility.

Psychological Empowerment: Competence and Meaning

How can we quantify psychological empowerment? Spreitzer (1995) identifies two measures (1) the extent to which one feels competent to discharge the job and (2) the level of meaning attained from the job. The overarching finding in relation to perceived competence is that most people gave positive self-reports, and there was generally a high level of confidence in participants' self-reported ability. For instance, Participant 52 asserted that he rates his competence at 100 percent. Others echoed this self-confidence:

> I do my work exceptionally well. I am from a background where you take accountability and responsibility. I don't like to be spoon-fed and to be watched.
>
> *(Participant 40, 55)*

> [My manager] rates me highly. He really values my input.
>
> *(Participant 40, 59)*

> If they leave it to me they can just walk away and they know it's done.
>
> *(Participant 4, 138)*

In addition to competence, Spreitzer (1995) identified the level of meaning one's job has as a critical attribute of psychological empowerment. Again, a number of participants reported elevated levels of meaning and enjoyment derived from the job:

> It is very important because it is something that I like and I have passion for.
>
> *(Participant 15, 33)*

> It is very important. It's actually challenging for me and in the past two years I have learnt a lot within the bank and grown.
>
> *(Participant 44, 37)*

Psychological Empowerment: Self-Determination and Impact

The additional dimensions of psychological empowerment espoused by Spreitzer (1995) are a sense of self-determination or autonomy in executing one's role and the sense of impact one feels he or she has within the organization.

> We are very flexible. I think most people in this department are in a position where they are trusted to do what they need to do . . . You can do more or less what you want.
>
> *(Participant 52, 33)*

There is no restriction in how you get it done.

(Participant 37, 89)

Participant 45 attributes her relative autonomy to a manager who encourages this self-determination as well as to her level of seniority, which comes with latitude for decision making.

It's quite high; my manager is quite hands off and is there when you need him, and that's one of the reasons I have job satisfaction.

(Participant 45, 123)

One of the negative discourses associated with employment equity is tokenism, in which designated groups are said to be undeserving of the roles to which they are appointed. An important check against this is the level of impact one believes he or she has within the organization. Participant 48 believes the team he heads has "exceptional" impact on the bank:

Oh, I tell you, [my team is] quite exceptional—because the output we produce has direct input into the capital structures of the bank.

(Participant 48, 38)

Participant 21 is a relatively young black female who heads a strategically important unit within the bank.

The work that we do has a profound influence on the bank.

(Participant 21, 95)

Conclusion

Despite the bad news about the pace of diversity in South Africa, when one turns the lens toward the individual, evidence reveals much that is positive about the changes employment equity legislation effected. Spreitzer (1995) and Zimmerman's (2000) concept of psychological empowerment can guide organizational leaders in ensuring substantial empowerment for all employees. The key learning for business leaders is that there are benefits to making a philosophical shift from seeing inclusion as externally imposed and encouraging tokenism to understanding it as an opportunity for promoting equal thriving. Employees thrive when they are empowered psychologically through self-determination, by contributing to the impact the organization makes, and when their sense of meaning and competence is bolstered. In a climate where high-performing black and female managers are well sought after in South Africa, leaders would do well to facilitate substantive psychological empowerment to promote recruitment and retention of valuable employees. Moreover, government officials with an interest in advancing equity should consider moving legislation from mere access toward measures for substantive empowerment (Goonesekere, 2007). This is the next frontier for altering the historical inequalities of the South African workplace. Beyond South Africa, countries with histories of marginalizing sections of their population, including Brazil, Malaysia, Canada, and the United States, will benefit from fostering practices of substantive empowerment. Significant scope remains for future research to identify examples of inclusion that also incorporate substantial empowerment efforts—both to identify best practices and to inspire those on the path to inclusion and substantial empowerment in their own organizations.

For Practitioners: Facilitating Inclusion

- Psychological empowerment can be facilitated by placing members of designated groups in roles with real power. For business leaders, this means that (1) support must be provided for these group members' success and (2) no structural rearrangements of roles should occur that could signal a lack of trust in one's capacity (e.g., appointing coleaders when a black person is appointed to a role but not when a white person is selected to lead).
- Human resources practitioners and leaders should regularly measure the psychological empowerment of employees (levels of meaning, competence, self-determination, and impact) and use this intelligence to make requisite supportive changes where possible.
- Research and monitoring agencies such as the Commission for Employment Equity should move beyond measuring access and toward engaging with notions of enhancing thriving.
- Business leaders and researchers should invest in studies to determine the relationship between substantial empowerment and retention of talented female, disabled, and black employees.
- Legislators in South Africa should craft legislation that bolsters substantial empowerment, thus moving from access to an expansive conceptualization of inclusion.

Note

1. Participants are named in the order in which their interviews were transcribed. Where direct quotations are presented, these are connoted with a line value (e.g., 88) as assigned by the ATLAS.ti program.

References

Bezuidenhout, A., Bischoff, C., Buhlungu, S., & Lewins, K. (2008). *Tracking progress on the implementation and impact of the employment equity act since its inception.* Sociology of Work Unit, Research Consortium, University of the Witwatersrand, Johannesburg, South Africa.

Cameron, K. (2005). Organizational effectiveness: Its demise and re-emergence through positive organizational scholarship. In M. A. Hitt & K. G. Smith (Eds.), *Handbook of management theory: The process of theory development.* London: Oxford University Press.

Cilliers, F., & May, M. (2010). The popularisation of positive psychology as a defence against behavioural complexity in research and organisations. *SA Journal of Industrial Psychology/SA Tydskrif vir Bedryfsielkunde, 36*(2), 1–10.

Conger, J. N., & Kanungo, R. N. (1988). The empowerment process: Integrating theory and practice. *Academy of Management Review, 13*(3), 471–482.

Crenshaw, K. (1999/2000). Playing race cards: Constructing a proactive defense of affirmative action. *National Black Law Journal, 16*(2), 196–214.

Commission for Employment Equity. (2007). *Commission for Employment Equity Annual Report 2006–2007.* Pretoria: South African Department of Labour.

Commission for Employment Equity. (2012). *12th Employment Equity Commission Report, 2011–2012.* Pretoria: South African Department of Labour.

Dutton, J. E., Glynn, M. A., & Spreitzer, G. (2006). Positive organizational scholarship. In J. Greenhaus & G. Callahan (Eds.), *Encyclopedia of career development.* Thousand Oaks, CA: Sage.

Friedman, J. (1992). *Empowerment: The politics of alternative development.* Oxford: Blackwell.

Goonesekere, S. W. E. (2007). *The concept of substantive equality and gender justice in South Asia.* Unpublished manuscript.

Guinier, L. (2003). Admissions rituals as political acts: Guardians at the gates of our democratic ideals. *Harvard Law Review, 117*, 113.

Habib, A., & Bentley, C. (Eds.). (2008). *Racial redress and citizenship in South Africa.* Human Science Research Council, Pretoria: HSRC Press.

Luthens, F. (2002). The need for and meaning of positive organizational behavior. *Journal of Organizational Behavior, 23*, 695–706.

Menon, S. T. (1999). Psychological empowerment: Definition, measurement and validation. *Canadian Journal of Behavioral Science, 31*(3), 161–4.

Modisha, G. (2007). A contradictory class location? The African corporate middle class and the burden of race in South Africa. *Transformation, 65*, 120–145.

Modisha, G. (2008). Affirmative action and cosmopolitan citizenship in South Africa. In A. Habib & C. Bentley (Eds.), *Racial redress and citizenship in South Africa* (pp. 153–178). Human Science Research Council, Pretoria: HSRC Press.

Nkomo, S. (2011). Moving from the letter of the law to the spirit of the law: The challenges of realising the intent of employment equity and affirmative action. *Transformation: Critical Perspectives on Southern Africa, 77*(1), 122–135.

Ramphele, M. (2008). *Laying ghosts to rest: Dilemmas of the transformation in South Africa.* Cape Town, South Africa: NB Publishers.

Rappaport, J. (1987). Terms of empowerment/exemplars of prevention: Toward a theory for community psychology. *American Journal of Community Psychology, 15*, 121–148.

Republic of South Africa. (1998a). Skills Development Act, No. 97. Pretoria, South Africa: Government Printer.

Republic of South Africa. (1998b). Employment Equity Act, No. 55. Government Gazette, No. 19370. Pretoria, South Africa: Government Printer.

Spreitzer, G. M. (1995). Psychological empowerment in the workplace. Dimensions, measurements and validation. *Academy of Management Journal, 39*(5), 1442–1465.

Zimmerman, M. A. (1995). Psychological empowerment. Issues and illustrations. *American Journal of Community of Psychology, 23*(5), 581–599.

Zimmerman, M. A. (2000). Empowerment theory: Psychological, organizational, and community levels of analysis. In J. Rappaport & E. Seidman (Eds.), *Handbook of community psychology* (pp. 43–63). New York. Kluwer Academic/Plenum Publishers.

21

ASSESSING ORGANIZATIONAL CULTURE AND ENGAGING FACULTY DIVERSITY IN HIGHER EDUCATION

Lamont A. Flowers, James L. Moore III,
Lawrence O. Flowers, and Tiffany A. Flowers

A college or university consists of academic units comprising faculty who interact with students, staff, and administrators as well as pursue the institution's primary functions, such as conducting research for economic and social purposes, educating its student population, and conferring degrees to students upon the successful completion of academic requirements. In light of complex interactions within higher education institutions, its faculty members work diligently to pursue important goals as well as manage the internal and external expectations of the institution and society (DiMaggio & Powell, 1983). Considering the impact of evolving social, economic, and technological conditions in higher education, Gappa, Austin, and Trice (2007) asserted, "To a significant extent, it is the faculty that enables higher education institutions to meet these numerous demands and fulfill their missions" (p. 4). Given this organizational reality, it is vital for higher education administrators to recognize the importance of applying comprehensive strategies to understand their institution's organizational culture (Maassen, 1996) and to develop an organization that fosters equity and inclusion among its faculty.

Diversity of the faculty reflects a value system for excellence in higher education. Stated differently, diversity "expands the teaching process, alters the application of an exclusionary curriculum, and incorporates competing mind-sets into the structure of knowledge" (Aguirre & Martinez, 2002, p. 55). Though not specifically referring to racial diversity among college faculty, Wooten (2006) acknowledged the benefits of racial and cultural diversity within an organization and acknowledged the importance of maximizing it. Her article explores the diversity landscape in organizations and describes the necessity of integrating diverse individuals and perspectives within the organization. Despite its importance, however, Wooten found that few companies had changed or modified their human resource policies and practices to leverage diversity in their organization. As a result, she advocated for a systemic approach to integrate and nurture divergent perspectives, ideas, and individuals in the workplace that utilizes the principles of Positive Organizational Scholarship as a means to foster inclusion and achieve organizational objectives.

One strategy for pursuing diversity-centered strategic goals in colleges and universities is to encourage productive and meaningful human-centered interactions among college faculty that foster productive work environments. Thoughtful considerations of these connections are critical to comprehending how and why individuals are productive at the workplace (Dutton & Heaphy, 2003). For example, higher education institutions may enhance the quality and effectiveness of the units within their organizations by advancing the capacity of their human resources to collaborate and solve problems through a coordinated system that equitably rewards productivity and celebrates an inclusive workforce. While pursuing these goals, units and departments on college campuses should evaluate their organizational cultures to ensure they value and acknowledge their faculty's contributions. In essence, assessing the organizational culture requires an understanding of the social and cultural dynamics of the units within the institution and the entire campus community with respect to social interactions, communication practices, and administrative functions that constitute the particular mission, objectives, and professional activities of each organizational unit. This goal resonates with Keeton and Mengistu (1992), who acknowledged, "an assessment of an organization's culture and the mapping of possible differences in perceptions of that culture are equally important and therefore should be included in any organizational development and change endeavor" (p. 206). Related to these concepts, Bond and Haynes (2014) also highlighted the importance of the interrelationship between diversity issues and organizational culture.

Several factors influence the current percentages of students and faculty who are "underrepresented" in higher education—that is, from racial groups historically discriminated against and whose representation on many college campuses is not proportional to their representation in America. Understanding the historical legacy of discriminatory admissions and hiring practices may provide insights for university administrators seeking to assess the organizational culture from a diversity and inclusion perspective. These insights may enable higher education administrators on college campuses to better comprehend the experiences of underrepresented faculty and strategically incorporate approaches to enhance the campus climate. Moreover, enabling underrepresented faculty members to pursue their teaching, research, and service activities in a supportive and professional environment increases the likelihood of positive faculty outcomes and institutional effectiveness.

Assessing Organizational Culture

Analyzing the organizational culture is critical to enabling innovation (Büschgens, Bausch, & Balkin, 2013). Using this information to better understand and support individuals from racially diverse groups to induce organizational effectiveness is equally important (Stevens, Plaut, & Sanchez-Burks, 2008). Organizational culture constitutes the individuals and structures that represent the organization and their complex interactions (Hatch, 1993), as well as the strategies and activities members within the organization pursue to reinforce the goals and structure of the organization (Masland, 1985). Among faculty in higher education, it is widely known that a common barrier to institutional effectiveness is the organizational culture in which the institution exists. Therefore, it is important for administrators to monitor the extent to which individuals in the organization have a common set of beliefs regarding the organization's vision, purpose, and status (Keeton & Mengistu, 1992). By extension, it is reasonable to suggest that within such organizational structures, the degree to which underrepresented faculty view the organizational culture as supportive and welcoming may affect their performance in the areas of teaching, research, and service. Accordingly, higher education administrators may need to implement an innovative set of management philosophies, policies, and practices that consider the benefits of utilizing underrepresented faculty to inform decision-making processes.

To be sure, colleges and universities are comprehensive organizations, and they comprise a diverse workforce. According to the National Center for Education Statistics (Kena et al., 2014), Asian/Pacific Islander, African American, and Hispanic faculty comprise approximately 9 percent, 6 percent, and 4 percent, respectively, of college and university faculty, and approximately 1 percent are American Indian/ Alaska Native. To better accommodate the organizational complexity and disparate missions within colleges and universities, publications from leading positive organizational scholars (Dutton & Heaphy, 2003; Wooten, 2006) suggest that colleges and universities can maximize their effectiveness by galvanizing the experiences and talents of their underrepresented faculty and enabling the development of meaningful interactions among all faculty. By implementing inclusive processes, programs, and policies that allow underrepresented faculty to influence the institution's strategic objectives, colleges and universities are in the best position to engage the unique perspectives of underrepresented faculty to inform institutional decision-making. To advance these objectives, higher education administrators may benefit from understanding the impact of organizational culture on the experiences and outcomes of underrepresented faculty on college campuses.

Ouchi and Wilkins (1985), in an extensive review describing the historical and contemporary study of organizational culture, noted that the field includes scholars who view it as an extension of organizational elements and processes that influence organizational outcomes. These conceptualizations are equally valid in particular contexts, but we believe that, in institutions of higher education, organizational culture can be best understood by examining the prevailing organizational sentiments, activities, and products. Consistent with this belief, we subscribe to an article by Tierney (1988) regarding organizational culture and higher education in which he noted, "An organization's culture is reflected in what is done, how it is done, and who is involved in doing it. It concerns decisions, actions, and communication both on an instrumental and a symbolic level" (p. 3). Tierney also acknowledged the importance of postsecondary institutions assessing their organizational culture. Furthermore, extant research on organizational culture has greater implications for higher education administrators attempting to change or enhance the social and political climate to promote diversity. Viewed collectively, research suggests that the organizational culture of colleges and universities may influence their ability to achieve institutional outcomes.

Engaging Faculty Diversity in Higher Education

Colleges and universities tend to reflect the aspirations, views, and intentions of society (DiMaggio & Powell, 1983). These beliefs and attitudes allow colleges and universities to remain relatively unchanged and free from public interference and societal intervention. As a result, many colleges and universities are able to influence—and preserve—their internal environment (Birnbaum, 1988), which may help to explain why the composition of faculty at these institutions do not reflect the racial demographics of America. Notwithstanding, engaging faculty diversity in higher education requires administrators to understand the racial composition of their faculty as well as the experiences of its underrepresented faculty. Moreover, higher education administrators should recognize the potential of the underrepresented faculty within their span of leadership to help the organization achieve its mission.

Assessing and monitoring the organizational culture of the institution is one way for higher education administrators to examine issues having an impact on underrepresented faculty. In addition, they should explore strategies that enable underrepresented faculty to serve in leadership positions on campus. Moreover, administrators need to understand the role of Positive Organizational Scholarship in facilitating the development of measurable and comprehensive plans that actively engage and support underrepresented faculty. Finally, higher education administrators should consider employing human-centered approaches (Dutton & Heaphy, 2003) to utilize underrepresented faculty to achieve the institution's evolving objectives, while also increasing the ability of underrepresented faculty to support student development, produce research, pursue leadership experiences, and engage in collaborative scholarly activities.

For Practitioners: Assessing Organizational Culture and Engaging Faculty Diversity in Higher Education

Ten Tips for Assessing Organizational Culture

1. Utilize surveys to identify and learn about the organizational culture at the institution.
2. Collect quantitative and qualitative data on the dispositions and experiences of underrepresented faculty on campus.

3. Conduct a comprehensive review of campus hiring practices of faculty, staff, and administrators from historically underrepresented groups on campus.
4. Conduct follow-up surveys and exit interviews with underrepresented faculty and staff that left the institution in the past 10 years.
5. Review and evaluate marketing and media materials to ensure that they reflect the accomplishments of underrepresented faculty.
6. Examine the history of the institution in terms of its treatment of underrepresented student groups on campus as it relates to student enrollment and students' experiences on campus.
7. Meet with parents of current and former underrepresented students to assess their perceptions of their child's educational and social experiences on campus.
8. Study the campus climate at the institution to identify potential and current issues that may affect underrepresented faculty.
9. Review and monitor the workload of underrepresented faculty to ensure fairness with respect to expectations and evaluation criteria.
10. Produce an annual report highlighting the total number of non-tenure track faculty, tenure-track faculty, tenured faculty, and administrators from underrepresented groups.

Ten Tips for Engaging Faculty Diversity

1. Conduct studies of faculty pay equity by race and gender.
2. Examine faculty promotion and merit pay outcomes by race and gender.
3. Ensure diverse faculty representation among all of the academic departments.
4. Ensure that university committees include underrepresented faculty.
5. In all policy-related and practical matters affecting faculty, understand that racial insensitivity may permeate the higher education environment and have a negative impact on the experiences of underrepresented faculty.
6. Conduct job satisfaction studies among underrepresented faculty on campus.
7. Develop future faculty programs designed to encourage underrepresented doctoral students to pursue faculty careers.
8. Evaluate higher education administrators with regard to hiring, retaining, and promoting underrepresented faculty.
9. Highlight and profile the work of underrepresented faculty through alumni magazines, Web-based information, and social media.
10. Establish and adequately fund a committee to enhance the recruitment and retention of underrepresented faculty.

References

Aguirre, A., Jr., & Martinez, R. (2002). Leadership practices and diversity in higher education: Transitional and transformational frameworks. *Journal of Leadership Studies, 8*(3), 53–62.

Birnbaum, R. (1988). *How colleges work: The cybernetics of academic organization and leadership.* San Francisco, CA: Jossey-Bass.

Bond, M. A., & Haynes, M. C. (2014). Workplace diversity: A social–ecological framework and policy implications. *Social Issues and Policy Review, 8,* 167–201.

Büschgens, T., Bausch, A., & Balkin, D. B. (2013). Organizational culture and innovation: A meta-analytic review. *Journal of Product Innovation Management, 30,* 763–781.

DiMaggio, P. J., & Powell, W. W. (1983). The iron cage revisited: Institutional isomorphism and collective rationality in organizational fields. *American Sociological Review, 48,* 147–160.

Dutton, J. E., & Heaphy, E. D. (2003). The power of high-quality connections. In Cameron, K. S., Dutton, J. E. & Quinn, R. E. (Eds.), *Positive organizational scholarship: Foundations of a new discipline* (pp. 263–278). San Francisco, CA: Berrett-Koehler.

Gappa, J. M., Austin, A. E., & Trice, A. G. (2007). *Rethinking faculty work: Higher education's strategic imperative.* San Francisco, CA: Jossey-Bass.

Hatch, M. J. (1993). The dynamics of organizational culture. *Academy of Management Review, 18,* 657–693.

Keeton, K. B., & Mengistu, B. (1992). The perception of organizational culture by management level: Implications for training and development. *Public Productivity & Management Review, 16,* 205–213.

Kena, G., Aud, S., Johnson, F., Wang, X., Zhang, J., Rathbun, A., . . . Kristapovich, P. (2014). *The Condition of Education 2014* (NCES 2014–083). Washington, DC: U.S. Department of Education, National Center for Education Statistics.

Maassen, P. A. M. (1996). The concept of culture and higher education. *Tertiary Education and Management, 1,* 153–159.

Masland, A. T. (1985). Organizational culture in the study of higher education. *Review of Higher Education, 8,* 157–168.

Ouchi, W. G., & Wilkins, A. L. (1985). Organizational culture. *Annual Review of Sociology, 11,* 457–483.

Stevens, F. G., Plaut, V. C., & Sanchez-Burks, J. (2008). Unlocking the benefits of diversity: All-inclusive multiculturalism and positive organizational change. *Journal of Applied Behavioral Science, 44,* 116–133.

Tierney, W. (1988). Organizational culture in higher education: Defining the essentials. *Journal of Higher Education, 59,* 2–21.

Wooten, L. P. (2006). Charting a change course for effective diversity management. *Human Factor, 1*(2), 46–53.

22

LEARNING TOGETHER

A Positive Approach to Diversity and Inclusion Education

Vicki J. Rosenberg

In 2013, U.S. foundations gave over $50 billion in grants to support charitable efforts to alleviate poverty and improve people's lives. By funding a variety of activities and causes that included research, health, education, and the arts, foundations serve as a "bellwether" for society; the effectiveness of their support can make or break nonprofit organizations and the well-being of the communities they serve (Capek & Mead, 2006).

Despite a demonstrated commitment to those communities, the philanthropic sector has been slow to employ Diversity and Inclusion practices that would improve organizational effectiveness. While a select group of funders has embraced Diversity and Inclusion, for most foundations these issues have been seen as important in principle, but not critical in practice (Bearman et al., 2010).

In 2007, the Council of Michigan Foundations (CMF) launched an initiative designed to "catalyze positive social change" by promoting Diversity and Inclusion as a means to increase the effectiveness of organized philanthropy in the state. As part of this effort, CMF designed and tested a new curriculum for Diversity and Inclusion education based on Appreciative Inquiry practices.

In this chapter, I describe our experience of developing and implementing this pilot program and reveal what we learned from it that may have implications for Positive Organizational Scholarship theory and research.

An Appreciative Inquiry Approach

Looking at the diversity training programs available to CMF's members in 2010, we noted many "antiracism" curricula focused on eradicating negative behaviors. Reasoning that a more effective method would be one that appealed to and built on foundations' intent to create positive social change, we invited two consultants to develop a new program using an Appreciative Inquiry process.

Appreciative Inquiry is defined as "change practices based on the assumption that organizations have a positive core that, if revealed and tapped, unleashes positive energy and positive improvement" (Cameron et al., 2003). As such, it provided a positive base for an educational program that promoted the organizational development benefits of Diversity and Inclusion.

Research has shown that the most inclusive organizations adopt a "learning and integration" perspective that values people's diverse backgrounds as a source of insight that can be used to improve organizational performance (Ely & Thomas, 1996), and that diversity education focused on historically marginalized groups can have the unintended effect of perpetuating negative stereotypes (Fiol et al., 2009). People in a learning and integration context described the value of "learning how not to be afraid of differences, learning about conflict, and learning to be willing to go toward it and trying to talk about hard things" (Ely & Thomas, 1996).

In fall 2010, CMF enrolled its first cohort in a pilot program that provided a safe place for foundations to "talk about hard things" with each other in a deep-engagement peer-learning curriculum.

Improving Intercultural Competency

A year-long series of seminars conducted by expert facilitators took CEO-led teams from member organizations through an intensive immersion in "intercultural competency," a concept pioneered by communications studies professor Milton Bennett (Bennett, 2004). Bennett's "Intercultural Development Continuum" (Figure 22.1) plots five stages from "denial" to "adaptation" that reflect an increasingly complex understanding of cultural differences. Each stage is linked to a specific set of behaviors displayed when people interact with different demographic groups.

In preparation for the first session, we administered the Intercultural Development Inventory (IDI) to assess participants' current locations on the continuum, as individuals and as groups. In addition, we assessed each foundation's entire employee population to achieve an organizational measurement. Since the IDI measures both "perceived" and "developmental" orientations, we were able to use Appreciative Inquiry techniques to create a learning culture that accommodated participants at their unique starting points and move them closer to their desired states. Program facilitators conducted coaching sessions with participants to help them understand their IDI results and develop and successfully complete action learning plans for further developing intercultural competency.

Day-long seminars brought participating teams from family, community, and private foundations across the state together to complete and discuss developmental exercises and report on their action learning projects. In the second seminar, each team completed an Appreciative Inquiry chart documented by a graphic recorder for sharing with others within their organizations (Figure 22.2).

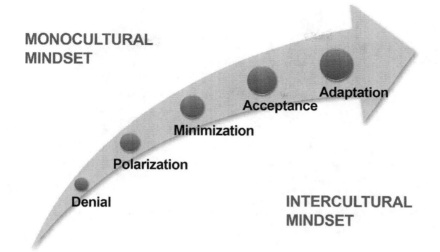

MONOCULTURAL MINDSET

Adaptation

Acceptance

Minimization

Polarization

Denial

INTERCULTURAL MINDSET

FIGURE 22.1 The Intercultural Development Continuum

Source: Mitchell R. Hammer, PhD.

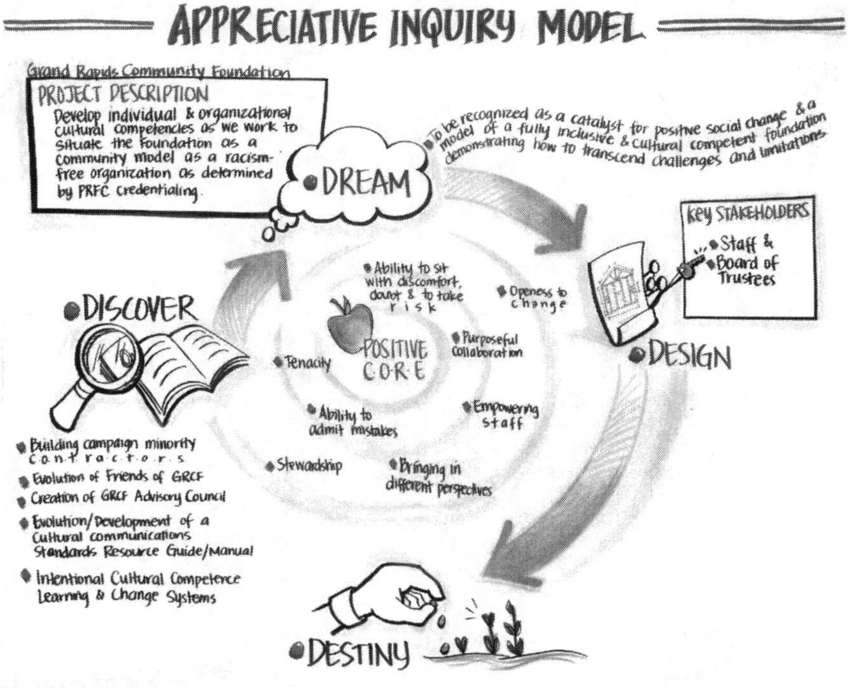

= APPRECIATIVE INQUIRY MODEL =

Grand Rapids Community Foundation

PROJECT DESCRIPTION
Develop individual & organizational cultural competencies as we work to situate the Foundation as a community model as a racism-free organization as determined by PRFC credentialing.

•DREAM

To be recognized as a catalyst for positive social change & a model of a fully inclusive & cultural competent foundation demonstrating how to transcend challenges and limitations

KEY STAKEHOLDERS
• Staff & Board of Trustees

•DISCOVER

• Ability to sit with discomfort, doubt & to take risk
• Openness to change
• Purposeful collaboration
• Tenacity
POSITIVE CORE
• Empowering staff
• Ability to admit mistakes
• Stewardship
• Bringing in different perspectives

•DESIGN

• Building campaign minority contractors
• Evolution of Friends of GRCF
• Creation of GRCF Advisory Council
• Evolution/Development of a Cultural communications Standards Resource Guide/Manual
• Intentional Cultural Competence Learning & Change Systems

•DESTINY

FIGURE 22.2 An Appreciative Inquiry chart

Source: Grand Rapids Community Foundation. Used with permission.

Learning from the Pilot

As part of the evaluation process, CMF commissioned a yearly report from the Community Research Center at the Johnson Center for Philanthropy and Non-profit Leadership at Grand Valley State University. The research, which pulled data from member surveys and interviews with program participants, found overwhelming support and acclaim for the learning pilot's curriculum and developmental framework (Johnson Center for Philanthropy, 2013).

Through postprogram IDI testing, we were able to document that every organization that participated in the pilot jumped a full level in the five-stage intercultural development scale, most of them moving from "minimization" to "acceptance."

We also conducted in-depth case studies with three member participants (Rosenberg, 2013) to learn more about the personal and organizational effects of the program. Many people we interviewed spoke about its transformative effect on their personal lives as well as their organizations' culture and grant-making practices.

Through the case studies, we found anecdotal evidence supporting the program's positive approach to Diversity and Inclusion. Participants noted that Appreciative Inquiry and the developmental model offered by the IDI assessment provided a common method and language for discussing cultural differences. For example, one community foundation vice president said that, while earlier anti-racism training his organization had been through "sent some people backwards into a place of shame and guilt for being white—really frozen in their ability to say anything," CMF's peer-learning program gave the foundation's management and staff "the understanding and vocabulary to talk about cultural differences in a nonthreatening way" (Rosenberg, 2013).

Other anecdotal evidence of the program's effectiveness:

- Eight of the 10 participating organizations sent multiple teams to the program over its four-year implementation phase, even after the registration costs doubled.
- Several of the organizations went through CEO changes during the four years of the program, and in each case, continued to participate, citing the positive benefits of the program as the compelling factor in the decision to remain.
- Many of the participating organizations hired program faculty to lead their boards of trustees through the IDI and some of the program exercises.

We have seen significant "ripple effects" from the program on the work of the participating foundations, with several developing capacity-building programs for grantees that use the same model. One foundation went on to provide a grant to the state of Michigan to engage cabinet members and members of the governor's executive office in IDI testing and customized training built on the Appreciative Inquiry approach.

Although we originally anticipated that the pilot program would attract different participants from our membership each year, this did not prove to be the case. Instead, the cohort of leading-edge foundations that began the program continued to send teams each year. While this had the happy outcome of developing a group of very advanced practitioners in Michigan, CMF was not meeting its goal of increasing the number of member organizations engaged in Diversity and Inclusion (Rosenberg, 2014).

Responses from member organizations indicating that "Diversity and Inclusion" is simply not an issue for their constituents leads us to question whether the language itself has unintended connotations. "Diversity" may be weighted with connections to racial discrimination and implications of negative behaviors that must be "fixed" before an organization can enjoy its benefits.

Building on findings that diversity leads to better organizational performance or individual outcomes only "when accompanied by an integration-and-learning perspective about diversity and the relevance of diversity to the organization's work" (Ramarajan & Thomas, 2011), CMF is testing out new language that puts a positive emphasis on the value of "differences" that go beyond racial and ethnic identities to encompass differences in economic status, thinking style, personality traits, and other factors. Recent scholarship suggests that combining a "focus on appreciation of different others with a more explicit focus on the value of diversity as a work group characteristic" may actually improve how well diverse groups work together (Van Knippenberg et al., 2007).

Going forward, CMF will be framing its learning service offerings as programs designed to help its members "leverage the power of differences." As part of this effort, CMF is introducing a new discussion guide and self-assessment tool that members will be able to use to evaluate their organization's current level of understanding and commitment to leveraging the power of differences and find learning services offerings that can help them move forward (Rosenberg, 2014).

Conclusion

Conceptually, "leveraging the power of differences" effectively blends two areas of study—Diversity and Inclusion and Positive Organizational Scholarship. CMF drew from both in its Appreciative Inquiry approach to designing and implementing a peer learning–based program for its members. This Diversity and Inclusion program yielded significant improvements in organizational intercultural competency that had positive effects on how the participant organizations functioned, which in turn had cascading effects on their grantees, partners, and colleagues. CMF discovered the importance of using positive framing and language when trying to engage its membership in learning about Diversity and Inclusion. Appreciative inquiry and the Intercultural Development Inventory worked well together in the nonprofit environment to create a supportive, aspirational learning culture and community. Further study of this combined approach, viewed through the dual lens of Diversity and Inclusion and Positive Organizational Scholarship, could examine its effectiveness in other areas such as business and education.

For Practitioners: Using Appreciative Inquiry to Guide Cultural Change

The PALN program used the Appreciative Inquiry Model (Discover, Dream, Design, and Deliver) to help teams discover their organization's "positive core" and define goals and action plans for achieving organizational culture change.

In preparation for engaging in a 90-minute Appreciative Inquiry exercise, participants learned about intercultural competency, organizational culture, and systems change.

Using a customized, artist-developed template, teams spent 90 minutes discussing and reaching consensus on each stage of the Appreciative Inquiry journey:

- **Discover** what is best about the organization and its culture.
- **Dream** about "what could be," using the elements of systems change.
- **Design** an action plan for achieving the dream.
- **Deliver** on that plan by taking action.

The Council of Michigan Foundations (CMF) hired a graphic recorder to create a customized illustration of each team's action plan (Figure 22.2). Many participants posted these graphics in their offices, presented them to their boards of trustees, and used them in staff sessions.

In subsequent seminars, CMF provided multiple supports to each team to achieve its "dream state," including:

- Monthly coaching calls to encourage teams to continue working and help them overcome obstacles
- Time for the team to work during each seminar, with faculty support and technical assistance
- Peer sharing at each seminar to learn about others' approaches and what was and was not working
- Team presentations during the final seminar, followed by a celebration.

Research conducted three years after the program began indicates that real progress is being made toward achieving the positive cultural change the PALN teams defined through the Appreciative Inquiry process.

References

Bearman, J., Ramos, H. A. J., & Pond, A.-S. (2010). Moving diversity up the agenda: Lessons and next steps from the diversity in philanthropy project. *Foundation Review, 2*(2), 85–99.

Bennett, M. (2004). Becoming interculturally competent. In J. Wurzel (Ed.), *Toward multiculturalism: A reader in multicultural education* (2nd ed., pp. 62–77). Newton, MA: Intercultural Resource Corporation.

Cameron, K. S., Dutton, J. E., & Quinn, R. E. (2003). *Positive organizational scholarship* (pp. 3–13) San Francisco, CA: Berrett-Koehler.

Capek, M.E.S., & Mead, M. (2006). Effective philanthropy: Organizational success through deep diversity and gender equality. Cambridge, MA: Massachusetts Institute of Technology (vs MIT) Press.

Fiol, C. M., O'Connor, E. J., & Pratt, M. G. (2009). *Managing intractable identity conflicts* (pp. 132–155). Briarcliff, NY: Academy of Management.

Johnson Center for Philanthropy. (2013). *Transforming philanthropy through diversity and inclusion, 2012 evaluation report.* Community Research Institute.

Rarmarajan, L., & Thomas, D. (2011). A positive approach to studying diversity in organizations. In G. M. Spreitzer & K. S. Cameron (Eds.), *The Oxford handbook of positive organizational scholarship* (pp. 552–565). Oxford: Oxford University Press.

Rosenberg, V. (Ed.). (2013). *Learning together: The peer action learning network for diversity and inclusion, stories of change.* Grand Haven, MI: Council of Michigan Foundations.

Rosenberg, V. (Ed.). (2014). *Leveraging differences: A pilot program in learning at the Council of Michigan Foundations.* Grand Haven, MI: Council of Michigan Foundations.

Thomas, D. A., & Ely, J. E. (1996, September/October). Making differences matter: A new paradigm for managing diversity. *Harvard Business Review* 74(5), 79–90. Cambridge, MA:

Van Knippenberg, D., Hasiam, S. A., & Platow, M. J. (2007). Unity through diversity: Value-in-diversity beliefs, work group diversity, and group identification. *ERIM Report Series Research in Management.* Rotterdam, The Netherlands: Erasmus Research Institute of Management RSM Erasmus University/Erasmus School of Economics Erasmus Universiteit Rotterdam.

23

ORGANIZATIONAL SUPPORT AND EMPOWERMENT OF DIVERSITY IN WORK–LIFE IDENTITIES

Ellen Ernst Kossek

Prologue: Three Vignettes of Work–Life Diversity

The Integrator. "My son has some learning issues. I spend time taking him to the occupational . . . and the group therapist; and I spend a lot more time overseeing him in a way that I didn't have to do with my older kids when they were nine . . . Right now that's probably the main thing that I don't have any control over that makes my work-life balance more difficult because it adds more things to my day . . . I have too many things that I need to deal with throughout the day . . . you know, e-mails that come in. Some of them are school-related and some of them are work-related and they all come to my work account so . . . I'm reading them and registering things . . . so I'm pretty integrated right now. I would say other years when I have had less . . . to handle, I tended to be more separated. I would want to go home, not think about work and just focus on home, for . . . the evening and . . . That's less and less possible because even once I go home I still check the [smart phone]. I still usually have something to read that somebody's given me as I'm walking out the door. I may not get all the way through it, but at least I get started on it in the evening and then finish it up the next morning when I'm on the exercise bike."

—"Mary," a director at a financial services firm with a child with special learning needs[1]

The Separator. "My manager would frequently call me at home asking questions on things that could have waited till the morning. These were not urgent matters and I felt that he was demanding too much of my time. I spend 10 hours to 11 hours at the plant, try to sleep seven hours a night, spend an hour getting ready, and an hour driving. I try to make my personal time free from nonessential work demands."

—*"Sam," an unmarried human resources manager*
who supports a 24–7 plant

The Cycler. "I normally travel . . . two weeks out of the month . . . and (if) I'm in a hotel room, I don't mind working until ten o'clock at night . . . because I can get caught up. And then on the weeks I'm back . . . I want to be home . . . and I want to be with [my children] and so I kind of just give myself some boundaries about that."

—*"Sandy," a director in a health care company with two children*

Integrating work and family throughout the day; *separating* work and private life as much as possible; or *cycling* with wildly divergent work and home boundary patterns from week to week. Employees' work-life demands and boundary management styles—the ways in which individuals synthesize work and nonwork identities are diverse, and so are the expectations for how organizations can best support individuals to enable greater control over and engagement in both work and personal life (Kossek & Lautsch, 2008, 2012). Unfortunately, research has shown that work–life policies generally have not had a major impact in ways that support diversity in work–life identities. Why does a gap persist between the rhetoric of work-life research and the implementation of positive work–life programs into practice (Kossek, Baltes, & Mathews, 2011)? Why have positive gains for employees and employers not been fully realized given all the available work–life programs (Kossek, 2005)? My research suggests that organizational work–life programs would be more effective if they were implemented as positive workplace initiatives designed to support diversity in work–life inclusion. By work–life inclusion, I mean having a workplace culture and structure (e.g., HR policies and practices) that support and empower employees to synthesize personal identities (e.g., wife, mother, daughter, friend) with work demands in ways that enable them to fully contribute to and participate in organizational life.

In the remainder of this chapter, I will: (1) identify issues that must be addressed to more effectively implement work-life initiatives by incorporating a diversity perspective on work–life identities into positive organizing; (2) describe indicators of a work–life inclusive organization, and 3) discuss positive organizational strategies to support and empower employees with diverse work–life identities.

Incorporating a Diversity Perspective into Work–Life Initiatives

Evidence is growing that most employees working today, regardless of personal background, value positive organizational support to help synthesize work–life identities. With the rise of 24–7 connectivity, many people are working longer due to increased life expectancy, and the rise of women and dual career families in the workforce, most managers and scholars would agree that there is a growing need for employers to improve effectiveness of organizational support of positive work–life programs for their work force. National studies show that employees of all backgrounds—single and married; old and young; those who care for elders, children, both (sandwiched) or neither; heterosexuals and lesbian, gay, bisexual, transgender, and queer (LGBTQ); active in the community or not—value employer support of work–life demands. Survey data from the National Study of the Changing Workforce (Galinsky, Aumann, & Bond, 2009) highlights transforming workforce trends that suggest that for the first time in the United States, women and men (age 29 and under) equally value challenging jobs. Further, around the globe, men and women of all generations increasingly report growing levels of work–life conflict regardless of national culture or career stage (Greenhaus & Kossek, 2014). Yet there is a workforce workplace mismatch: Employers have lagged in viewing diversity in work–life identities as an inclusion challenge.

Toward a Work–Life Inclusive Organization

A work–life inclusive organization has four cultural attributes (Ryan and Kossek, 2008): (1) it values individual and intergroup differences in the primacy of work and other life roles; (2) it supports variation in domestic background and blending of work and nonwork roles; (3) it does not view differing nonwork or caregiving identities as barriers to contributing fully to work and nonwork roles and fulfilling one's potential at work; and (4) it promotes organizational involvement of all employees regardless of their nonwork demands and preferences. Thus, a work–life inclusive organization takes a broad perspective on what a work–life issue is, to include the nonwork needs of all employees—not just individuals with salient work–life needs (e.g., a baby or an elderly parent). It moves away from a one-size-fits-all approach to work–life support and offers a menu of options. It sees employees as "whole people" and values positive involvement in both work and personal life; being successful in personal life balance is not seen as a detriment to success at work. A work–life inclusive organization strives to enable all workers to fully participate contribute to the organization's effectiveness to the maximum of their potential.

Organizational Strategies for Work–Life Inclusion: Support and Control

Work–life initiatives are more likely to promote a culture of inclusion if they are implemented in ways that increase employee perceptions of positive control and social support to reveal diversity in work–life identities without stigmatization. Organizational strategies for increasing work–life inclusion that take two forms which are not necessarily mutually exclusive: (1) initiatives that increase *work–life control* and (2) those that increase *positive social support* for a wide diversity of employee backgrounds that impact the work–home boundary. These strategies are successful to the extent to which they increase employee perceptions that they have the organizational support to be able carry out their job demands in ways that do not harm and even enrich personal and family well-being.

When employees have work–life control, they perceive that they are empowered through job resources to have control over where, when, or how work is done in ways that are compatible with personal lives (Kossek, Lautsch & Eaton, 2006). This can be achieved through either (1) autonomy in job design or (2) formal or informal work–life flexibility. An example of autonomous job design is where job characteristics allow for a lot of independence and daily choice to decide the timing and location of work. Formal flexibility refers to organizational policies such as telework or flextime where an employee has some predictable control to restructure and customize work arrangements. Informal flexibility may come from the ability to use informal practices such as having the ability to decide to telecommute at the last minute instead of getting snarled in a messy commute during a snow day.

It is important to note that work–life control may look different for different types of jobs or employee backgrounds. A professional may want to have a "no e-mail" vacation to get away from electronic communication and recover. A person working in a plant may want the ability to trade shifts without penalty to be able to take a child to the doctor at the last minute. The goal is to provide some schedule control for all jobs in whatever form is possible given job demands.

Social support refers to employees' feeling they are supported by peers, managers, or coworkers to live their lives in ways that fit their most salient personal identities (e.g., wife, mother, leader, LGBTQ) without having to sacrifice one for the other. Social support involves access to social resources from peers or managers that affirm an individual's ability to enact nonwork identities in relation to their professional persona without feeling stigmatized. Sometimes it can involve *not pointing out* that someone is working in different ways from the majority. For example, a manager or coworker *doesn't* make remarks about a lack of face time should a colleague leave the office "early" to pick up a child and decide to work at home at night to finish up the day. Or a supervisor doesn't judge an individual's performance by how much he or she is seen sitting at a desk in the office (known as "presenteeism") rather than the results achieved. The research I conducted as part of a study called the Work Family Health Network referred to this kind of unsupportive talk that focuses on diversity in face time over results "sludge."

In sum, organizations need to develop flexible processes and norms regarding the social construction of "ideal workers" that address variation in employee needs for support and abilities to control work–life demands across a wide range of personal life and job contexts. By "ideal workers" (cf. Williams, 2000), I mean that many organizations have preferred norms and career and human resource systems for how to enact work and nonwork roles, often in standardized ways. My research shows it is the customization of work–life interventions that allows capture of varying needs for social support or job and family/personal life control for many different types of workers who are nested in diverse nonwork and employment contexts (Kossek, Hammer, Kelly, & Moen, 2014). By customization, I mean that the principles of control and support are the same in terms of change targets but how they are designed must be tailored to organizational context and employee job and demographic groups and at different levels of analysis. Organizations need evidence-based tools such as validated leader behavior support (Hammer, Kossek, Bodner, Anger, & Zimmerman, 2011) and boundary management training (Kossek, Ruderman, Braddy, & Hannum, 2012) to implement change in ways that address the work–life implementation gaps across multiple levels (individual, leader and team, organizational).

Confronting the Barriers to Work–Life Initiatives

What's keeping work–life initiatives from moving from the margins to the mainstream of organizational life (Kossek, Lewis, & Hammer, 2010)? Key obstacles relate to an implementation gap in how they are viewed, designed, and put into practice. Work–life policies aren't viewed as mainstreamed resources for positive organizing in an increasingly diverse and volatile world. What can be done?

First, we must first close the gap to address how most work–life initiatives are disconnected from organizational goals related to business strategy and performance—or worse yet, seen as the economic scapegoat. An illustration is Yahoo! executive Marissa Mayer's recent banning of telework, viewing work–life flexibility as the poster child for productivity problems. Instead, a positive perspective on organizing would view flexibility as a lever for improving employee engagement and performance (Kossek, 2013).

Second, we must stop viewing work–life initiatives as reactive "special" programs to accommodate work–family conflict from "specific" problems (e.g., childbirth recovery; disability after a heart attack; assisting a declining elderly parent; child-rearing), but rather a broad diversity initiative to support a plethora of work–life identities. We must recognize that employees' work–life identities are a mainstreamed issue: Individuals prefer and need to manage work–life boundaries over the life course, whether separator, integrator, cycler, or any other type of work–life balance. How one works is less important than the ability to provide sustained results. Why not refocus work–life initiatives on providing long-term work force sustainability that supports *all* workers to be productive on and off the job over the course of their working lives (Kossek, Valcour, & Lirio, 2014)?

Third, let's tackle the problem that work–life policies generally do not address the "big" work-life issues today such as the increasing "precariousness" of the workplace (Kalleberg, 2009), evident in loosening ties and a weakening social contract of mutual caring between employees and employers. Why not refocus work–life initiatives to provide stability, predictability, and a better buffer for employees from "life spillovers" (Ragins, Lyness, Williams, & Winkel, 2014)? For example, combating the cascading effects of the mortgage and financial crisis (Ragins et al.,

2014) or the transferring of market risk from unpredictable labor demand, costs, and schedules onto workers (Lambert, 2008).

Fourth, let's redesign initiatives to solve the problem that many do not address—unequal access and distribution of work–life programs across the workforce. We need to address the problem of "organizational stratification" (Waxman & Lambert, 2005); that is, the persistent silos in employee opportunities to use work–life policies. If you are lucky enough to have a supportive supervisor, you likely have greater access to work–life supports. But if you are assigned a supervisor who does not value work–life inclusion, you are out of luck. What about addressing unequal access in job type, which is often correlated with socioeconomic class, gender, and ethnicity? Highly educated professionals are more likely to be in jobs designed with greater autonomy or that regularly use computers, which facilitates telecommuting. These individuals, right from the starting gate, have greater access to work–life resources and control over where, when and how they work than employees with contrasting job characteristics. My research suggests that a way to begin to address the gaps of unequal access is to learn from the disciplinary approach taken in occupational health psychology and safety, which strives to protect workers from occupational risk exposures on the job. Working as a founding investigator on the National Work, Family and Health Network, I have found that a helpful strategy to increase the effectiveness of work–life initiatives is to implement them as part of an entire worksite-based change effort that is integrated into the work environment to *prevent* work–family conflict from occurring by focusing on how jobs are designed and managed (Kossek, Hammer, Kelly & Moen, 2014).

Fifth, let's close the career usability gap (Eaton, 2003) between the availability of policies and their actual use to countervail stigma or backlash. Most work–life flexibility policies are discretionary, allowing employees to request to telework, work part-time, use flextime, or take leaves of absence for personal and family needs (Kossek, 2005; Kossek & Thompson, 2015). But when these options are actually used, employees can sometimes face negative repercussions related to such things as pay, promotion, and job loss (Williams & Segal, 2003). Career-oriented employees underuse policies that appear on the corporate books for fear of not looking like a dedicated professional and experiencing backlash.

Let's put it out in the open that using work–life policies has potential risk because it visibly challenges corporate social structures reifying work as the primary role identity. Research shows that if managers think you are using flexibility for personal and not performance reasons, you are more likely to be seen negatively by them (Leslie, Manchester, Park, & Mehng, 2012). Why not educate managers on the research showing that all employees increasingly "want a life," and that there is growing diversity in work–life needs to reduce fear of using work–life supports? Why not normalize the use of work–life policies by everyone? It starts with educating others on what a work–life inclusive organization looks like.

Future research and practice can build on existing management development and organizational interventions designed based on the Positive Organizational

Scholarship principles to evaluate their effectiveness in creating an inclusive culture. Studies might build on research with the National Work Family Health Network that shows that training leaders to increase family social supportive behaviors (e.g., emotional and instrumental support, role modeling and creative problem-solving) (Kossek & Hammer, 2008) not only increases employee perceptions that their organizations are seen as supportive (Kossek et al., 2011), but also results in lower work–family conflict, lower turnover, and higher satisfaction (Kossek & Hammer, 2008). Similarly, research might build on whether training employees and teams on how to increase boundary control to better align their work–life identities with their jobs could lead to a more inclusive workplace (Kossek et al., 2012).

For Practitioners: Are You Work–Life Inclusive?

- What is your own work–life boundary management style, and has it been supported effectively by your manager or organization?
- Do you know which employees are Integrators, Separators, and Cyclers and the different ways leaders might adjust styles to support each boundary style?
- How does diversity in work–life identities and preferences for boundary management styles affect your work group's effectiveness in meeting objectives?
- What are examples of current cultural assumptions in your organization about "ideal workers" that are barriers to work–life inclusion of different types of workers?
- What are examples of policies or practices or leadership actions that could be implemented to increase work–life control and social support of employees in your organization?
- What are strategies leaders and organizations can take to increase support to close the gap in how lower paid workers are supported in meeting their work–life needs compared to higher-paid employees?
- What actions could be taken to move your organization to support different employees' needs to have time to separate or detach from work to be able to give focused energy and time to meaningful nonwork identities?

Note

1. The quotations and information come from case studies written by Dana Henessey in 2010 as part of a graduate assistantship with Ellen Ernst Kossek at Michigan State University.

References

Eaton, S. C. (2003). If you can use them: Flexibility policies, organizational commitment, and perceived performance. *Industrial Relations, 42*(2), 145–167.

Galinsky, E., Aumann, K., & Bond, J. T. (2009). Times are changing: Gender and generation at work and at home. http://familiesandwork.org/site/research/reports/Times_Are_ Changing.pdf

Greenhaus, J., & Kossek, E. (2014). The contemporary career: A work-home perspective. *Annual Review of Organizational Behavior, 1*, 361–388.

Hammer, L. B., Kossek, E. E., Bodner, T., Anger, K., & Zimmerman, K. (2011). Clarifying work-family intervention processes: The roles of work-family conflict and family supportive supervisor behaviors. *Journal of Applied Psychology, 96*(1), 134–150.

Kalleberg, A. L. (2009). Precarious work, insecure workers: Employment relations in transition. *American Sociological Review, 74*(1), 1–22.

Kossek, E. E. (2005). Workplace policies and practices to support work and families. In S. Bianchi, L. Casper, & R. King (Eds.), *Work, family, health, and well-being* (pp. 97–116). Mahwah, NJ: Lawrence Erlbaum.

Kossek, E. E. (2013). Allow Yahoo workers to work at home. http://www.cnn.com/2013/02/27/opinion/kossek-yahoo-mayer/

Kossek, E., Baltes, B., & Matthews, R. (2011). How work-family research can finally have an impact in organizations. *Industrial and Organizational Psychology: Perspectives on Science and Practice, 4*, 352–369.

Kossek, E., & Hammer, L. (2008, November). Work/life training for supervisors gets big results, *Harvard Business Review*, 36.

Kossek, E., Hammer, L., Kelly, E., & Moen, P. (2014). Designing organizational work, family & health organizational change initiatives. *Organizational Dynamics, 43*, 253–263.

Kossek, E., & Lautsch, B. (2008). *CEO of me: Creating a life that works in the flexible job age.* Philadelphia, PA: Wharton School.

Kossek, E., & Lautsch, B. (2012). Work-family boundary management styles in organizations: A cross-level model. *Organizational Psychology Review, 2*(2), 152–171.

Kossek, E. E., Lautsch, B. A., & Eaton, S. C. (2006). Telecommuting, control, and boundary management: Correlates of policy use and practice, job control, and work–family effectiveness. *Journal of Vocational Behavior, 68*(2), 347–367.

Kossek, E., Lewis, S., & Hammer, L. (2010). Work family initiatives and organizational change: Mixed messages in moving from the margins to the mainstream. *Human Relations, 61*(3), 3–19.

Kossek, E., Pichler, S., Bodner, T., & Hammer, L. (2011). Workplace social support and work-family conflict: A meta-analysis clarifying the influence of general and work-family specific supervisor and organizational support. *Personnel Psychology, 64*(2), 289–313.

Kossek, E., Ruderman, M., Braddy, P., & Hannum, K. (2012). Work-nonwork boundary management profiles: A person-centered approach. *Journal of Vocational Behavior, 81*(1), 112–128. doi:10.1016/j.jvb.2012.04.003

Kossek, E., & Thompson, R. (In press). Workplace flexibility: Integrating employer and employee perspectives to close the research-practice implementation gap. In L. Eby & T. Allen (Eds.), *Oxford handbook of work and family*. New York: Oxford.

Kossek, E., Valcour, M., & Lirio, P. (2014). The sustainable workforce: Organizational strategies for promoting work-life balance and well-being. In C. Cooper & P. Chen (Eds.), *Wellbeing in the workplace: From stress to happiness* (pp. 295–319). Oxford: Wiley-Blackwell.

Lambert, S. (2008). Passing the buck: Labor flexibility practices that transfer risk onto hourly workers. *Human Relations, 61*(9), 1203–1227.

Leslie, L., Manchester, C., Park, T., & Mehng, S. A. (2012). Flexibility practices: A source of career premiums or penalties? *Academy of Management Journal, 55*(6), 1407–1428.

Ragins, B., Lyness, K., Williams, L., & Winkel, D. (2014). Life spillovers: The spillover of fear of home foreclosure to the workplace. *Personnel Psychology, 67*(4), 763–800.

Ryan, A., & Kossek, E. (2008). Work-life policy implementation: Breaking down or creating barriers to inclusiveness? *Human Resource Management, 47*(2), 295–310.

Waxman, E., & Lambert, S. (2005). Organizational stratification: Distributing opportunities for work life balance. In E. Kossek & S. Lambert (Eds.), *Work and life integration: Organizational, cultural and individual perspectives* (pp. 103–126). Mahwah, NJ: Lawrence Erlbaum Associates.

Williams, J. C. (2000). *Unbending gender.* New York: Oxford University Press.

Williams, J. C., & Segal, N. (2003). Beyond the maternal wall: Relief for family caregivers who are discriminated against on the job. *Harvard Women's Law Journal, 26*, 77.

SECTION VI
Innovative Thinking
Section Introduction

Amy Lemley, Lynn Perry Wooten, Martin N. Davidson, and Laura Morgan Roberts

For L'Oréal USA, it's all about the formula—whether for health and beauty products or for a thriving, multicultural workforce. With "Diversity Plus Inclusion Equals Innovation and Success®" as its trademarked stance, the organization monitors its internal progress using its own "Diversity Balance Sheet," an up-to-the-minute tool that allows its locations and subsidiaries to compare notes on what D&I efforts are working and where they need to improve (Egan, 2011). But L'Oréal USA and its parent company L'Oréal Paris's D&I commitment extends far beyond its employment practices and work culture. A defender of diversity and inclusion for consumers, too, L'Oréal presents a world of options for all skin types and colors, hair textures, ages, genders, and cultural expressions. In turn, the world presents options to L'Oréal—new ideas, new products, promising acquisitions with international potential.

With 77,000 employees of 156 nationalities and a presence in 130 countries, L'Oréal is constantly exposed to myriad health and beauty traditions and challenges, any of which can spark an innovation. For example, in India, women's haircare is somewhat of a ritual, with the shampoo preceded by a scalp massage with nourishing oil—a custom interpreted by subsidiary Garnier Fructis as the 2-in-1 Shampoo and Hair Care Oil. In Brazil, L'Oréal saw what natural elements— sun and humidity—as well as cultural ones—straightening treatments and heat styling—were doing to women's long curly hair. The solution? Elsève Total Reparação 5, an instant success that soon expanded into Latin America and Europe. In the United States, L'Oréal's Milani cosmetics expanded its offerings to women of color with True Texture, a line of products for naturally curly hairstyles based on a study conducted at the company's Institute for Ethnic Hair and Skin Research. In addition to this facility, which is devoted solely to black, Asian, and Hispanic hair and skin, L'Oréal maintains research centers in Asia, Europe, and North America.

Throughout the world, the company looks to what it calls "geocosmetics" to engage with diversity from behind a one-way mirror. Inside "bathroom laboratories," study subjects go about their normal skin care, makeup, or hair styling routines, just as they would any other day. Yet what researchers observe—a cultural practice, a tradition, a shortcut, an unmet need—may well lead to the next big thing in cosmetics, skin care, hair care in a region, a nation, on a continent, or around the world.

By definition, diversity brings together individuals whose perspectives, values, knowledge, and skill level may differ—and that can cause friction. DeGraff and Mueller's chapter, "Constructive Conflict: The Essential Role of Diversity in Organizational Innovation" suggests welcoming this friction as a constructive element required to create the friction that produces innovation. Far from being negatives, we learn, divergence and dissimilarity are key elements for creating novel products, services, and solutions.

The next chapter is "The Benefits of Diversity for Innovation in Academic Research." Kamimura and Posselt describe how, in a research environment, diverse cognitive roles provide fodder for innovation when the group discovers synergies in its functional and knowledge diversity. Once certain communication processes are in place, the stage is set for innovative thinking.

Strengths, opportunities, aspirations, and results are the elements of the "SOAR" profile, which is the focus of the next chapter by Stavros and Cole, "Promoting the Positive Effects of Team Diversity through SOAR: An Inclusive Approach for Strategic Thinking, Planning, and Leading." Traditional strategic approaches focus on an organization's problems. But SOAR takes a strengths-based inclusive approach that is particularly effective in diverse teams and organizations. This chapter includes a real-life example of how the process and outcomes of using the SOAR profile led to inclusivity and innovation.

"Life on the Edge: How Weird People Thrive in Organizations (and What They Can Teach Us about Diversity and Inclusion)" is this section's final chapter. In it, Davidson posits that there is such a thing as "positive weird"—characterized by a person in a group who is discounted, ignored, or marginalized but, once welcomed, can invigorate a team or organization by prompting those in the mainstream to think a little differently. The result? New and better organizations and communities that bring out the best from both those in the margins and those in the center.

Reference

Egan, M. E. (2011, July). L'Oréal USA: Harnessing employees' diverse perspectives for innovation. In Global diversity and inclusion: Fostering innovation through a diverse workforce. *Forbes Insights.* http://images.forbes.com/forbesinsights/StudyPDFs/Inno vation_Through_Diversity.pdf

24

CONSTRUCTIVE CONFLICT

The Essential Role of Diversity in Organizational Innovation

Jeff DeGraff and Chris Mueller

Darwin, Marx, and Freud, largely credited with our current conception of modernity, framed the concept of progress as the result of the generative power of competitive forces to produce hybrid variations. This constructive conflict emerging across time is the basis for our contemporary understanding of the conditions that advance the development of innovations (Bacevice & DeGraff, 2013; Danneels, 2008; Leonard & Sensiper, 1998; Ogle, 2007). Diversity in its many forms produces the essential variation and associated friction that ignites innovation, which is taken here to mean useful novelty in its many forms, including products, services, and solutions, as well as types of creative experiences and inventive means of expression such as fashion or design. This places divergence and dissimilarity among the key elements necessary to spark the combustion of innovativeness. Within the vernacular of Positive Organizational Scholarship, this element of divergence is referred to as *positive deviance* (Spreitzer & Sonenshein, 2004). But within the temporal framework of innovation, deviance is more than a departure from the normative. It is the dynamic synthesis of countervailing impulses in a perpetual state of emergence (DeGraff & Nathan-Roberts, 2011). In other words, deviance itself is a relative designation that exists in relationship to competing anomalous beliefs and behaviors.

There Are No Data on the Future

Innovation is a time-bound concept and is inseparably linked to a future state for which we currently have no data. Because an innovation only remains as such for a limited period, innovation is inextricably connected to time and timing. Given a competitive milieu, it will succumb to better and new innovations and will eventually be relegated to the status of a commodity. For example, what were once miracle drugs can now be routinely purchased as over-the-counter medicines. The relative speed of development, distribution, and adoption of an innovation will determine its common designation as evolutionary or revolutionary. More so, arriving too early or too late to an intended market or audience will jeopardize its efficacy and lifespan. Therefore, extending the planning cycle or excessive data collection are both classic errors of innovation management, for they fail to produce any more information about the highly variable and ambiguous future.

Magnitude, meaning the level of deviance from the situational norm, is the second primary dimension of innovation. Ranging from imperceptible incremental changes to radical disruptions, innovations occur in a comparatively smaller or larger degree at any given moment. For example, pharmaceutical professionals may achieve incremental improvements by reengineering an existing medicine, whereas, a venture capitalist may prompt the discovery of a miracle drug by giving money to a dozen biotech start-up firms all with widely different therapies for the exact same disease. While this may seem wasteful, the venture capitalist is diversifying his or her portfolio to accelerate the inevitable failure cycle that determines what therapies prove to be the most promising in the real world. Real insight must be gained through experiments and the knowledge these experiences bring. The strong survive this staged competition and subsume the positive attributes of the lesser competitors. The extent of the diversity of rivals will largely determine the width of the array of possible solutions.

Constructive Conflict

Conflict and competition are not traditionally essential dynamics of Positive Organizational Scholarship. In fact, it is a common misconception in human potential and performance literature that positivity is associated with happiness or success and negativity with discontent and failure. Yet, dissatisfaction is a key driver of the impulse to create. So positivity within this conception of innovation simply means moving from a current state to a future desirable one. This description does not assume the inspiration to create is a reaction to negative circumstances, as is the case in problem solving, but instead suggests that innovativeness involves moving toward an intended outcome produced by the dynamics of positive tensions (Dougherty, 2001; Lawrence & Lorsch, 1967; McEvily & Zaheer, 1999; Mintzberg, 1989; Vogus & Welbourne, 2003; Weick, 1979). Therefore, as with Positive Organizational Scholarship, innovation is conceived of here not as a reaction to deficiency but rather a desire for abundance.

Types of Diversity

The Competing Values Framework (Cameron, Quinn, DeGraff, & Thakor, 2006; O'Neill & Quinn, 1993; Quinn & Rohrbaugh, 1983) is a theory that unites management, culture, and competency development and change and innovation

strategy to predict value creation. It is commonly used to describe cultural variations and other types of diversity within organizations and beyond. The framework was the result of research on organizational effectiveness that described how
leaders differ in their definitions of effectiveness and success. These differences go
well beyond management style, for they characterize the substantive destruction
of value. For example, an automobile manufacturer may seek to produce quality
by eliminating variation in its manufacturing operations through the introduction
of a strict production process. Using this same process in the vehicle design will
eliminate the variation required for new product innovation, and bolder rivals will
take the lead. This conflict of interests and values is often destructive, but if constructively engaged, produces positive results such as hybrid solutions and other
breakthroughs. The practical application of the Competing Values Framework
(Figure 24.1) has made it a cornerstone of many corporate change and innovation
programs and methodologies.

Each of the following profile types in the Competing Values Framework
represents a diverse approach to value creation occurring at three observable
levels: strategic, communal, and personal. These are more than stylistic differences. They represent the creation and displacement of value propositions (Figure 24.2).

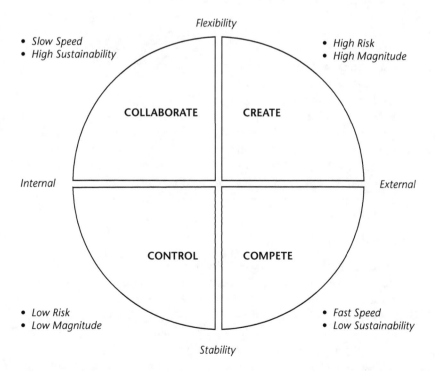

FIGURE 24.1 The Competing Values Framework

	Oppositional Pairing: Time		Oppositional Pairing: Magnitude	
	COLLABORATE	COMPETE	CREATE	CONTROL
Archetype	Sage	Athlete	Artist	Engineer
Domain	Social	Business	Generative	Technical
Gift	Empathy	Courage	Imagination	Discipline
Central question	Is it ethical?	Is it valuable?	Is it beautiful?	Is it functional?
Experience of time	Natural	Man-made	Eternal	Sequential
Experience of space	Balanced	Aligned	Integrated	Structured
Experience of energy	Gathering	Pursuing	Expanding	Focusing
What they seek	Harmony	Power	Transcendence	Perfection
How they seek it	Reflection	Challenge	Experimentation	Observation
What they value	Integrity	Winning	Novelty	Standards
How they learn	Dialogue	Competition	Synthesis	Analysis
How they create	Values	Goals	Vision	Process

FIGURE 24.2 The Competing Values Matrix of Diverse Preferences.

The *Collaborate* Profile

The Collaborate profile encompasses the kinds of people who believe in something greater than the business itself and run their businesses to reflect those values. This is the profile associated with creating a great place to work and learn.

People in the Collaborate profile are committed to their community and focused on shared values and communication. Their culture strives to learn over time, and once a set of competencies is established, the amount of time required to understand a situation and act appropriately is shortened. They are likely to believe that innovation should be timeless. Collaborate companies seek to create something sound that is appreciated by the community. Driving purposes are community and knowledge, achieved by drawing on communication, cooperation, and learning-oriented partnerships. Leaders build the organization by encouraging trust, commitment, and relationships, and by nurturing a community of empowered individuals. Their unified behavior produces a strong organizational image in the marketplace. Customers may be considered partners in an extended community. The Collaborate profile taken to an extreme becomes a party.

The *Compete* Profile

The Compete profile encompasses the kinds of people and practices that many people associate with Wall Street. This is a profile that shows the intensity of competition and achievement—everyone is either a winner or a loser.

Individuals with the Compete profile are focused on performance and goals. Their culture emphasizes these results and the discipline necessary to create them. People with the Compete profile are competitive and love a good challenge, which motivates them toward a speedy and profitable outcome. Compete companies seek to create quickly, before competitors can. Driving purposes are profits, through market share, revenues, and brand equity or speed of response. Leaders build the organization by clarifying objectives and improving the firm's competitive position through hard work and productivity. These companies seek to deliver results to stakeholders as quickly as possible. Beating the competition is a matter of not only strategy but also pride. The Compete profile taken to an extreme becomes a sweatshop.

Oppositions of Time

There is a tension between the Collaborate and Compete forms of innovation that shows up as every day tradeoffs regarding how fast an organization, team, or leader must move to act upon innovation. The question "How fast?" is key to this positive tension. Do we pursue sustainable organizational competencies and culture, which take time to develop, or do we pursue a short-term opportunity, which must be acted upon quickly? This temporal element of innovation determines which projects are funded, who leads these efforts, and what strategic horizon the organization will focus on.

The *Create* Profile

The Create profile encompasses the kinds of purposes and practices that many people think of first when they hear the word "creativity." This is the profile of radical breaks with the past and breakthrough ideas that can change the marketplace.

Individuals with the Create profile tend to be generalists or "artists" who enjoy exploring and easily change direction when solving a problem. The culture that supports their work is characterized by experimentation and speculation; the focus is on generating ideas. This group is often in R&D units or entrepreneurial activities. Create companies seek to create something new that has been previously thought impossible. Driving purposes are innovation or growth. They strive to orient their products, services, and ideas to the future. Leaders build the organization by developing a compelling vision and emphasizing new ideas and technologies, flexibility, and adaptability. Create companies capitalize on turbulent environments. The Create profile taken to an extreme becomes chaotic.

The *Control* Profile

The Control profile represents incremental innovation—taking something that exists and modifying it to make it better. This is the profile of large complex organizations that create products and services that must not fail.

People in the Control profile are systematic, careful, and practical. Their culture focuses on planning, creating systems and processes, and enforcing compliance. Control people seek to keep things running and efficient. Control companies seek to create something better so that they can build upon the present. Driving purposes are quality, efficiency, and predictability. Leaders build the organization by optimizing processes, cutting costs, and establishing rules and procedures. Role definition is important here. These companies tend to elaborate or extend existing products with minor variations. The Control profile taken to an extreme becomes a bureaucracy.

Oppositions of Magnitude

A second tension involving the Create and Control approaches is based on the magnitude and commensurate risk to be assumed in pursuit of innovation. The question "How much?" defines the center of this positive tension. Do we pursue revolutionary innovation, which brings great risk and expense, or do we pursue incremental and scalable innovation, which has less risk but often lacks sufficient inventiveness to develop new markets? The level of ambition, and corresponding risk, often determines the course of action a firm will take. For example, a start-up biotech firm will typically develop very novel therapies because it lacks the resources to compete on scope or scale. An incumbent pharmaceutical company, however, will develop relatively minor enhancements to an existing medication to extend the life of its patents and revenues.

Connecting the Dots

Innovation may be understood as a form of positive deviance. Therefore, the effectiveness of innovation leadership is not determined by the practices used to maintain the equilibrium of the organization but rather those that disrupt the status quo. Effective innovation leadership produces variation and accelerates the failure cycle to incite the constructive conflict that creates hybrid solutions. The competing values contained within these diverse perspectives, cultures, and competencies provide the necessary constructive conflict to produce innovation in all its forms. The key role of an innovation leader is not to make the complex simple but rather to understand how to lead effectively in complex situations. One size never fits all.

For Practitioners: Harnessing the Power of Competing Values

The generative power of the competing values may be effectively harnessed to make conflict constructive in several ways:

- Partnering with other people and communities who are strong in areas where you are weak
- Purposefully engaging these people and communities in constructive conflict to evoke new hybrid solutions

- Managing these people and communities differently, like a portfolio, recognizing that each has its own unique abilities and needs to produce specific intended outcomes
- Developing the appropriate culture and competency, and associated methodologies, for the desired result.

The key role of an innovation leader is not to make the complex simple but rather to understand how to lead effectively in complex situations.

References

Bacevice, P., & DeGraff, J. (2013). Leading innovation in a creative milieu. *Kindai Management Review, 1*(1), 118–131.

Cameron, K. S., Quinn, R. E., DeGraff, J., & Thakor, A. V. (2006). *Competing values leadership: Creating value in organizations.* Northampton, MA: Edward Elgar.

Danneels, E. (2008). Organizational antecedents of second-order competencies. *Strategic Management Journal, 29*(5), 519–543.

DeGraff, J., & Nathan-Roberts, D. (2011). Innovativeness as positive deviance: Identifying and operationalizing the attributes, functions and dynamics that create growth. In K. Cameron & G. Spreitzer (Eds.), *The Oxford handbook of Positive Organizational Scholarship* (pp. 703–714). New York: Oxford University Press.

Dougherty, D. (2001). Reimagining the differentiation and integration of work for sustained product innovation. *Organization Science, 12*(5), 612–631.

Lawrence, P. R., & Lorsch, J. W. (1967). Differentiation and integration in complex organizations. *Administrative Science Quarterly, 12*(1), 1–47.

Leonard, D., & Sensiper, S. (1998). The role of tacit knowledge in group innovation. *California Management Review, 40*(3), 112–132.

McEvily, B., & Zaheer, A. (1999). Bridging ties: A source of firm heterogeneity in competitive capabilities. *Strategic Management Journal, 20*(12), 1133–1156.

Mintzberg, H. (1989). *Mintzberg on management: Inside our strange world of organizations.* New York: Free Press.

O'Neill, R. M., & Quinn, R. E. (1993). Editors' note: Applications of the Competing Values Framework. *Human Resource Management, 32*(1), 1–7.

Ogle, R. (2007). *Smart world: Breakthrough creativity and the new science of ideas.* Boston, MA: Harvard Business School Press.

Quinn, R. E., & Rohrbaugh, J. (1983). A spatial model of effectiveness criteria: Towards a competing values approach to organizational analysis. *Management Science, 29*(3), 363–377.

Spreitzer, G. M., & Sonenshein, S. (2004). Toward the construct definition of positive deviance. *American Behavioral Scientist, 47*(6), 828–847.

Vogus, T. J., & Welbourne, T. M. (2003). Structuring for high reliability: HR practices and mindful processes in reliability-seeking organizations. *Journal of Organizational Behavior, 24*(7), 877–903.

Weick, K. E. (1979). *The social psychology of organizing* (2nd ed.). New York: Addison-Wesley.

25

THE BENEFITS OF DIVERSITY FOR INNOVATION IN ACADEMIC RESEARCH

Aurora Kamimura and Julie R. Posselt

Whether assessing a society, school, or business, organizational experts often point to innovation—the development of concepts into new/refined products, services, or processes—as a key indicator of growth. How might organizational diversity be related to innovation, and how does it affect research innovations, specifically? Prior work has shown that compositionally diverse teams (i.e., those whose members have diverse identities) have more innovative approaches to problem solving, and that this can enhance organizations' competitive advantage (Hambrick, Cho, & Chen, 1996; Page, 2008). Dramatic demographic shifts and growth in women's labor market participation would therefore seem to poise the United States for an historic era of knowledge innovation. In this chapter, we explore this emerging perspective on diversity in the academy, where intellectual innovations often occur through collaborative effort by teams of researchers, including graduate and, increasingly, undergraduate students.

By synthesizing empirical research and established ideas from organizational scholarship, we integrate multiple perspectives—including absorptive capacity, functional diversity, and cognitive complexity—to propose a model that represents how diverse identities shape knowledge creation through specific communication processes. We then offer a brief example of one engineering professor's experience with the relationship of diversity and innovation in his research team.

Absorptive Capacity

Cohen and Levinthal's absorptive capacity (AC) framework unpacks diversity's impact on learning, innovation, and knowledge generation. They defined AC as "the ability of an [organization] to recognize the value of new, external information, assimilate it, and apply it" (Cohen & Levinthal, 1990). AC enables group members to make linkages between prior and different perspectives, develop insight from those points of connectivity, and thus generate new knowledge. Diversity of knowledge provides the optimal environment in which to create new knowledge—that is, to innovate. Clear communication is required for group members to make more "novel associations and linkages" across their varied experiences and knowledge bases (Cohen & Levinthal, 1989, 1990).

Exposure to diverse external sources of knowledge is central to the conceptualization of AC that scholars currently use (Zahra & George, 2002). This exposure increases a team's ability to link to prior knowledge and experiences, which allows them to innovate. AC affects not only the pace of innovation, but also its frequency and magnitude, which collectively generate a stronger knowledge base for the organization (Lane, Koka, & Pathak, 2006). Thus AC strengthens a diverse team's capacity to innovate and grow over time.

Functional Diversity: More Angles on the Problems and Solutions

Whereas AC emphasizes the broader range of knowledge available to diverse groups, research by Page (2008) emphasizes diverse groups' varied approaches to using knowledge (i.e., heuristics). Functional diversity, defined as heterogeneous ways of representing and solving problems, is both a characteristic of some groups and a mechanism of innovation. Diverse teams are more likely to innovate by bringing both more perspectives to bear on problems and more ways of searching for solutions, so that heterogeneous groups of amateurs have been found to actually outperform homogenous groups of experts in problem solving and prediction—two fundamental research tasks (Hong & Page, 2004; Mannix & Neale, 2005; Page, 2008). From a positive organizational perspective, this work is vital in demonstrating that cultural difference on teams is an asset, not a liability (Stahl, Makela, Zander, & Maznevski, 2010).

Cognitive Roles and Communication Processes: Coordinating Diverse Perspectives

Amid the complexity that comes with compositional, knowledge, and functional diversity, coordination is critical to a team's effectiveness. Neumann (1991) identified eight cognitive roles on administrative teams: "the Definer, the Analyst, the Interpreter, the Critic, the Synthesizer, the Disparity Monitor, the Task Monitor, and the Emotional Monitor". In a research context, diverse cognitive roles may enhance team effectiveness by finding synergies in the group's functional and knowledge diversity, and by enacting communication processes that AC theory asserts are central to innovation. For example, interpreters assimilate information by translating the multiple meanings a group's members may perceive, while synthesizers negotiate ambiguities and encourage compromise across multiple meanings and interpretations (Neumann, 1991). The diversity of roles allows members to make distinct contributions when their strengths may be best utilized and to take turns leading during the research process.

An Illustration from Engineering

We turn now to a brief description of one professor and his research team's commitment to diversity and how it has encouraged innovation. If there is any corner of academia that values innovation, it is engineering, yet it remains one of the most homogeneous academic fields, with 64 percent of doctoral degrees awarded to white students and 70 percent to men (NSF, 2008). In this context, James[1] is an Ivy League–trained engineering professor from an underrepresented racial/ethnic background. He is committed to diversity in higher education as both a social good and intellectual opportunity, unlike most of his colleagues whom he characterized as "nod[ding] politely whenever the term diversity comes up." In a recent interview, he exchanged a calm, serious demeanor for passion as he expressed ideas about America's past and future, emphasizing how he has "seen firsthand [his] lab benefit from the creativity that diversity brings." This lab consists of 10 to 15 graduate students, professional researchers, and undergraduates, whose identities and strengths he proudly described:

> I have underrepresented minorities, I have women, I have Americans who were born outside the U.S. . . . So I have a very diverse group of folk in my lab, but they all have just very high intelligence and excitement . . . They're interested in the field and are freaks about it just like me *[laughter]* . . . They're also balanced and very good communicators.

In discussing his group's success over the years—their advancements for the field, awards, and productivity—James identified both their talents as individuals and the talent of "the collective—how well they work together, the communication, the diversity." The team's compositional diversity elicits cognitive diversity, he said:

> [W]hen we have our lab meetings, my students rotate and give presentations at those meetings. And I can see the dude who was born in Africa comes out from left field from the person who was born in China. It's just really amazing . . . I don't think you would capture the diversity of ideas if you didn't have people with different life experiences, different cultures, different backgrounds coming together. You know, some of the most brilliant work that's come out of my group has been because of that. Sort of like jazz, the influence of different things coming together to create something new.

In research, as in jazz, group members' unique perspectives may not always array cleanly. Fresh ideas, like improvisations, may include a few discordant notes and awkward transitions, for example. But it also involves careful communication and a willingness to take turns with the limelight so every voice can shine for a time and contribute to creating something new. James's narrative offers a very brief example of how a compositionally diverse team generates cognitive diversity that is instrumental to innovation.

Innovation through Collaborative Research

The elements represented in Figure 25.1 and echoed in James's story represent conditions through which social diversity can be leveraged for a type of organizational performance that higher education values—innovation through collaborative research. The research opportunities that a scholar sees are inextricable from one's identity and experiences—and those of one's colleagues. For example, at our institution, the University of Michigan, new technologies have been developed for streetlights and sanitation as a result of students who grew up in nearby Detroit seeing the need for improvements in these areas. Among students growing up in wealthier environments, where streetlights and sanitation services are taken for granted, these needs may have been blind spots.

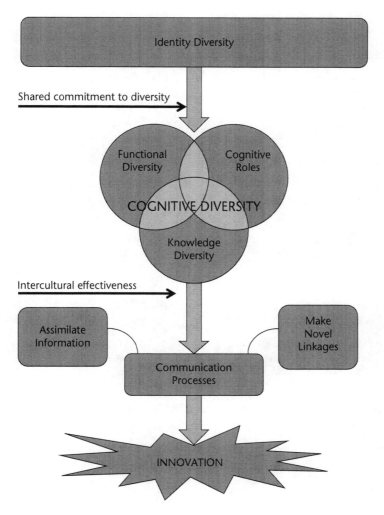

FIGURE 25.1 Conceptual framework representing diversity and research innovation

This process has relevance for other types of team-based work as well. Irrespective of context, compositionally diverse groups contribute richer knowledge, more ways of thinking about problems and their solutions, and a broader range of cognitive roles. These roles feed cognitive diversity and enhance group performance by facilitating communication, which absorptive capacity theory claims is a critical precondition of innovation. Those responsible for cultivating diversity in higher education—especially faculty, who select the graduate students who so often serve as research collaborators—can take from this work a new perspective on the importance of factoring diversity considerations into the admissions process. Those responsible for managing diversity for innovation—faculty, staff, and others—should be mindful, however, that it is not only the presence of heterogeneity that matters. Shared commitment to diversity and the development of intercultural effectiveness both shape the possibility that diversity can realize its potential in sparking creativity and innovation.

For Practitioners: Do You Recognize These Cognitive Roles in Your Administrative Teams? (From Neumann, 1991)

Do you have a team member who . . . ?

Contributions to the Team
Definer: Identifies and proposes problems and topics for the team to attend to. Sets the team agenda.
Analyst: Examines the problem from multiple angles. Explains the problem's multiple facets and their interrelationships. Contributes depth of understanding on the topic at hand.
Interpreter: Predicts how outside constituencies will view the team members and their work. Offers new ways of understanding actions and events that may appear as unidimensional. Keeps an appreciation for multiple ways of understanding the situation alive in the organization.
Critic: Proposes revisions to the agenda, interpretations, and perceptions. Plays devil's advocate by challenging established understandings. Provides alternative understandings.
Synthesizer: Develops summaries from the team's diverse perspectives and contributions. Plays arbitrator or compromiser among diverse team members. Elicits team members' role contributions and uses these as strengths to further the agenda.
Disparity Monitor: Collects and conveys facts about what outsiders are doing, saying, and feeling about the team's actions. Helps provide corrective action when needed. Provides checks and balances between the team's perception and reality.
Task monitor: Helps facilitate the team's progress and completion of the agenda. Provides other team members with backup when and where needed.
Emotional Monitor: Aware of teamwork's humanistic dimensions, this individual may offer comic relief, encouragement, and/or mediation that facilitates the work.

Note

1. Name has been changed to protect confidentiality.

References

Cohen, W. M., & Levinthal, D. A. (1989). Innovation and learning: The two faces of R&D. *The Economic Journal, 99*(397), 569–596.

Cohen, W. M., & Levinthal, D. A. (1990). Absorptive capacity: A new perspective on learning and innovation. *Administrative Science Quarterly, 35*(1), 128–152.

Hambrick, D. C., Cho, T. S., & Chen. M. (1996). The influence of top management team heterogeneity on firms' competitive moves. *Administrative Science Quarterly, 41*(4), 659–684.

Hong, L., & Page, S. E. (2004). Groups of diverse problem solvers can outperform groups of high-ability problem solvers. *Proceedings of the National Academy of Sciences, 101*(46), 16385–16389.

Lane, P. J., Koka, B. R., & Pathak, S. (2006). The reification of absorptive capacity: A critical review and rejuvenation of the construct. *Academy of Management Review, 31*(4), 833–863.

Mannix, E., & Neale, M. A. (2005). What differences make a difference? The promise and reality of diverse teams in organizations. *Psychological Science in the Public Interest, 6*(2), 31–55.

National Science Foundation. (2008). Racial and ethnic diversity among U.S.-educated science, engineering, and health doctorate recipients. http://www.nsf.gov/statistics/infbrief/nsf12304/#fig2

Neumann, A. (1991). The thinking team: toward a cognitive model of administrative teamwork in higher education. *Journal of Higher Education, 62*(5), 485–513.

Page, S. E. (2008). *The difference: How the power of diversity creates better groups, firms, schools, and societies.* Princeton, NJ: Princeton University Press.

Stahl, G. K., Makela, K., Zander, L., & Maznevski, M. L. (2010). A look at the bright side of team diversity. *Scandinavian Journal of Management, 26*(4), 439–447.

Zahra, S. A., & George, G. (2002). Absorptive capacity: A review, reconceptualization, and extension. *Academy of Management Review, 27*(2), 185–203.

26

PROMOTING THE POSITIVE EFFECTS OF TEAM DIVERSITY THROUGH SOAR

An Inclusive Approach for Strategic Thinking, Planning, and Leading

Jacqueline M. Stavros and Matthew L. Cole

The global workforce of the 21st century can be characterized by increased numbers of women, minorities, age groups, and ethnic backgrounds with a wide range of personalities, attitudes, beliefs, and values. Heterogeneous groups have the potential for broad task-relevant knowledge, skills, abilities, and viewpoints leading to increased creativity and innovation (Pieterse, van Knippenberg, & van Dierendonck, 2013; Roberge & van Dick, 2010). As teams become a central structural unit, organizations are paying close attention to understanding the effects of diversity on team performance. To leverage the potential benefits of diversity, organizations are becoming more interested in creating inclusive environments in which team members are valued, respected, and supported. But building inclusive environments that promote the positive effects of team diversity can be challenging for professionals and for researchers. This chapter describes how a new practice-oriented tool, the SOAR Profile, helps individuals understand their natural capacity for strategic thinking, planning, and leading. It illustrates how SOAR promotes an inclusive environment that facilitates positive performance among diverse teams in which strategy is a dynamic and generative process that focuses on strengths, whole system solutions, and stakeholder inclusion.

SOAR is a strengths-based framework with a whole system approach to strategic thinking, planning, and leading that focuses on strengths, opportunities, aspirations, and results (Table 26.1) (Stavros & Cole, 2013). Traditional approaches to strategy, such as SWOT, tend to focus on organizational problems via an exclusive approach that links strategic thinking with upper management. In contrast, SOAR advocates for strategy to be innovative, invigorating, and inclusive via a "strengths-based framework with a participatory approach to strategic thinking that allows an organization's stakeholders to co-construct its future through collaboration, shared understanding, and a commitment to action" (Stavros & Wooten, 2012, p. 826).

TABLE 26.1 Typical SOAR Questions

Strengths	Opportunities
What are we most proud of as an organization?	What are the best possible opportunities?
What are our greatest assets?	How might we best partner with others?
Aspirations	**Results**
What do we care deeply about?	How do we know we are succeeding?
What is our preferred future?	What are our measurable results?

Source: Adapted from Stavros, Cooperrider, & Kelley (2007).

The SOAR Profile was designed from the theory and empirical research on SOAR and offers researchers and practitioners the ability to measure and understand an individual's natural capacity for SOAR-based strategic thinking, planning, and leading (Cole & Stavros, 2014). The profile draws from the fields of strategy, organization development and change, and Appreciative Inquiry (AI), and is positioned through the lens of Positive Organizational Scholarship with its focus on generative dynamics of how teams in organizations are social systems that build on strengths and aspirations of members to achieve positive results. AI is vital to the emergence of SOAR due to its engagement of people at all levels of an organization in an inquiry into the organization's positive core. This positive approach embraces inclusion and diversity and leads to changes in the organization based on images of the best possible future as articulated and visualized by the people who make up its human system (Cooperrider, Whitney, & Stavros, 2008). Additionally, research suggests that when positive factors are given attention, individual and team performance tends to flourish (Fredrickson, 2009).

To explore how SOAR has the potential to promote the positive effects of diversity in teams by maximizing collaborative strategies that are inclusive, we begin this chapter by addressing the importance of diversity and inclusion initiatives on team performance. Next, we demonstrate that SOAR is an inclusive approach to strategic thinking, planning, and leading. Finally, we briefly describe an empirical study in which the SOAR Profile was used in an investigation of the relationship among SOAR, team diversity, and team performance.

Understanding Diversity and Inclusion in Teams

Teams in organizations have become increasingly diverse in terms of surface-level diversity (e.g., age, gender, ethnicity) and deep-level diversity (e.g., attitudes, beliefs, values), and they will continue to become more diverse in years to come (Roberg & van Dick, 2010). Although diverse teams as compared to homogenous teams may have more conflicts and misunderstandings that contribute to poor collaboration and threaten team performance, diversity in teams has the potential to affect a wide range of positive team outcomes, such as creativity, innovation, and exchange of different perspectives and ideas that can enhance team performance (Homan & Greer, 2013). To help leverage diversity as a positive resource, organizations aim to achieve inclusion. Inclusion signifies involvement and engagement and suggests ongoing commitment to knowledge sharing in the development of collaborative strategies within the team (Roberson, 2006). SOAR is a framework that can help organizations achieve inclusion through a dialogic process that supports the full utilization of a social system to understand, at a deeper level, where unique contributions can make a difference for positive change (Stavros & Hinrichs, 2009).

An Inclusive Approach to Strategic Thinking, Planning, and Leading

SOAR evolved from strategy research, Positive Organizational Scholarship, and Appreciative Inquiry to engage all stakeholders of a team and organization in strategic thinking, planning, and leading to create a desired future. Strategic thinking encourages an open exchange of ideas and solutions to meet the dynamic challenges in today's economy (Haycock, Cheadle, & Bluestone, 2012). Strategic planning establishes strategic targets to ensure competitive success (Collins & Rukstad, 2008). Finally, strategic leading articulates goal formation and implements the strategic plan. Strategic leadership is demonstrated by the ability to influence others to make decisions that lead to the organization's long-term growth and positive results (Rowe & Nejad, 2009).

At the heart of SOAR is an inclusive approach that inspires individuals and teams to reach for aspirations and results, and helps team members to frame strategy by inquiring into the team's positive core—the sum total of the team's unique strengths, assets, networks, resources, and capabilities—to create a desired future (Cooperrider et al., 2008). Inquiry into the team's positive core requires members to engage in strategic conversations that are multidirectional communication mechanisms for framing the strategic intent of the team. SOAR focuses on identifying strengths, building creativity in the form of opportunities, encouraging individuals and teams to share aspirations, and determining measured results focused on a holistic view of team goals. Theoretically, is SOAR the mechanism by which the positive effects of team-based diversity on team performance are promoted? For the practitioner, is SOAR an inclusive approach to strategic thinking, leading, and planning that can promote diversity in teams and ultimately increase team performance? To answer these questions, we conducted an empirical study on the relationship among SOAR, team diversity, and team performance.

Empirical Study on Diversity in Teams

To explore how SOAR might promote the positive effects of team diversity, we conducted an empirical study that examined SOAR as a mediator of the

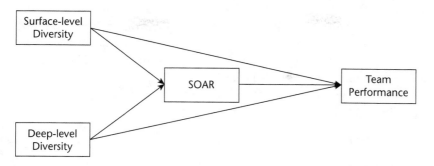

FIGURE 26.1 SOAR as a mediator of the relationship between diversity and team performance.

positive effect that team diversity has on team performance (Figure 26.1). Using a sample of 65 graduate architecture students working in 12 teams comprising five to six members per team, we defined team diversity in terms of surface-level diversity (gender and age of students) and deep-level diversity (students' creative problem-solving style and personality type). To measure team performance, we used the final project score, and to measure SOAR, we used the SOAR Profile. Analytically, we conducted a mediation path model using structural equation modeling to test for an indirect effect of SOAR on the relationship between diversity and performance. The results of the analysis found surface-level diversity had no impact on team performance, deep-level diversity had a positive impact on team performance, and SOAR mediated the relationship between overall team diversity and team performance. These findings suggest that SOAR is an underlying process that may explain how team diversity has a positive impact on team performance.

Recommendations and Conclusion

For an organization to *positively transform* and *change*, it must take advantage of opportunities, leverage internal strengths, and optimize its human capital for building a sustainable organization. The Center for Positive Organizations (www.centerforpos.org) has been on a mission to promote positive states of organizing in which solution generation is a function of positive aspects of strategy and strategic thinking and planning. In this chapter, we have described how SOAR, as measured by the SOAR Profile, can promote the positive effects of team diversity through self-awareness of natural capacity for SOAR-based thinking, planning, and leading.

We propose that the efficacy of SOAR in promoting the positive effects of team diversity can be summarized in three main target areas (see following callout box). First, by targeting individual strengths and positive core, SOAR helps to create a results-driven outcome for the team that is based on members' individual strengths rather than weaknesses. Second, SOAR leverages whole system and solution-oriented thinking that can help team members focus on solutions that positively affect the entire organization. Finally, by encouraging the inclusion of all team members in strategic thinking, planning, and leading, SOAR enhances team relationships founded on trust, collaboration, and mutual respect. We recommend that organizations utilize the SOAR framework to create an inclusive environment that promotes the positive effects of team diversity.

For Practitioners: The SOAR Framework

The SOAR Framework

Strengths: Capabilities to do something well—*What can we build on?*
Opportunities: Innovations to achieve results—*What are our stakeholders asking for?*
Aspirations: Strong desires to achieve results—*What do we care deeply about and for whom?*
Results: Outcomes achieved to meet goals—*What are the indicators to know we are succeeding?*

How Does SOAR Promote the Positive Effects of Team Diversity?

Strengths and positive core—*Creates results-driven outcomes based on individual strengths rather than weaknesses*
Whole system and solutions—*Focuses on solutions that impact the entire organization rather than specific departments*
Inclusion of all team members—*Enhances team relationships founded on participation, trust, collaboration, and mutual respect*

References

Cole, M. L., & Stavros, J. M. (2014). *Psychometric properties of the SOAR Profile.* Paper session presented at Lawrence Tech Research Day 2014, Southfield, MI.

Collins, D. J., & Rukstad, M. G. (2008). Can you say what your strategy is? *Harvard Business Review, 86*(4), 82–90.

Cooperrider, D., Whitney, D., & Stavros, J. (2008). *Appreciative inquiry handbook: For leaders of change.* Brunswick, OH: Crown Custom.

Fredrickson, B. (2009). *Positivity: Groundbreaking research reveals how to embrace the hidden strength of positive emotions, overcome negativity, and thrive.* New York: Crown.

Haycock, K., Cheadle, A., & Bluestone, K. S. (2012). Strategic thinking: Lessons for leadership from the literature. *Library Leadership & Management, 26*(3/4), 1–23.

Homan, A. C., & Greer, L. (2013). Considering diversity: The positive effects of considerate leadership in diverse teams. *Group Processes & Intergroup Relations, 16*(1), 105–125.

Pieterse, A. N., van Knippenberg, D., & van Dierendonch, D. (2013). Cultural diversity and team performance: the role of team member goal orientation. *Academy of Management Journal, 56*(3), 782–804.

Roberge, M.-E., & van Dick, R. (2010). Recognizing the benefits of diversity: When and how does diversity increase group performance. *Human Resource Management Review, 20,* 295–308.

Roberson, Q. M. (2006). Disentangling the meanings of diversity and inclusion in organizations. *Group & Organization Management, 31*(2), 212–236.

Rowe, G., & Nejad, M. H. (2009, September/October). Strategic leadership: Short-term stability and long-term viability, *Ivey Business Journal,* 1–9.

Stavros, J. M., & Cole, M. L. (2013). SOARing towards positive transformation and change. *ABAC ODI Visions. Action. Outcome, 1*(1), 10–34.

Stavros, J. M., Cooperrider, D., & Kelley, L. (2007). SOAR: A new approach to strategic planning. In P. Homan, T. Devane, & S. Cady (Eds.), *The change handbook: The definitive resource on today's best methods for engaging whole systems* (2nd ed., pp. 375–380). San Francisco, CA: Berrett-Koehler.

Stavros, J., & Hinrichs, G. (2009). *Thin book of SOAR: Building strengths-based strategy.* Bend, OR: Thin Book.

Stavros, J., & Wooten, L. (2012). Positive strategy: Creating and sustaining strengths-based strategy that SOARs and performs. In K. Cameron & G. Spreitzer (Eds.), *The Oxford handbook of positive organizational scholarship* (pp. 825–838). Oxford: Oxford University Press.

27

LIFE ON THE EDGE

How Weird People Thrive in Organizations (and What They Can Teach Us about Diversity and Inclusion)

Martin N. Davidson

Take from the margin to rethink the whole.

—*Susan Sturm & Lani Guinier (1996)*

At the core of all Diversity and Inclusion (D&I) work is a focus on the marginalized. An underlying aspiration of most D&I initiatives is to create organizations and communities that engage members of both marginal and dominant groups. But in practice, the primary focus of D&I is to bring those on the margin more to the center. Remedies such as affirmative action and D&I recruiting and retention programs are designed to provide underrepresented people a "seat at the table" (Joshi, 2014). But as Sturm and Guinier (1996) suggest in their seminal article on affirmative action, simply providing access for those who are different to enter into the established center is not nearly ambitious enough. What if sitting at the table is *not* the best place to be? What if the most generative space for both marginal and dominant people to come together is actually somewhere between the margin and the center, standing in a circle, speaking together in small pods, or even dancing together? And what can people in the center learn by allowing themselves to step *out* to the margin?

With this desire to explore the margin more deeply, my colleagues and I began to talk to weird people. "Weird" is an intentionally loaded term. We define it as that which is counternormative—different—relative to the context in which it is situated. Moreover, the word connotes an extreme degree of difference. As our preliminary inquiries revealed, weird people aren't just interesting to be around. Rather they frequently tend to generate aversive responses from those in the center. Often, weird people are the ones about whom the majority will say "if only so-and-so weren't on the team, this would be an excellent team. We would get so much done!" To be clear, sometimes those sentiments are spot on. Teammates may have that "if only" reaction because the weird person continues to impede progress, diminish productivity, and contribute to a climate that destroys, rather than creates, value. This type of weirdness is problematic and must be assessed and dealt with. But too often, this destructive weird is confused with productive, generative, and life-affirming weird. This "positive weird" will be the focus of this chapter as we seek to understand how to create better organizations and communities that bring out the best in both marginal and dominant members.

Lessons Learned from Positive Weirdness

We realized first that weirdness is context-dependent. Almost anyone can quickly conjure an image of someone they might deem weird—socially awkward, disheveled, or even creepy. But even people fitting that description have their own havens of like individuals. In those places, these individuals are not weird at all. By the same token, organizations and teams develop norms that define what is acceptable and common behavior, but those norms can vary widely. Normal in an investment bank in Germany—attire, behavior, emotional expressiveness—looks quite different from normal in a start-up venture in Hanoi. In this exploratory research, we solicited ratings from managers of intact teams across multiple organizations spanning multiple industries. We asked these informants to identify individuals they would describe as significant outliers in the team or working group. We interviewed the individuals they identified, inquiring about (1) role and work history; (2) perception of the culture of the organization and team; and (3) experience of work, including their most successful outcomes. We asked them about their perception of similarities and differences among their peers, and inquired about times in which they went against the grain at work. Finally, we asked them for personal stories that would help us understand "who they are as a person." By virtue of our selection process, the people we interviewed skewed toward positive weird. All of them were described by their managers as high performers, though they were described often as individuals who were difficult to manage. Two critical themes are emerging from our interviews so far.

First, being weird is not easy. Our initial findings suggest that these people often struggle as a result of their weirdness. Prevailing norms and dominant ways of thinking continue to exert pressure on weird people to conform to conventional standards of behavior. Many of the people we interviewed pushed back on the assumption that being different is a choice. They highlighted the ways in which their very sense of who they are as individuals was deeply intertwined with the way they experienced the world. While some behaviors are clearly the product of choice, there remained this strong sense that conforming simply was not possible.

One exceptionally articulate respondent described how his style led others to undervalue his intellectual talent:

M.L.: I always come off a little bit as the C student in an A-student culture.

Another respondent captured the disconnection between motivational styles:

P.S.: I drive more from my gut than my head. More from my heart than my head, and [this company] is an excruciatingly rational and literal place and that is not something that I fit into.

Despite stories of not fitting in, the weird people we interviewed were far from miserable. Some found ways to reframe their counternormative behavior to make it seem like an asset rather than a liability to their colleagues. M.L. went on to describe how being a "C Student" worked out well sometimes:

M.L.: To some degree I've become this tangible vision of what people could be. So yesterday I was at the design off-site, you know, so 170 . . . 200 designers at an off-site and I talked to the organizer. She said, "Thank you." And I said, why? She said, "Well, you're embodying everything that we're trying to actually get this community to become." And actually having someone to point to and say, [you are] what we want to be . . . that's where it feels like I'm fitting. Like A students actually need C students.

A second theme emerging from the interviews is that there are different drivers of weirdness. One driver is a more habitual, ego-centered expression of weird. The motivation for counternormative behavior seems to be the desire to stand out from the crowd. These people act weird just to oppose the norm. It makes them feel good to be different, and any behavior that feeds that feeling is fair game. Ironically, this weird can have a certain predictability to it. It's as though the weird person is thinking, "Whatever you say or do, I'll say or do the opposite." In contrast, a more mission-driven weirdness emerges for some individuals. Here, weird people enact counternormative behavior in the service of a larger team or organization goal. They are trying to achieve that goal, and they can see that following a normal path won't get them there. Often these individuals display a certain tenacious humility. One respondent described a rejection of the organization's structure:

S.J.: I'm really anti-hierarchy, and I do call it out, and I have been called out for calling it out, and I do it because I think we need to recognize it so that we can . . . break it down. I think that if you're not going to acknowledge something that's happening, the politics, the hierarchy, the re-org that occurs in an organization, you're not being honest, and you're not gonna be able to effect the kind of change that you want.

Another respondent discussed the act of speaking about the "elephant in the room":

M. L.: I think I will always say the things that nobody else wants to say. So I'll be the first one to get into a room and see if there's an elephant in it and be like . . . point to it and start slapping it too. I'm willing to go after the elephant in the room or the sacred cow . . . and I always say, "I finally found the elephant in the room. It was hidden behind the sacred cow." When I joined, people said, "Oh, you're very snarky." Because I would question. My brand started becoming snark. And my director said, "You gotta be careful. You gotta find the right line between being snarky and actually being effective." And at first, people thought that I was snarky because I didn't fit in. They thought . . . I just left [my previous company], I'm here just for a few months or maybe a year and I'm not serious about the outcomes and I'm gonna leave eventually. And I had to prove that I have skin in the game and that actually when I'm being snarky about the organization, [it's] because I care, not because I'm making fun of it. I'm being snarky about the organization and when I am snarky, I'm gonna do something to change it. When I actually point to the elephant in the room, I don't just point and leave. I'll do everything to actually try to resolve that issue.

These are brief examples of generative paths of weirdness. As Sturm and Guinier (1996) argue, these marginal people can potentially help reframe the status quo in ways that create more powerful and positive lives for everyone. The challenge for organization leaders is to figure out how to support weird people so that they create—not destroy—value. Some of these people have stifled their offbeat creativity out of social fear, camouflaging their true selves because they think it's not appropriate at work to be as they really are. They leave essential parts of themselves at the office door.

Weirdness and Diversity and Inclusion

It should not be a stretch to see the parallels between the weird people in this study and members of traditionally underrepresented groups in organizations. While this research de-emphasizes social identity group diversity—the respondents are predominantly white, male, and U.S.-born—their stories resemble those frequently shared by women, people of color, differently abled people, and lesbian, gay, bisexual, trans, and queer colleagues. Even though norms of political correctness teach us the right words to use (just as I have carefully chosen in the previous sentence) the simple truth is that people in these groups are experienced as—and may feel—just as weird as the individuals in our study.

There's much more to learn about the weirdness factor. The question we continue to explore is why some people who stand out as weird thrive while other weird people wither. Whatever their path, people who are different can stimulate growth, foster learning, and catalyze innovation. Weird people can teach those of us who struggle to stand out and be noticed how do so more effectively.

And whenever we are tempted to succumb to the unexamined conclusion that a colleague or a peer is just too different and simply "cannot fit in here," it is worth considering the story of this individual: He ignored even the most basic tasks of self-maintenance. Not only did he bathe "very rarely," he rarely even changed clothes, sleeping in full regalia—shoes included. His assistant once complained that, "He has sometimes gone so long without taking (his shoes) off that then the skin came away, like a snake's, with the boots." He suffered from social awkwardness, was reluctant to interact with people, and tended to just walk away from a person in the middle of a conversation. He worked obsessively, to the sacrifice of absolutely everything else in his life (Arshad & Fitzgerald, 2004).

That focus allowed him to create this (Figure 27.1) . . .

FIGURE 27.1 Detail, Sistine Chapel, Michelangelo, painted 1508–1512
Source: Wikimedia Commons.

Michelangelo, historians believe, had autism before that diagnosis was known, and he may have come off as simply "weird" to his peers. The artist exemplifies a critical lesson: Weirdness can look like a problem but, in fact, it's quite often the solution.

For Practitioners: How Leaders Can Foster Positive Weirdness

- Remember that weirdness is a powerful path toward group creativity and innovation.
- Being weird is not easy. Be empathic toward those who are different.
- Adopt a learning orientation toward weird people. What do they see that you might be missing?
- Encourage mission-driven weirdness.
- Curtail ego-driven weirdness.
- Be open to exploring the ways in which you are weird. Reflect on how you are unusual and distinctive.
- Practice expressing your own positive weirdness—it provides permission for others to bring out their weird.

References

Arshad, M., & Fitzgerald, M. 2004. Did Michelangelo (1475–1564) have high-functioning autism? *Journal of Medical Biography, 12*(2), 115–120.

Joshi, Y. (2014). The trouble with inclusion. *Virginia Journal of Social Policy & the Law, 21*(2), 207–265.

Sturm, S., & Guinier, L. (1996). The future of affirmative action: Reclaiming the innovative ideal. *California Law Review, 84*(4), 953.

CONCLUSION

Building a Bridge to Positive Organizing

Laura Morgan Roberts, Lynn Perry Wooten,
and Martin N. Davidson

We began this book with an open-ended question: *What happens when thought leaders integrate Diversity, Inclusion, and Positive Organizational Scholarship?* Rather than providing definitive answers, these chapters have stimulated a host of new questions to guide our scholarship, teaching, and practices of positive organizing in our diverse society. By building conceptual, empirical, and experiential bridges between diversity, inclusion, and Positive Organizational Scholarship (POS), these chapters have laid the foundation for exciting paths of inquiry and potent tools for intervention. The voices represented in this book have revealed to us many things that POS scholars can learn from Diversity and Inclusion research, such as: how identities constitute sources of strength; how individuals and organizations build capacity through generative mechanisms of resilience, positive deviance, and inclusion; how to form and sustain high quality relationships across difference; and how to lead innovation and systemic change through engaging diverse perspectives. Likewise, we discover what Diversity and Inclusion scholars can learn from POS by examining six central, organizing themes that emerged from these chapters: the benefits of multiple identities, how to increase authenticity in diverse settings, how to cultivate resilience while facing diversity-related challenges, how to foster high-quality relationships across differences, how to sustain inclusive and equitable systems, and how to leverage diversity in order to spark innovative thinking. The bridges we have begun to build between POS, diversity, and inclusion beckon us to question critically several longstanding assumptions regarding the most "positive" ways to strengthen diverse organizations. Taken together, the chapters in this book represent a paradigm shift: Through deeply contextualized illustrations and rigorous theoretical substantiation, we step away from a dominant frame of "managing difference," which problematizes the experience and implications of diversity, and move toward a strengths-based view of diversity as an individual, group, or relational and organizational resource. In the following section, we will highlight several ways in which the "bridge-building" work of these chapters move the traditional deficit focus on Diversity and Inclusion to a vantage point from which we can illuminate new processes for enhancing inclusion and building capacity in diverse organizations.

Shifting the Deficit Focus

The vast majority of organizational research ignores diversity altogether. Some quantitative studies account for demographic composition as a control variable in statistical models; this analytical choice suggests that diversity is influential in organizational dynamics, but not worthy of theoretical examination. On the other hand, in-depth examinations of marginalization aptly document disparities in treatment, advancement, inclusion, and well-being for people who represent non-dominant identity groups within organizations. Yet the ongoing debate between "difference-blind" organizational theorists and diversity and inclusion researchers often revolves around a problem-based dialogue: the problems of marginalization, exclusion, and bias.

How does one introduce POS, which privileges the study of strengths, into this discourse, without overlooking the deficiencies in systems that promote inequality and injustice? Many diversity and inclusion scholars fear that strength-based perspectives, which are grounded in POS, will undermine the push for equality and empowerment by misrepresenting inequitable systems (and their leaders) in glowing terms. Many POS researchers fear that the examination of diversity and inclusion dynamics, especially the challenges, will detract from (and damper) the rich discovery of "pockets of goodness" (i.e., sources of strength and generative mechanisms), that enhance performance and well-being, and may even undergird positive transformations. The chapters in this book break through the de facto silos that represent ideological barriers between Diversity and Inclusion and POS research. In so doing, these chapters indicate clearly that diversity—that is, differences—are not the issue. The contributors recognize that organizational leaders and members face complex contextual challenges in the form of "wicked problems" (Chrobot-Mason et al.), a flat world (Blake-Beard et al.), and demands for continuous innovation (DeGraff & Mueller). Even while diversity may manifest or exacerbate such complex challenges, it is also a strategic resource that is essential for individuals and organizations who must navigate these challenges. In other words, the answers to positive organizing in the 21st century lie in the sophisticated understanding and engagement of diversity and inclusion processes.

Viewing multiple (and marginalized) identities as resources vs. oppressive forces. As a parallel to the organizational diversity discourse, competing theories construe multiple identities as resources versus oppressive forces within individuals. The chapters in this book counter the presumption that multiple identities only create internal conflict, tension, confusion, and angst. Through a POS lens, these chapters present theoretical frameworks, empirical evidence, and rich illustrations of how individuals and organizations intentionally tap into the diversity *within* individuals to stimulate innovation, build relationships, refine strategic goals, and sustain one's sense of well-being. For instance, Wilder, Rao, and Donaldson exhort readers to rethink the concept of the "ideal worker" as singular in focus and homogenous in identity background; instead, we should reframe our views on marginalized identities to consider them assets rather than liabilities. Roberts and Cha, Ramarajan and LeRoux-Rutledge, and Atewologun provide substantive accounts of how multiple identities generate valuable nondominant cultural capital, catalyze global entrepreneurship, and expand relational and identity resources. Creary's discussion of social identity resourcing bridges the micro- and macro-level dynamics of Diversity and Inclusion; she explains how multiple identities also constitute organizational assets for creating a vision and strategy for global diversity management. Kamimura and Posselt also examine how diverse identities benefit organizations, particularly through shaping knowledge creation and stimulating research innovations. Atewologun incorporates ambivalence into her discussion of multiple identities and resources, detailing a process through which people increase comfort with their intersectionality and develop a more positive sense of self. Thus, the POS lens recognizes the challenges with navigating multiple identities, but focuses on how to overcome these challenges to harness the resources that lie within each individual as a function of one's intrapersonal diversity.

Encouraging deviance and distinctiveness versus conformity and assimilation. The "disappearing" of diversity in organizational research has reinforced the assumption that differences are responsible for deviance (which are considered problematic),

and that the role of an organizational researcher is to understand the normative (i.e., dominant) experience. Integrating POS, diversity, and inclusion turns
this construction of "deviance as problematic" versus "normality as desirable"
on its head. POS research, like positive scholarship in the psychology and asset-
based community development fields, illuminates how positive deviance promotes
human flourishing. Positive deviance, though an uncommon experience, is a distinctive act of departing from the norm in an honorable way. Several chapters
in this book, especially those by Canham, Wasserman, Stavros, Rosenberg, and
Davidson, explain how positive deviance counters the status quo in a way that acts
as a force for positive change. For instance, DeGraff and Mueller define diversity
as essential variation and associated friction that ignites innovation; this view of
diversity as positive deviance explains how both dissatisfaction and inspiration
may drive creativity. Other chapters in this book examine authentic expressions as
forms of positive deviance. By recognizing the existence of dominant and marginalized subcultures within organizations, Hewlin and Opie suggest that inclusion
and integrity involve welcoming authentic expressions of marginalized and mainstream personal and cultural values and practices. It is noteworthy that none of the
chapters in this book encouraged conformity or assimilation as effective means
for managing diversity; rather than minimize differences, POS and Diversity and
Inclusion research shed light on the value of differences in perspectives, expertise,
identities, values, and cultural expressions.

Building high quality connections across differences, not based on similarities. The integration of POS and Diversity and Inclusion in this book identifies the relational
benefits of understanding differences. While psychological and organizational
theories have documented the default preferences for similarity, the chapters in
this book counter the assumption that only similarity improves relationship quality. For example, Blake-Beard et al. propose that when people "bring identity into"
mentoring interactions, they are better positioned to build higher-quality relationships across differences. Chrobot-Mason et al.'s chapter on boundary spanning
encourages leaders not to conform to polarized views of "us versus them" and
dichotomies of "either/or"; instead, they propose a boundary-spanning mindset
that embraces paradoxes of "both/and" and values the "me" within "we." Simola's
chapter on a care-based approach to life story–telling and receiving proposes a
mechanism for building high-quality relationships by listening across difference.
Booysen's chapter cautions against idealizing views of collectivism that fail to
account for oppressive actions; she offers a rich discussion of how *Ubuntu*, when
practiced in an inclusive way, ties into a relational view of leadership that bridges
individual and collective orientations.

Reframing discomfort as a barrier vs. necessary and productive. Throughout this book,
readers are reminded that bridging POS and Diversity and Inclusion involves
becoming more comfortable with discomfort. As Ferdman notes, inclusion means
that discomfort is distributed more evenly; to build inclusive organizations we
must all become "outsiders." Menon and Chakravarti's chapter on social resilience

addresses how people move beyond first impressions and persist in discomfort to build stronger relationships. Atewologun's chapter on intersectionality accounts for the ambivalence people may feel about their personal identities as relevant resources that can enhance their professional effectiveness; as they work through this ambivalence, they cultivate more positive identities. Roberts, Wooten, Davidson, and Lemley's chapter on authentic affirmation emphasizes what we can learn from discomfort with strengths-based development that can deepen the cross-cultural impact of POS. Davidson highlights the reframing that "positively weird" people undertake that helps them shift from chronic discomfort to a sense of optimism and possibility. Thus, the POS lens on Diversity and Inclusion helps to explain the processes by which diverse groups work through the necessary and productive experiences of discomfort with differences.

Moreover a POS lens on Diversity and Inclusion endows us with a perspective for reimagining the discomforts associated with the management of diversity and inclusion, such as it is a nuisance, just an act of compliance, or a state of paralysis to an opportunity for birthing, nurturing, and leveraging Diversity and Inclusion practices. For instance, the chapter written by Wooten, Parsons, Griswold, and Welch highlights the generative mechanisms that can be leveraged by moving beyond the "business case" for diversity to the strategic and positively deviant management of diversity. Similarly, Flowers et al.'s chapter calls for organizations to reframe human resource management practices, strategically thinking about the management of diversity by aligning it with the organization's culture and the engagement of underrepresented stakeholders. Building on the importance of culture as a lens for reframing the discourse, Rosenberg's chapter exposes us to a ripple effect of positive outcomes that result when the practice of culturally competent organizational behavior is integrated with appreciative inquiry. Whereas Kossek's chapter invites us to rethink work–life initiatives from the margins to the mainstream of organizational life by connecting them to organizational goals, equal access, and the customization of social support. And, for a strategic thinking view of reframing Diversity and Inclusion with POS, Stavros and Cole's chapter presents SOAR, an inclusive process for engaging in conversations that focus on identifying *strengths*, seizing *opportunities*, encouraging shared *aspirations*, and a holistic view for establishing measured *results* for the goals of a group.

Cultivating resilience versus surrendering to the adversity of discrimination. Consistent with decades of diversity research, the chapters in this book acknowledge the challenges that surface from discriminatory attitudes and actions in diverse organizations. Those who have less power and status, often due to identity characteristics, face psychological, social, and career obstacles. The POS lens sharpens our understanding of the adversity of discrimination, by illuminating the processes by which marginalized people cultivate resilience against the damaging effects of discrimination on individuals and groups. A key insight in the chapters regarding resilience is the importance of building social and familial support throughout one's life span to equip people with the psychological and social resources required for buffering the deleterious impact of discrimination. Henderson and Bell's chapter explains how racial socialization messages that build pride in one's identity help to prepare African Americans to develop resilience in the face of racial bias. Giscombe's chapter on resilience emphasizes the importance of overcoming maladaptive self-protective mechanisms, such as hiding vulnerability, to defend oneself from bias; instead, people who cultivate resilience are better able to learn from failure and thus counteract maladaptive coping mechanisms. Menon and Chakravarti's chapter on social resilience also acknowledges the implicit biases toward in-group preferences, which affect the diversity of friendship networks, and discusses how to cultivate resilience that can counteract these tendencies in favor of pursuing more interactions with diverse others.

Reenergizing diversity discourse versus succumbing to resistance and fatigue. The tone of the chapters in this book is strikingly optimistic; even as they acknowledge the complexity of diversity, they offer evidence-based insight for increasing capacity building and flourishing. For example, Wasserman contrasted the public discourse of diversity discouragement and fatigue against her experiences of using POS principles with clients who "came alive" through engaging with different narratives. Wishik also writes about her field experiences with using a Leveraging Difference framework, explaining how it opened up new forms of communication and helped diverse groups to understand the broader relevance of diversity discussions. The conceptual linkages between diversity, inclusion, resources, and creativity also infuse scholarship and practice with fresh insight and energy, by pointing to the untapped potential that exists within diverse organizations.

Continuing to Build Bridges in Scholarship: Implications for Integrating POS and Diversity and Inclusion

In sum, we learn from this volume that longstanding assumptions that have anchored predominant views on Diversity and Inclusion and POS must be challenged to build conceptual, empirical, and practical bridges between these fields. Differences are not the sources of problems, but are the engines and conduits for capacity building. Tapping into differences doesn't drain organizational systems of focus and engagement. Instead, differences energize human and organizational transformation. Bridges across differences are built on the pillars of resilience, authenticity, productive discomfort, innovating thinking, and ongoing inquiry.

Certainly, there are other pillars beyond those that emerged from the chapters in this book. For instance, germane topics in Diversity and Inclusion research that can also be enriched through POS perspectives include empowerment, social justice and activism, counteracting implicit biases, challenging the dominance of gendered and social class hierarchies, and eliminating performance/achievement gaps. A much deeper exploration of global diversity will also further develop the U.S.-based focus of many of the issues in this volume. Likewise, POS topics that have gained considerable attention in academic journals and popular outlets can benefit from a more systematic, contextualized examination of diversity influences. POS studies can build bridges by emphasizing more complex stories that take into account the context of a globally diverse society. Rather than use a broad brush and assume that "one size fits all" for processes and outcomes, POS studies can further consider the impact of proposed generative mechanisms for diverse groups. In so doing, POS can provide more differentiation in how various strength-based theories apply to various identity groups and the management of diversity and inclusion. For example, how are virtues and character strengths such as authenticity, compassion, courage, and humility construed and enacted differently by prototypical leaders versus nonprototypical leaders? What does the successful bridging of connections across difference reveal about how high quality connections are established and nurtured? How are positive deviance and exemplary performance the result of extraordinary diversity management practices? Where are there opportunities to link the long-term sustainability or thriving of people, organizations, and society to acts of inclusion and the capacity to embrace diversity? What are the cognitive, affective, and relational mechanisms that bring out the best in individuals, teams, and organizations?

We conclude this book with even greater excitement for deeper dialogues around the synergies and contradictions between Diversity and Inclusion and POS. During our workshop with 75-plus Academy of Management members in 2010, we pondered whether the enterprise of POS, at its broadest, may be quite similar to the enterprise of Diversity and Inclusion at its broadest? Both perspectives can offer scholars and practitioners scholarship that is generative and transformational, both for the Academy and in the field. Both Diversity and Inclusion and POS have been juxtaposed against traditional organizational and psychological scholarship, which focus primarily on the problems faced by dominant, majority-group organizational members (e.g., white heterosexual males in the United States). Prior to this compilation, however, these shared enterprises have been approached from very different angles, and with little overlap between leading voices in D&I scholarship and leading voices in POS. This gap creates an implicit contradiction between the proposed aims of inclusion, justice, virtuousness, extraordinary leadership, and flourishing, and the lack of representation of a diversity of experiences. Our book begins to lay the groundwork for building stronger bridges between D&I and POS. As our Academy of Management workshop participants noted, we often write about similar concepts but use different language to describe them (e.g., flourishing, striving, and resource) based upon our disciplinary backgrounds and orientations toward inquiry. The chapters in this book initiate the process of creating a common vocabulary to draw upon in future work. We hope that this book will stimulate further interest in convening D&I and POS scholars, inviting all to build a bridge that leads to new findings, effective practices, and unseen possibilities for individuals and organizations.

Taking Action: Practical Implications of Bridging Diversity, Inclusion, and POS

The chapters were written to not only bridge the disciplinary divide between diversity, inclusion, and POS research, but also to engage scholar practitioners who are doing the field work to bridge the principles of POS to Diversity and Inclusion dynamics in social systems. While you are engaging in this capacity building, consider the featured case studies, tools, and frameworks as catalysts for your work. For example, the chapter written by Giscombe provides us with inclusive practices for establishing norms that encourage people to learn from their mistakes, and Simola's chapter shares discussion points to encourage people to bring more of themselves to work through life story–telling. In addition, there are thought-provoking resources for incorporating Diversity and Inclusion with an organization's strategic planning process (Creary; Stavros; Wasserman; & Wooten et al.). If you are capacity building in the area of innovation, the chapters written by Ramarajan and LeRoux, Stavros and Cole, and DeGraff and Muller highlight specific ways to leverage diversity for generating new ideas. Several chapters also provide suggestions for inclusive approaches to capacity building via performance and talent management (Hewlin; Kossek; Opie; Roberts & Cha; Roberts, Wooten, Davidson, & Lemley). Last, but not least, most chapters in the book remind us that the bridges we build between Diversity, Inclusion, and POS begin with ourselves. This book provides concrete suggestions for managing our personal identities, assumptions, and behaviors in ways that will help us to focus on the diverse strengths within ourselves and in others, and to welcome opportunities to practice inclusion for personal, relational, and organizational growth.

INDEX

Note: Page numbers with *f* indicate figures; those with *t* indicate tables.